FEMININE VISIBILITY IN CONTEMPORARY IRAN

Studies in Critical Social Sciences Book Series

Haymarket Books is proud to be working with Brill Academic Publishers (www.brill.nl) to republish the *Studies in Critical Social Sciences* book series in paperback editions. This peer-reviewed book series offers insights into our current reality by exploring the content and consequences of power relationships under capitalism, and by considering the spaces of opposition and resistance to these changes that have been defining our new age. Our full catalog of *SCSS* volumes can be viewed at https://www.haymarketbooks .org/series_collections/4-studies-in-critical-social-sciences.

Feminine Visibility in Contemporary Iran

Women, Religion, Culture and the State

Edited by
Esmaeil Zeiny
Seyed Javad Miri

Haymarket Books
Chicago, IL

First published in 2024 by Brill Academic Publishers, The Netherlands
© 2024 Koninklijke Brill NV, Leiden, The Netherlands

Published in paperback in 2025 by
Haymarket Books
P.O. Box 180165
Chicago, IL 60618
773-583-7884
www.haymarketbooks.org

ISBN: 979-8-88890-514-2

Distributed to the trade in the US through Consortium Book Sales and
Distribution (www.cbsd.com) and internationally through Ingram Publisher
Services International (www.ingramcontent.com).

This book was published with the generous support of Lannan Foundation,
Wallace Action Fund, and the Marguerite Casey Foundation.

Special discounts are available for bulk purchases by organizations and
institutions. Please call 773-583-7884 or email info@haymarketbooks.org for more
information.

Cover design by Jamie Kerry and Ragina Johnson.

Printed in the United States.

Library of Congress Cataloging-in-Publication data is available.

Contents

Acknowledgments

First and foremost, we would like to thank our contributors who have worked diligently and patiently in the editorial process of this collection. Their contributions made it possible for this volume to bring "Feminine Visibility" in Iran to the fore. While in the making, this volume benefitted from the expertise and help of a number of individuals. For her helpful comments and help, we wish to thank Afsaneh Tavassoli. At Brill, we are grateful to the editorial and production staff, in particular Katie Short, whose hard work saw this volume reach completion. Our heartfelt thanks go to Professor Dr. David Fasenfest, the series editor of the Studies in Critical Social Sciences for all his support. For the intellectual and financial support, we would like to express our gratitude to Xiamen University Malaysia. This project was supported by Xiamen University Malaysia Research Fund (Grant No: XMUMRF/2023-C11/IELL/0002). We would also like to express our appreciation to the Institute of Humanities and Cultural Studies in Tehran for their constant support.

Figures and Tables

Figures

Tables

Notes on Contributors

Maliheh Abedi
is a Ph.D. Candidate in Sociology at Payame Noor University (PNU). She received her Master's degree in Sociology and Bachelor's degree in Social Research from Alzahra University. In addition to conducting research on Iranian education, she teaches different courses in sociology. She has published articles in various journals and conference proceedings in the field of women's studies. Her research interests are feminist theories and critics, gender studies, women in education, sociology of family, and women's health. She has conducted many research projects in sociology and women's health.

Hamideh Dabbaghi
is an Assistant Professor of Women's Studies at Allameh Tabataba'i University. She writes on women's issues, especially employment, work-life balance, the division of domestic work, and Female Entrepreneurship. Some of her publications include: "Tourism and the Empowerment of Women in Iran" (Routledge, 2018), "A Multiple Narrative of the Work-Life Relationships of Academic Women" (*Iranian Journal of Anthropology*, 221), and "Infertility and Women's Suffer: A Review of the Psychological, Social & Economic Problems of Infertility" (*Social Sciences*, 2023).

Zahra Karimi
is an Associate Professor at the University of Mazandaran, Iran. Her fields of research are Development economics, Institutional Economics, and labor market. Some of her Publications are "The Effects of International Trade on Gender Inequality in Iran: Women Carpet Weavers of Iran" (*SSRN*, 2008), "The Role of Credit in Women's Employment; The Case of Women's Cooperatives in Iran" (*Iranian Economic Review*, 2013), and "Iran Labour Market Under the Sanction" (*International Journal of New Political Economy*, 2022).

Teo Lee Ken
was a postdoctoral fellow at Alzahra University, Tehran, where his research project focused on intellectual thought and movements in Iran, particularly religious intellectualism and the women's movement. He received his Ph.D. from the Department of Malay Studies, National University of Singapore (NUS). He also holds a Master of Laws (LLM) specializing in Asian Legal Studies from the same university. He has previously been a visiting researcher at the

Department of Pacific and Asian History in the School of Culture, History and Language at the Australian National University (ANU), and has presented academic and social research papers in Singapore, Japan, Turkey, Iran, Indonesia, Germany and the United States. His research interests include the sociology of knowledge and culture, political history, comparative politics, and political history.

Zahra Mirhosseini
is an Assistant Professor of Women and Family Studies at Alzahra University, where she has served as the department head since 2019. She earned her Ph.D. and Master's degree in Sociology from the University of Tehran and has been teaching a variety of courses, including gender sociology, family sociology, women's social issues, and family social policy for over seven years. She is particularly interested in qualitative research and believes that it provides a more comprehensive understanding of women's issues. Her work has been published in several journals, including her most recent article, "Women, Sexual Harassment, and Coping Strategies: A Descriptive Analysis", which was co-authored with her colleagues and published in 2023. Other articles she has authored include "Qualitative Evaluation of Women's Problems and Life Challenges during the COVID-19 Pandemic," and "Identifying the Context of Designing a Model for Successful Social Integration of Offender Women: A Grounded Theory Approach."

Seyed Javad Miri
Ph.D. (2000), is a Professor of Sociology and History of Religions at the Institute of Humanities and Cultural Studies in Tehran. He has published more than 50 books and 100 articles on various issues related to philosophy, religion, sociology and social theory. His publications appear in Oxford University Press and Brill.

Marzieh Mohases
is an Associate Professor at the Faculty of Theology and Religions, Shahid Beheshti University. She received her Ph.D. in Quranic Science and Hadith. The main field of her research is women and gender studies from the perspective of the Qur'an and authentic Islamic texts. For the last 13 years, she has been studying and researching the fundamental issues of women, and has authored several scientific articles and books. She is the translator of several English books in the field of gender studies in Persian.

Samaa Naissi

has received her MA degree in Women's Studies from Alzahra University and another MA degree in Political Geography from Tarbiat Modares University. She enjoys a profound understanding of the economic and political outlook of Iran in the region and beyond. It also provided her with analytical skills in geo-strategic affairs and in applied fields like journalism. Women Studies allowed her to have depth understanding of the problems and injustice against women, and provide solutions for empowering women. She is very much interested in gender equality and the empowerment of women in her country. She is currently reflecting on a project to provide social assistance and working skills for young girls in need.

Zahra Nejadbahram

has a Ph.D. in Political and Communication Science. She is a political scientist. She teaches communication, news journalism, public opinion and administrative rights. She is also a researcher and journalist. She was the head of the political committee of the Women Journalists' Association. From 2001 to 2004, she was the first woman deputy governor in Tehran. In 2004–5, she served as the first woman to occupy the position of the director of the social and electoral affairs of Tehran province. Dr. Nejadbahram has also been active in several NGOs as civil society organizations. She is the author of some books including *The Obstacles to Women's Political Participation in Iran* and *A Comparative Study of Women's Economic Participation in Iran, Malaysia and Turkey*.

Zeinab Shariatnia

is a Ph.D. Candidate in Islamic Mysticism at the Institute of Imam Khomeini, Iran. Her research interests are Islam and Zoroastrianism, and Sufism and Islamic mysticism. She also writes on the history of religions and Sufism, the psychology of religion and mysticism, and sociology of religion. She is currently writing a book about the "Philosophical and mystical thoughts of Shah Ismail."

Afsaneh Tavassoli

is an Associate Professor of Sociology at Alzahra University. She received her Ph.D. and MA degrees in Sociology. Since then, feminist theoretical thought and the sociology of family have become the main focus of her research. She conducts her research and training in an interdisciplinary manner. She has been teaching at the Department of Women and Family Studies at Alzahra University for more than 16 years. Her research interests are Feminist theories and the critics, gender studies, women in education, sociology of family, women's health and sociology of sport. She has published several research papers in well-known journals and has written many books in the field of women's studies with the sociological approach in Persian and English. She has conducted many research projects on women and family.

Saideh Torab

is a Ph.D. candidate in the History of the Islamic Revolution of Iran at the Islamic Revolution Research Institute. She has been teaching at Jiroft University since 2013. Her research expertise is Persian Gulf studies, and the political and social life of Iranian women. She also writes on the history of the Persian Gulf, the Iran-Iraq war and Iran's foreign relations with the Arab countries. Gender studies and the pioneers of women's rights movements are among her research interests as well. She has written on Persian Gulf Maritime trade, and women in contemporary Iranian history. She gave a talk on the relations between Iranian parties and women's organizations and associations (in the 1940s) at the University of St. Andrews. Currently, she is writing about the life of Zandakh Shirazi, one of the activists of women's rights during the Pahlavi era.

Esmaeil Zeiny

Ph.D. (2013), is an Assistant Professor of Literature and Cultural Studies at Xiamen University Malaysia. He was previously a Research Fellow at the Department of English Language and Literature, Kharazmi University, and the Institute of Malaysian and International Studies, the National University of Malaysia (UKM). His areas of specialization include Postcolonial Literature, Middle Eastern Studies, Women's Studies, and Cultural Studies. His essays have been published in *Interventions* (Taylor & Francis), and *Asian Journal of Social Science* (Brill). His most recent edited volume is entitled *The Rest Write Back: Discourse and Decolonization* (Brill, 2019).

CHAPTER 1

Introduction: Iranian Women and Sociopolitical Change

Esmaeil Zeiny and Seyed Javad Miri

Iran has witnessed a decades-long history of women's roles in bringing about sociopolitical change, promoting women's rights, pursuing a vision of equality, and interrogating patriarchal and discriminatory rules and regulations. Iranian women had prominent and often decisive participation in political and social movements such as the 1905–11 Constitutional Revolution and the 1979 Iranian Revolution. Scattered through the different eras of Iranian history, Iranian women's roles changed and their objectives evolved but they have always played an integral part in refashioning the sociopolitical, economic and cultural arenas of the country. However, their significant roles have historically fallen victim to disregard not only in the West but also in Iran. In the West, the historical depiction of Iranian women as passive, inferior and veiled victims of their religion and society, has, indeed, resurfaced after 9/11. These sorts of stereotypes have preserved their predominance with the political and media miseducation in the West and through the narratives of Muslim women in the diaspora narrating their stories of victimhood, seclusion, and oppression in Islamic society. This was a post-9/11 strategy to persuade people in the West that the Middle East and its people, especially women, are in dire need of the West for liberation; and it justified the project of "white men saving brown women from brown men." One of the most evident ramifications of 9/11 is the bolstering of Oriental fantasies about Muslim women. Despite Iranian women's heavy engagement in sociopolitical activities and developments, such orientalist assumptions still prevailed. More often than not, the predominant image of a typical Muslim Iranian woman in the West blended powerlessness and passivity overlooking decades of Iranian women's activities, movements, and achievements. In asking Western adults about Muslim women, one might be still greeted with the cliché responses of "submissive to men, not well educated, covered faces and bodies with hijab or burka, no rights, fragile, and separated from men." Such widely held miss-imagined assumptions demonstrate little understanding of the degrees of diversity in spiritual, political and cultural practices amongst Muslim women, reduce all diversities of Muslim women to a single image, and ignore all their movements and accomplishments in changing the patriarchal/*Sharia* rules and regulations.

Throughout the Iranian history, women have always held sway in the country. Pari Khan Khanum, the daughter of the Safavid Shah Tahmasb I (1548–1578), Khayr al-Nisa Beigum, the mother of Shah Abbas the Great (1549–1579) and Malek Jahan Khanum (1805–1873), Bibi Khanum Astarabadi (1858–1921) and Taj-al-Saltanah (1883–1936) are only a few prominent women who exerted serious sociopolitical influences in Iran. The annals of Qajar courts and memoirs reveal that there were well-educated women and women of great stature who wrote poetry and prose, were well-versed in Ottoman Turkish and French, and had their own library and female scribes.[1] Bibi Khanum Astarabadi was one such influential woman playing a key role in increasing women's self-awareness and gaining women's rights. She penned *Ma 'aayeb al-rejaal* (Vices of Men) (1894) to depict many social issues, men's inappropriate behaviors, and the plights of Iranian women. In the book, she advised women that "no man is superior to women and no woman is inferior to a man." This was written as a rebuttal to the misogynist text of *Ta'dib al-Niswan* (Disciplining Women) which was a crude manifestation of patriarchy and male chauvinism. *Ta'dib al-Niswan* advised men how to treat their wives and daughters. The book made it a point to emphasize that a woman's salvation depends on pure obedience to her husband. Bibi Kahum Asterabadi's devotion to educating women to fight for their rights led to the establishment of the first school for girls in 1906. While women did not have much presence in public life and enjoyed only a few rights, she set up a school for girls and paved the way for sociopolitical transformation.

In Iran, the proclivity to trivialize such women's roles and movements and the consequent disregarding of their rights have been rife. For instance, during the Constitutional Revolution of 1905–1911, Iranian women organized many clandestine associations and meetings in support of the nationalist and anti-imperialist movement, initiated street riots and strikes, participated in fights against foreign forces, boycotted the importation of foreign goods, and raised funds for the establishment of the National Bank but they were not included in the definition of "citizen" in the constitution demanding the "equality of all citizens in law." The male constitutionalists and the religious leaders denied these women also the voting rights on the grounds that they lacked political and social insights overlooking their heavy involvement in political activities such as the Tobacco Protest (1891–1892) that culminated in the Constitutional Revolution and their movements which led to the writing

---

1   Safa Altaf and G.N. Khaki, "QAJAR WOMEN: The Pioneers of Modern Women Education in Persia." *The Journal of Central Asian Studies*; Srinagar 23 (1) (2016): 65–81.

of the first constitution. Much to the male constitutionalists' chagrin, however, the outcome of the constitution prompted the female constitutional activists to organize many more semi-clandestine associations to modify the situation, improve their socio-political status and further their goals through publishing and education. Despite facing ulama's fierce opposition, these women succeeded in opening up schools and associations in major cities such as Tehran, Tabriz, Mashhad, Rasht, Hamadan and many other cities across the country within a short period.

All the women's socio-political movements and later Reza Shah's (1925–1941) policies of modernization tremendously altered the lives of Iranian women. A number of women "entered into the modern sectors of the economy, public and non-sex segregated schools were established, family laws were modified ..." and "women officially entered institutions of higher education and taught."[2] Women did gain some rights in various social arenas but Reza Shah forcefully closed their independent organizations and developed a state-sponsored women's association of *Kanoon-e Banovan* (The Ladies' Center) in 1934, headed by his daughter Ashraf Pahlavi. Pursuant to Reza Shah's modernization policies was the 1936 Unveiling Act which prohibited women from appearing veiled in public. Dressing up for modernity has been fashioned through unveiling women.[3] Whereas this forced unveiling was not well-received amongst a great number of Iranian women, particularly the lower-middle-class women, the dominant feminists of the time celebrated this law of unveiling despite the violence of this action.[4] They were persuaded that it was a "progressive" measure necessary for confronting clerical misogynistic approaches to women's concerns. This forceful act of unveiling was applauded by the *Kanoon-e Banovan* as an epitome of social progress. The *Kanoon* was, indeed, the key organization in bolstering the underpinnings of the state's preferred image for the "modern" Iranian woman. This Unveiling Act "ostensibly liberated women while denying them the freedom to choose how to present themselves in public."[5] The Unveiling Act was later abolished and the ban was lifted with the 1941 Reza Shah's coerced abdication and enthroning of his son Mohammad Reza Shah. This became a period when women formed many women's organizations and associations for their political and cultural demands, of which the following were the most influential: *Jamiat-e Nesvan-eVatankhaah-e*

2 Hamideh Sedghi, *Women and Politics in Iran: Veiling, Unveiling and Reveiling.* (Cambridge University Press, 2007), 61.

3 Ibid.

4 Nima Naghibi, *Rethinking Global Sisterhood: Western Feminism and Iran.* (London: University of Minnesota Press, 2007), 44.

5 Ibid., 45.

Iran (The Patriotic Women's League of Iran), *Tashkilat-e Zanan- e Iran* (The Organization of Iranian Women), *Hezb-e Zanan* (Women's Party), and *Jamiat-e Zanan* (Women's League).[6] They developed close ties with different political parties as well. Women were now involved in politics and directed institutes and organizations. Their involvement became more conspicuous in 1963 when 6 women were elected as deputies in the Parliament, and in 1965 when a woman was appointed as a minister. The presence of these women in the legislative body of the government paved the way for the 1967 Family Protection Law which transmuted several aspects of law in favor of women.

Another episode that is illustrative of women's significant role in refashioning the country is the participation of women in the Iranian revolution of 1979 which was historically unparalleled, both in terms of the depth and breadth of their commitment. As socio-political and economic discontent escalated in the country in the late 70s, many women participated in strikes and demonstrations against the Shah. To mobilize a strong force against the Pahlavi regime, the *ulama* asked women to participate in the demonstrations.[7] Seeing the massive outpouring of women against the Shah, many young and secular Iranian women voluntarily wore *chador* in symbolic defiance of the Shah's Westernization policies and participated in the demonstrations.[8] For these women, *chador* became the mark of resistance, agency and cultural membership.[9] Soon women from all walks of life, veiled and unveiled, with different ideological inclinations participated in these anti-Shah demonstrations. These strikes and anti-Shah demonstrations led to the overthrowing of the Shah in 1979. The "participation of women in the Iranian revolution of 1979 was historically unparalleled, both in terms of the depth and breadth of their commitment."[10] Yet, their achievements in the immediate post-revolution period were far away from their expectations. Immediately after the establishment of Mehdi Bazargan's Interim Government, Ayatollah Khomeini demanded the abolition of the Family Protection Act, ordered the implementation of *Sharia* and issued a decree demanding women not to wear miniskirts

6   Ruth F. Woodsmall, *Women and the New East*. Washington, D.C.: Middle East Institute, 1960.

7   Mehrangiz Kar, *Hoqooqe Siyaasi-ye Zanaane Iran (Political Rights of Iranian Women)*. Tehran: Roshangaran & Women Studies Publishing, 1997.

8   Farah Azari, "The Post-Revolutionary Women's Movement in Iran," in *Women of Iran. The Conflict with the Fundamentalist Islam*, ed. Farah Azari. London: Ithaca Press, 1983.

9   Naghibi, *Rethinking Global Sisterhood*.

10   Ali Akbar Mahdi, "The Iranian Women's Movement: A Century Long Struggle." *The Muslim World*, 94 (2004): 435.

to work and wear the Islamic form of modest dress to which women responded massively and angrily. Hundreds of thousands of women poured into the streets and chanted slogans against the forced *hijab* and the abolition of the Family Protection Act. All these demonstrations and activities of women made the government retreat and caused a delay in enforcing the Veiling Act. However, in 1983, Ayatollah Khomeini ratified the Veiling Act which forbade women to appear unveiled in public. Women, who played a significant role in the 1979 Revolution were no longer free to choose either to veil or not to veil. Since then, the Islamic revolution has been described as turning the clock back on women and returning them to a shrouded life "like a pearl in its shell."[11]

The sentiment of historical disregard in Iran, and Western orientalist stereotypes changed after the death of Mahsa Amini which triggered the largest protest movement in decades against discriminatory rules. The movement of "Women, Life, Freedom" brought women again to the fore. This movement and concomitant protests are solid proof that the imposed restrictions and discriminatory regulations that have been constructed over centuries of patriarchy do not have the same potency that they once possessed. The undermining of these discriminatory regulations stems from decades of Iranian women's resistance, achievements, and their role as a visible sociopolitical force mostly unknown and ignored. Being at the forefront of demonstrations and protests chanting "Women, Life, Freedom," Iranian women are now countering the orientalist assumptions about women in Iran and questioning the discriminatory and patriarchal rules. Anchored within such discourse and in line with bringing women to the fore, this volume creates a space that empowers an alternative way of knowing, filtered through what Barbara Harlow describes as specific "conditions of observation"[12] and others refer to as experience. This edited volume offers fresh perspectives and an on-the-ground understanding of the shift in Iranian women's experiences. While introducing alternative thoughts, visions and perspectives, "Feminine Visibility" explores how the imposed restrictions and discriminatory regulations that have been constructed over centuries of patriarchy do not have the same potency that they once possessed. Irrespective of the fact that many of the Iranian women's social conduct and professional progress are regularly undermined, it is difficult to ignore their resistance, achievements, and their role as a visible political and social force.

---

11   "Like a pearl in its shell" was a revolutionary slogan that encouraged women to veil and wear chador in the immediate post-revolution Iran.

12   Barbera Harlow, "Introduction," in *The Colonial Harem*, Malek Alloula. Trans. Myrna Godzich & Wlad Godzich. (Minneapolis: University of Minnesota Press, 1986), xxii.

The essays in this volume explore how high women leaped over the hurdles obstructing their progress and how far they have achieved to renegotiate the women's roles demanded by Iranian society. While in dialogue with and adding to the already existing scholarship on Iranian women, this volume approaches this topic from the vantage point of an insider account. Covering diverse issues like socio-economic and political developments, the role of religion, employment, education, politics, law, literature and war, this collection aims to disturb the dominant discourse and furnish an alternative lens through which readers are invited to reconsider the stereotypical representation of Iranian women and learn more about Iranian women's resistance, movements, progress, and achievements. A timely contribution, this volume brings to light Iranian women's developments, accomplishments and movements that interrogate the patriarchal regulations, and orientalist assumptions. A depiction of Iranian women's important roles and bravery in refashioning the country's religion, economy, politics and culture will speak volumes of the feminine power of the nation, and it will challenge the Western rhetoric of "saving Muslim women." By focusing on the broad theme of "feminine visibility," this volume seeks an interdisciplinary re-thinking of the sociopolitical, cultural and religious issues concerning women in Iran. This collection demonstrates the Iranian women's roles and movements that led to a breakthrough in societal attitudes towards women, and has positive implications for the future of Iran. It reveals that Iranian women's willpower to refashion the country is shaping the democratic aspirations of the nation in content, method and philosophy and challenges the Western rhetoric of "saving Muslim women." The essays in this volume not only threaten the historical stereotypical representations perpetuated and controlled by the conditioned way of seeing but also produce and reinforce a new way of seeing women as visible agents of sociopolitical changes. This positive shift in vision will produce a positive social change as well.

Bibliography

Azari, Farah. (1983). "The Post-Revolutionary Women's Movement in Iran." In *Women of Iran. The Conflict with the Fundamentalist Islam*, edited by Farah Azari. (190–225). London: Ithaca Press.

Altaf, S. & Khaki, G.N. (2016). "Qajar Women: The Pioneers of Modern Women Education in Persia." *The Journal of Central Asian Studies*; Srinagar 23 (1), 65–81.

Harlow, Barbera. (1986). "Introduction." In *The Colonial Harem*, Malek Alloula. (Myrna Godzich & Wlad Godzich, Trans.). (ix–xxii). Minneapolis: University of Minnesota Press.

Kar, Mehrangiz. (1997). *Hoqooqe Siyaasi-ye Zanaane Iran* (*Political Rights of Iranian Women*). Tehran: Roshangaran & Women Studies Publishing.

Mahdi, Ali Akbar. (2004). "The Iranian Women's Movement: A Century Long Struggle." *The Muslim World*, 94, 427–448.

Naghibi, Nima. (2007). *Rethinking Global Sisterhood: Western Feminism and Iran.* London: University of Minnesota Press.

Sedghi, Hamideh. (2007). *Women and Politics in Iran: Veiling, Unveiling and Reveiling.* Cambridge University Press.

Woodsmall, Ruth F. (1960). *Women and the New East.* Washington, D.C.: Middle East Institute.

CHAPTER 2

Rethinking Female Resistance: Women in the Division of Domestic Labor

Hamideh Dabbaghi

1 Introduction

Family has had a flexible and changeable structure in the past, and based on its economic structure and social context, it has experienced quantitative and qualitative changes. Social and economic contexts at any time have influenced the type of relationships and interactions between men and women and their gender-based roles in the family have regulated their relationships.

According to Chafetz, there is a gender-based division of labor in which women have mainly different tasks and responsibilities than men.[1] However, the division of tasks between men and women is a function of the characteristics and nature of that labor. Long commutes and exposure to danger while working are among the features that can cause a task and labor to be assigned to men instead of women. As a result, the same work, such as shepherding may be given to women in one place and men in another.[2]

However, regardless of characteristics such as the labor nature, the gender division of labor in the family has experienced a trend until today. In fact, from the Industrial Revolution onwards, the presence of women in the field of employment, their duties, and gender roles was questioned and reconsidered. The "traditional" gender division of labor, due to the assignment of paid productive work to men, and several feminist researchers have always presented reproductive work and unpaid domestic work to women as the leading cause of women's social and economic inequality.[3] The gendered division of labor, which is highly propagated based on gender ideals and reinforced by numerous

1 Janet Saltzman Chafetz, "The Gender Division of Labor and the Reproduction of Female Disadvantage: Toward an Integrated Theory." *Journal of Family Issues*, 9 (1) (1988): 108–131.

2 Michale Burton, Lilyan A. Brudner, & Douglas White, "A Model of The Sexual Division of Labor." *American Ethnologist*, 4 (2) (1977): 227–251.

3 Nancy Fraser, *Gender Equity and the Welfare State: A Postindustrial Thought Experiment, Democracy and Difference*. Princeton: Princeton University Press, 1996; Diemut Bubeck, *Care, Gender and Justice*. Oxford: Oxford University Press, 1995; Susan Moller Okin, *Justice, Gender and the Family*. New York: Basic Books, 1989.

social and legal norms, has shaped women's lives; and even after women enter the labor market, there is still the belief that women are always responsible for performing household and family duties.[4] According to this view, to balance their personal and professional lives, most women choose part-time jobs or even quit their jobs at times, especially when their children are young. This position leads women to unstable, less profitable careers. Its consequence is not having enough and reliable, independent income. Thus, the risk of being dominated in married life and poverty after losing their spouse increases.[5]

In the last two decades, we have seen a kind of change in the relationship between husbands and wives, which somehow helped them not to do all the household duties and to move away from the women's traditional division of labor. Perhaps this change in the traditional division of labor can be seen as the consequence of two fundamental ideas: gender equality, and women's activism. Gender equality means women and men, girls and boys, have similar conditions, treatment, and opportunities to fully realize their potential and dignity, and participate in economic, social, cultural, and political development. Gender equality is the new behavior of a society toward the similarities and differences of men and women and the roles they play, and in a way, it values equality against these differences. So, men and women are full partners in the home and society. Equality does not mean that men and women are the same, but the rights, responsibilities, and opportunities of men and women do not depend on their gender. In gender equality, the interests, needs, and priorities of men and women, and girls and boys, should be considered. It is related to human rights and is considered a precondition and indicator of sustainable people-centered development. Therefore, in recent decades, the emphasis on the idea of gender equality in the context of the current era, along with the progress of technology, women's abilities, the increase in education, and the possibility of women working outside the home, has changed the type of gender division of labor in the family resulting in different narratives of interactions between men and women in the family.

Moreover, the idea of women's agency and active confrontation with their gender roles can be an important factor in women's resistance and bargaining against playing gender roles. This has led to the redefinition of gender roles. Chandra Mohanty (1991) argues that, for a long time, women in the Third World were not treated as agents but as victims. Even in feminist studies, an average of one-third of the world's women have experienced a life based on ignorance,

---

4   Arlie Hochschild, *The Second Shift*. London: Penguin Books, 1989.
5   Julieta Elgarte, "Basic Income and the Gendered Division of Labour." *Basic Income Studies*, 3(3) (2008): 1–7.

poverty, illiteracy, dependence on tradition, and family-centeredness. This victimization in the Third World, or what Mohanty terms as "structures of victimization" impacted the lives of women of the pre-democratic era and caused domestic violence, or unemployment.[6] Nevertheless, women acted differently than before in various socio-political fields due to the formation of women's agency, which meant the ability to change, commit to change, or create a challenge for women against inequality. Although agency, by definition, is inevitably ambiguous due to its contradictory aspects, it refers to specific bargaining strategies that women may use in their relationships to moderate family relationships.

The ideas presented in the articles and research also refer to these factors. For example, Reece Garcia and Jennifer Tomlinson in an article entitled "Rethinking the Domestic Division of Labor" deal with changes in the division of domestic labor and negotiation between couples.[7] Using a qualitative and longitudinal research design, this article enjoyed bargaining theory and relative resources, and showed the various effects of the negotiation process, "silent bargaining," and "collaborative decision making." According to the research results, despite supporting egalitarian attitudes, couples participate in negotiation and bargaining differently. Women's contribution to the division of labor is usually more, even in cases where the men are highly involved. Moreover, in the absence of explicit negotiation, a range of implicit strategies for resistance, even tactics clearly at odds with the traditional division of labor, are used by women. Bargaining and women's agency are related to structural contexts in society or culture.

In changing the traditional division of labor, other background factors such as increasing the education of women in Iran and their employment can be named as facilitating causes in this process of resistance against the traditional division of labor. The increase in women's education in and of itself has become an intensifying factor of women's mistrust of traditional doctrines and has prompted them to believe in more equality in the division of labor in raising their children. They try to teach their children, especially their sons, to cooperate in household affairs. In addition, in most middle-class families, there is a belief that girls should have a comfortable life in their father's house and not do domestic labor because later, after marriage, they have to do much of the chores in their husband's houses.

---

6   Chandra Mohanty, Ann Russo & Lourdes Torres (Eds.), *Third World Women and the Politics of Feminism* (Vol. 632). Indiana University Press, 1991.

7   Reece Garcia & Jennifer Tomlinson, "Rethinking the Domestic Division of Labor: Exploring Change and Continuity in the Context of Redundancy." *Sociology*, 55 (2) (2020):300–318.

The above discussion shows that there seems to be a kind of rethinking and change in women's beliefs about the traditional division of labor. As a result, it is no longer possible to deal with the traditional narrative of gender division of labor in the family: the idea mixed with patriarchy, traditional values, and norms in which the woman plays the nurturing role in the family. Redefining this traditional view has led to a range of narratives about the division of household labor, which I intend to review in this chapter. This chapter accommodates accounts and semi-in-depth interviews with women in traditional groups, homemakers, and working women with different levels of education and number of children. These accounts detail the nature of gender division of labor in Iranian families. Moreover, I am trying to depict women's agency through small and hidden resistances and explicit challenges. Before delving into the nature of gender division of labor and modes of resistance, an explanation of concepts such as the relative resources, the power in marital relationships, and the resistance to the gender division of labor is in order.

2 The Concept of Relative Resource

According to the relative resource theory, one spouse's more excellent socioeconomic resources such as income, occupational position, and education level can secure more authority and less work than the other spouse.[8] In other words, the smaller the difference between spouses' incomes, the more equal the division of domestic labor will be. This theory, readily accepted in many sociological studies, suggests that husbands have more socioeconomic resources and generally more power and authority than their wives. This power distribution is more pronounced when the woman is merely a housewife and does not have a job outside the home.[9]

In a longitudinal study of the division of domestic labor over thirty years in Sweden and the United States, Evertsson & Nermo (2004) found a linear relationship in a Swedish sample i.e., when women are less economically dependent on their husbands, they do less work in the house. On the other hand, American women spend their time on domestic labor when their husbands are more economically dependent on them.[10]

---

8   Robert Oscar Blood & Donald M. Wolfe, *Husbands and Wives: The Dynamics of Family Living*. Free Press Glencoe, 1960.

9   Paula England, *Households, Employment, and Gender: A Social, Economic and Demographic View*. Routledge, 2017.

10   See Marie Evertsson & Magnus Nermo, "Dependence within Families and the Division of Labour: Comparing Sweden and the United States." *Journal of Marriage and the Family*, 66 (5) (2004): 1272–1286.

3   The Concept of Power in Marital Relations

Power in marital life plays an essential role in family dynamics and has always been the subject of much research. For example, the qualitative study of Quek and Knudson-Martin (2008) on Singaporean couples is one such study that shows the power shift in the home. Power tends toward equality and is more structurally formed; men make the final decision, and women find ways to influence them.[11] In another study entitled "Wives, Husband, and Hidden Power in Marriage," Zipp et al. (2004) found out that even if women have more income than their husbands, it is still the women who are affected by the decisions and strategies of their husbands.[12] Another research conducted by Kulik (2002) on power relations between husband and wife shows that variables such as resources available to the individual, the emotional involvement of spouses, and background factors strongly influence power relations in the family.[13] In other words, the more help and socioeconomic opportunities each spouse has, the better they can use them to exercise power over the other. In Iran, the labor division pattern is also affected by the woman's education, employment status, and age of the spouses.

One of the explanatory theories of power in the family is Steven Lukes' "three-dimensional" theory (2006),[14] which allows using the power dynamics embedded in broader cultural ideologies, for example, power in the marital negotiation process and the division of household affairs. In the first and most obvious sense, marital power states that a spouse can apply his spouse's apparent power to do something. For example, when a husband successfully forces his wife to do domestic labor by protesting and getting angry at his wife's request for help, he uses his apparent power. The second dimension of this issue is latent. This dimension is related to the ability to suppress problems or potential problems. This type of power manifests itself in successfully resolving conflicts in ways that prevent similar contests from occurring in the future. In the previous example, if the woman accepts the unequal share of the work, despite the initial reluctance, and avoids raising the issue due to the fear of renewed conflict, the husband has shown his latent power towards his wife.

---

11   See Karen Mui-Teng Quek & Carmen Knudson-Martin, "Reshaping Marital Power: How Dual-career Newlywed Couples Create Equality in Singapore." *Journal of Social and Personal Relationships*, 25 (3) (2008): 511–532.

12   John F. Zipp, Ariane Prohaska & Michelle Bemiller, "Wives, Husbands, and Hidden Power in Marriage." *Journal of Family Issues*, 25(7) (2004): 923–948.

13   Liat Kulik, "Marital Equality and the Quality of Long-term Marriage in Later Life." *Ageing & Society*, 22(4) (2002): 459–481.

14   Steven Lukes, *Power: A Radical View*. second edition. Basingstoke: Palgrave Macmillan, 2005.

The last, and perhaps the subtlest type of power exercise is a hidden power.[15] It refers to the ability to ensure obedience by shaping beliefs and desires in such a way that the dominated person looks at the constructed categories from the viewpoint of the dominant person, and considers it natural, beneficial and logical. A power that the actors themselves are unaware of having. The previous example does not deal with domestic labor because the woman thinks that she must do the domestic labor under any circumstances, and explanations based on "inherent nature"—such as what a woman is made to do—may be used. In this sense, the husband has benefited from the hidden power.[16]

4   The Resistance to the Gender Division of Labor

In the theoretical literature, there are different gender roles for men and women. Women are considered suitable for the "expressive role" (nurturing role at home) and men are suitable for the "instrumental role" (which is more suitable for the breadwinner). The roles are complementary, and the division of household work results from consensus and economic efficiency. Nowadays families believe in gender equality in their attitudes towards domestic labor, caregiving, and unpaid work, but there are significant differences in attitudes towards the division of domestic labor across and within countries and by age and gender.[17] Women's participation in the labor market and the growth in the number of couples who earn do not always affect their share of domestic labor and care work. Even though there have been changes in the traditional model of the breadwinner, internal resistance from men and women can be seen on inequalities in couple's relationships.[18] This indicates that the hours that men with two jobs and breadwinner women work at home affect this division of household work.[19]

---

15   Pierre Bourdieu, *Masculine Domination*. Stanford: Stanford University Press, 2001.

16   Aafke Komter, "Hidden Power in Marriage." *Gender and Society*, 3 (2) (1989): 197–216.

17   Jacqueline O'Reilly, Tiziana Nazio & Jose Manuel Roche, "Compromising Conventions: Attitudes of Dissonance and Indifference towards Full-time Maternal Employment in Denmark, Spain, Poland and the UK." *Work, Employment & Society* 28(2) (2014): 168–188.

18   Martina Dieckhoff, Vanessa Gash, Antje Mertens, & Laura Romeu Gordo, "A Stalled Revolution? What Can We Learn from Women's Drop-out to Part-time Jobs: A Comparative Analysis of Germany and the UK." *Research in Social Stratification and Mobility*, 46 (part B) (2016): 129–140.

19   Jennifer Tomlinson, Wendy Olsen & Kingsley Purdam, "Women Returners and Potential Returners: Employment Profiles and Labour Market Opportunities—A Case Study of the UK." *European Sociological Review*, 24(2) (2009): 1–15.

Furthermore, despite women's increased participation in paid work, they also do a disproportionate share of unpaid work and are often responsible for caregiving and nurturing duties. In contrast, the relative resource bargaining perspective focuses on the importance of power and interpersonal preferences. The bargaining perspective assumes that the partner with the most resources and economic power (based on actual or potential income, hours of paid work, and educational attainment) as opposed to the partner with less income can determine his or her role in the family.[20] There are more factors than just self-interest in decisions and division of domestic labor.[21] For example, moral judgments, values, and political views can influence people's decisions. In other words, it is questionable that people can withdraw from domestic labor just because they have more relative resources. Studies show that in families where women earn as much as their husbands or more than them, they still do domestic labor.

However, many couples consciously or unconsciously adopt gender norms and behaviors, and even women, when their paid hours are equal to or greater than their husbands, may continue doing a disproportionate share of unpaid work.[22] For example, Wheelock (1990), in his study in the North of England, showed that most families had moved away from the traditional division of labor to varying degrees, without an equal division of domestic labor and childcare.[23] The fact that women continue to take on a more significant share of unpaid work when men are unemployed is usually attributed to the entrenchment of the male breadwinner ideology. Male breadwinner, and Masculinity, is a hegemonic idea that has affected the gender division of labor. However, the new conditions of income generation in the family can lead to changes in the gender division of labor. This change can be welcomed or resisted when a man loses his Job. Therefore, men's and women's adopted strategies are different now. For example, Deutsch (1999) refers to "passive resistance," which means that men ignore their partner's requests for more involvement in the home.[24]

---

20   Rosemary Crompton, *Employment and the Family: The Reconfiguration of Work and Family Life in Contemporary Societies*. New York: Cambridge University Press, 2006.

21   Simon Duncan, Rosalind Edwards, Tracy Reynolds, & Pam Alldred, "Motherhood, Paid Work and Partnering: Values and Theories. *Work, Employment and Society*, 17(2) (2003): 309–330.

22   Ibid.

23   Jane Wheelock, "Capital Restructuring and the Domestic Economy: Family Self Respect and the Irrelevance of 'Rational Economic Man.'" *Capital & Class*, 14(2) (1990), 103–141.

24   See Francine M. Deutsch, *Halving It All: How Equally Shared Parenting Works*. Cambridge, MA: Harvard University Press, 1999.

Fox (2009) deals with "unpleasant compliance," which means that women do extra work themselves during changes instead of creating tension and engaging with their husbands.[25]

Other research has a predominantly male approach and deals with the concept of "strategic incompetence" in domestic labor. For example, according to a study by Deutsch (1999), women deliberately refrain from cooking, cleaning, and washing their husband's clothes—in order to spend less time on domestic labor, and on the other hand, they hope that the behavior of their husbands will change.[26] Mannino and Deutsch (2007) found that the more assertive women are in bringing about change, the higher the likelihood of change in the traditional division of labor.[27] However studies suggest that efforts to bring change do not necessarily lead to desirable results.[28] Strauss (1978) used the term "silent bargains" to show how people may be influential with the verbal exchange in situations with the potential for conflict (or explicit negotiation).[29] In other words, silent bargains are more common.[30] Researchers have also noted that power is not always explicitly visible in negotiations but is sometimes implicitly applied;[31] sometimes, the man or woman with less economic power may decide to change the gender division of labor. At this time, silent deals are used, which may lead to a negative response.

5 Methodology

This study used the interpretive paradigm and thematic analysis method. The interpretive paradigm focuses on the originality of human beings and the essence of human choice instead of causal determinism. This paradigm believes in the active role of human opinions and attitudes in the performance

25 Bonnie Fox, *When Couples Become Parents: The Creation of Gender in the Transition to Parenthood*. University of Toronto Press, 2009.

26 Deutsch, *Halving It All*.

27 Clelia Anna Mannino & Francine M. Deutsch, "Changing the Division of Household Labor: A Negotiated Process Between Partners". *Sex Roles* 56(5–6) (2007): 309–324.

28 See Ronald E. Bulanda, "Paternal Involvement with Children: The Influence of Gender Ideologies." *Journal of Marriage and Family*, 66(1) (2004): 40–45.

29 Anselm Leonard Strauss, *Negotiations: Varieties, Processes, Contexts, and Social Order*. San Francisco: Jossey-Bass, 1978.

30 Janet Finch & Jennifer Mason, *Negotiating Family Responsibilities*. London: Routledge. 2003.

31 Marion Collis, "Marital Conflict and Men's Leisure: How Women Negotiate Male Power in a Small Mining Community. *Journal of Sociology*, 35 (1) (1999): 60–76.

of human social actions. In addition, two points of view are significant in using the thematic analysis method. First, many analyses are certainly thematic—however, they are called by another name (for example, conversation analysis or content analysis).[32] In other words, the thematic analysis method is one of the primary qualitative methods. In the second perspective, the thematic analysis method is not considered a specific method at all—for example; the data will be qualitative in usually recurring themes. In this study, thematic analysis is presented as an analysis method used to identify, analyze and report patterns or themes in the data and describe and manage the data in a minimal organization in more detail.[33]

Moreover, this method is used to understand people's everyday experiences, with finer details than reality, and tries to understand the phenomenon. The technique of semi-in-depth and semi-structured qualitative interviews was used to collect the data. Then, the text of the interviews was analyzed using the theme analysis technique and MAXQDA 2018 qualitative data analysis software, and the final results were presented as a pattern of main and sub-themes. In this study, 23 working women/homemakers, married/single, with children/without children, religious/non-religious, literate/less literate, from the age groups of teenage, young, and middle-aged were interviewed. This diversity in the studied group of women helps to understand the studied subject better and obtain different conceptual parts. The interviews were semi-structured and lasted about two hours.

The researcher analyzed the research reliability. The objective was to reach the highest level of agreement between the coders; therefore, in the present article, re-coding was done on three interviews by the second independent coder, and the reliability of the interviews is as follows: the average reliability of the three interviews is 75.809%, which is more than 70%, and it is acceptable. In this qualitative research, coding was also semi-open; coding was formed between theory and data, establishing the research validity. In the following table, the information of the interviewees is included:

---

32 Tom Meehan, Cathryn Vermeer, & Carol Windsor, "Patients' Perceptions of Seclusion: A Qualitative Investigation." *Journal of Advanced Nursing*, 31(2) (2000): 370–377.

33 Richard E. Boyatzis, *Transforming Qualitative Information: Thematic Analysis and Code Development*. Sage.1998.

TABLE 2.1   Introduction of the interviewees

Code	Nickname	Age	The level of education	Number of children	Job
1	Nazanin	45	Bachelor's degree	1	Carpet weaving
2	Azam	51	Master's degree	2	Coach
3	Roghayeh	25	Bachelor's degree	2	Housewife
4	Sara	40	Master's degree	0	Employee
5	Nafiseh	45	Master's degree	1	Employee
6	Maryam	45	Master's degree	2	Employee
7	Fatemeh	28	Bachelor's degree	1	Housewife
8	Samaneh	31	Ph.D.	0	University Lecturer
9	Mahboobeh	30	Master's degree	2	Hair stylist
10	Shadi	40	Ph.D.	0	University Lecturer
11	Soraya	51	Master's degree	2	Teacher
12	Touba	40	Bachelor's degree	2	Teacher
13	Mahdiyeh	49	Bachelor's degree	2	Teacher
14	Raziyeh	42	High school	3	Carpet weaving
15	Mansoureh	31	Bachelor's degree	1	Graphic Designer
16	Soudabeh	56	Associate degree	2	Retired teacher
17	Jamileh	56	High school	4	Restaurant worker
18	Aida	28	Bachelor's degree	1	Tailor
19	Esmat	49	High school	4	Retired service force
20	Yeganeh	23	Diploma	2	Hair stylist
21	Asal	39	Master's degree	1	Employee
22	Shohreh	38	Bachelor's degree	1	Employee
23	Najibeh	40	Bachelor's degree	1	Housewife

6   Research Results

Women in terms of Age: The women participants in this research can be divided into four age groups: 20–30 years old, 30–40 years old, 40–50 years old, and 50–60 years old. As shown in Figure 2.1, the age group of 40–50 (44%) constitutes this research's most significant number of interviewees.

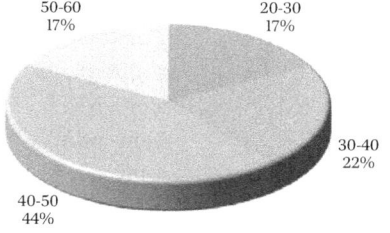

FIGURE 2.1
Frequency percentage of interviewees in terms of age

Women in terms of Education

According to Figure 2.2, most women have bachelor's and master's degrees, which constitute 70% of the research field of this study.

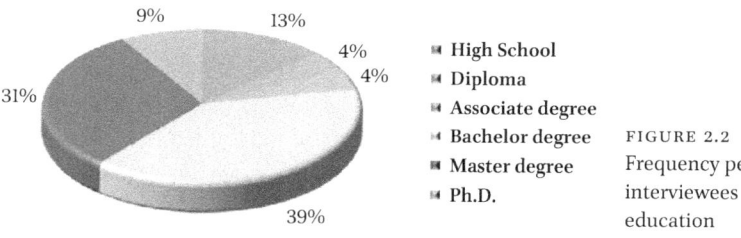

- ◄ High School
- ◄ Diploma
- ◄ Associate degree
- ◄ Bachelor degree
- ◄ Master degree
- ◄ Ph.D.

FIGURE 2.2
Frequency percentage of interviewees in terms of education

Women in terms of the Number of Children

Women with two children are the most significant number, equivalent to 39% in this research. After this group, women with one child are in the second place with a 35% frequency. (Figure 2.3)

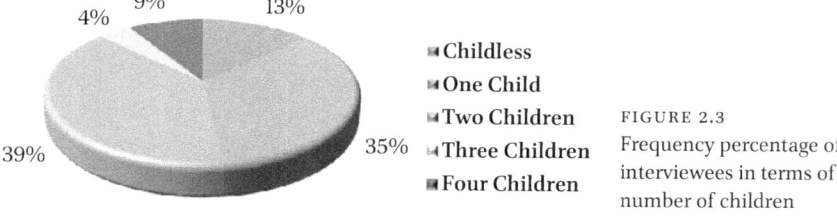

- ◄ Childless
- ◄ One Child
- ◄ Two Children
- ◄ Three Children
- ◄ Four Children

FIGURE 2.3
Frequency percentage of interviewees in terms of number of children

Women in terms of Job: Also, the most significant interviewees are female employees and teachers. (Figure 2.4)

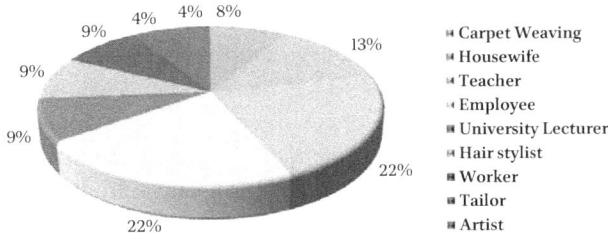

FIGURE 2.4 Frequency percentage of interviewees in terms of Job

7   Analytical Results

Let us now consider the division of labor in the Iranian family as a spectrum. There are two ends of the spectrum. One side is the participation of men in household work, or in other words, understanding the extended participation. On the other side is the traditional division of labor. However, several patterns can be observed as challenging actions against the traditional division of labor, and some patterns reveal rethinking this traditional division of labor.

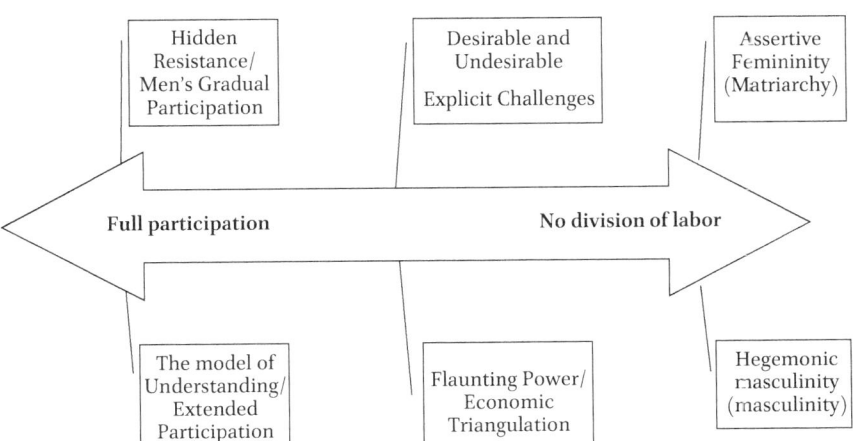

FIGURE 2.5 The levels of gender division of labor in the family

7.1   *Hegemonic Masculinity (Masculinity)*

At one end of the spectrum, there is no division of labor, and the family is based on hegemonic masculinity in which men are breadwinners and decision-makers. On this side, *women's gender roles* are defined as child care, reproduction, and housekeeping. In this type of Iranian family model, which has a long history in the world, the relationship between men and women in the family, according to Steven Lukes, is the expressive power that belongs to men.[34] This power is only given to men in the gender roles of the family, but society, culture, and religion also confirm this idea. Religion, and culture in the traditional society, and norms and values prefer male dominance over the family system, which is always supported by the traditional division of labor and assigns the gender roles of the breadwinner. According to Parsons, whereas men play an instrumental role in society, the role of nurturing and caregiving is given to women who play the expressive role.[35] Below is an account of what a number of women believe.

Soraya states:

> I have studied the Quran, and I can say from the point of view of Islam and religion that Islam has determined a place for everyone in the family, even a seven-year-old child. The position of mother and father in the home is significant, the mother is the means of strengthening the family, but on the condition that the manager—it means that the family man—should cooperate with her, so it is important how much the family man values the work of the family and considers her important role in the family.

Najiba states:

> My husband does not have much time to get to work at home, and he goes to work at 7 in the morning and comes back at 9 at night, and all the work related to my daughter and housework is my responsibility. It has become a habit for my husband, and there is No division of labor in our family.

Obviously, in this participant's unconscious, there are gender norms based on her cultural values. Cultural values are derived from religion, which is not only in Islam but can be found in other religions, which provide regulatory

---

34   Lukes, *A Radical View*.

35   See Talcott Parsons, Robert F. Bales, *Family: Socialization and Interaction Process* (1st ed.). Routledge, 1956.

principles for the relationship between men and women in the family. Here, values of religion have affected the gender's functions at home[36] and have caused women to do most of the domestic labor.[37] Moreover, the participant did not feel inequality to express and did not consider this type of labor division as an unfair relationship.

However, in contrast to the traditional gender division of labor (the breadwinner and the housewife), there are different types of agencies of Iranian women, with different degrees of resistance or involvement, including hidden and passive resistance, obvious challenge, and finally, assertive femininity. There is no challenge in assertive femininity as in hegemonic masculinity. Women and the family accept the male power and dominance. In assertive femininity, the woman's power is accepted, and both the husband and the children have no doubts about the centrality of the woman in the decisions.

7.2   *Assertive Femininity (Matriarchy)*

In contrast to patriarchy, there is another pattern with no division of labor, and women are responsible for the family. The author terms it as "assertive femininity," or in popular language, Matriarchy. The author insists on not using the word Matriarchy; because Matriarchy is a symbol of hegemonic domination and accepted power of women by society. However, in Iranian society, it cannot be said that women have achieved the stage of Matriarchy; instead, in a way, they have shown strong resistance or femininity in society. This female action can be considered a form of resistance, which the public has not yet fully accepted. The model of a woman breadwinner is not necessarily compatible with assertive femininity in the family. It is clear that assertive femininity is a kind of division of power in decision-making, and the woman breadwinner in the family indicates the change and displacement of gender roles in the family. Nevertheless, there are also families where women, despite breadwinning or economic participation in providing financial resources, still play roles such as hidden resistance or even understanding or persuasion.

Ayda states:

> My mother always makes the final decision at home. My father never interfered in doing things or making decisions. He was a harmless person. He didn't do anything to hurt my mother. My father did not take any

---

36   Sampson Lee Blair & Daniel T. Lichter, "Measuring the Division of Household Labor: Gender Segregation of Housework among American Couples." *Journal of Family Issues,* 12(1) (1991): 91–113.

37   See Harriet B. Presser, *"Employment Schedules among Dual-earner Spouses and the Division of Household Labor by Gender."* American Sociological Review, 59 (3) (1994): 348–364.

responsibility at home. My mother always did the housework and things related to the children. My mother always decided what we should do, where we should travel, how we should study, and where we should go to work.

7.3   *Desirable and Undesirable Explicit Challenges*

The third pattern is a kind of obvious challenge and struggle of women with the traditional division of labor. The third type, obvious challenge, can be divided into two types: compulsory self-sufficiency (undesired) and persuasion (desired). In the compulsory self-sufficiency model, women have a kind of compulsory independence. The men may have left the house, been imprisoned, or they are deceased. Thus, the woman is forced to accept guardianship and be a breadwinner in the family.

In persuasion, the woman has concluded based on reason and logic that the family man is not capable of handling affairs and making decisions and has removed him from the division of labor at home. In this model, the man may still be a breadwinner but he is not a decision-maker anymore. In this model, the woman takes the man's position as the head of the family and is responsible for his duties. The kind of power in this form of family is the woman's responsibility. The difference between compulsory self-sufficiency and persuasion is that in the former, the man is not present in the family, and the breadwinner and assertive femininity belong to the woman. However, in the persuasion, the family man may still be the breadwinner but unable and disabled; therefore, the woman is the decision-maker.

The explicit challenges imply the conflict between men and women in the family in defining the gender position and roles. In this model, men and women do not try to hide their pain and try not to be submissive and oppressed. The view of equalitarianism in this model is the ultimate goal of women, and preserving the manly position and dominance is the goal of men in the family. In this model, women in a position of power and domination do not hesitate to make their children and other relatives aware of this power shift. Women can desire this challenge, and women themselves have come to understand their husband's ability to take care of the family.

7.3.1   Desirable Explicit Challenge: Persuasion

In the persuasion model, men and women have agreed to work together, but the woman considers him worthy of reward due to persuasion and satisfaction with the man's performance in other areas and not in gender roles. Therefore, she sacrifices herself and reduces the man's duties. Some instances of such a model are accounted below.

Soudabeh states:

> According to Islam: both men and women should do housework. The man should do the hard and heavy work that a woman cannot do. But when a woman sees that her husband cares about his duty, he works outside the home. He loves his wife and child. Naturally, this woman does not allow her husband to do the household chores when he returns home. The woman knows that her husband's responsibility outside the home is too much, and he works very hard. So, she does not allow herself to assign tasks to her husband inside the house.

Yeganeh states:

> When I decided to work, I was supposed to do housework with my husband. Unfortunately, my husband is always at home because he was the first child in his family, did not take much responsibility, and did not know how to do anything. My husband is not social at all. If I want to take a loan or enroll my children in school, all the responsibilities are on me, and my husband doesn't take any more responsibility. It means he doesn't do the few things he used to do at home anymore. There is no division of labor in our house.

In the persuasion model, participation and cooperation in the division of labor and gender roles are floating and based on the woman's persuasion and satisfaction. Notably, this pattern in the Iranian family shows a clear difference from the study of Maret and Finlay (1984) and Evertsson & Nermo (2004) in Sweden.[38] They showed an indirect and negative relationship between women's economic independence and doing domestic labor. However, in persuasion, despite the woman's economic independence and work outside the home, other factors persuade her not to ask the man to participate in the housework. In other words, even the domestic labor of working women may be not only different from that of homemakers but also more because sometimes they also perform men's duties at home. This pattern is different from The Understanding or Extended Participation Model. In the second model, both men and women are satisfied with their conditions and understanding. Nevertheless, in the persuasion model, the woman convinces herself to accept

---

38   See Elizabeth Maret & Barbara Finlay, "The Distribution of Household Labor among Women in Dual-earner Families." *Journal of Marriage and the Family*, 46 (2) (1984): 357–364.; Evertsson & Nermo, "Dependence within Families."

the responsibility of the family based on the mandatory conditions. However, the family man also is not satisfied and happy with this situation.

7.3.2   Undesirable Explicit Challenge: Compulsive Self-Sufficiency Model
In some Iranian families, due to the absence of the family man, his illness, or his disability, the woman is forced to acquire capabilities that were not among her duties and gender roles in the past according to the conventional model. Of course, this model can also be actual for men, but men usually use auxiliary forces such as family (mother and sister or the service force) in emergencies when their spouse is sick or disabled or is not at home. They leave the duties of their wives to other women. One such example is detailed below.

Mahdieyeh states:

> From the first days of our marriage, I decided to learn to drive. My hus-band has cancer, and I was always worried about the future. So, I decided to take on all the responsibilities. Now I take my son and daughter to school myself. We live in the village, and it takes a long time to reach the city. However, I try to do all the housework in the evenings when I get home.

7.4   *Women's Hidden Resistance/Men's Gradual Participation*
7.4.1   Passive/Hidden Resistance
In this type of resistance, women gradually learn to avoid domestic labor. They direct their husband toward a situation where they have no choice but to cooperate.

Shadi states:

> When I saw that my husband didn't help at all with the housework, I gradually realized that I should do less housework. Of course, it's not that I'm a lazy person, but with studying and working outside, I didn't really get enough time. At first, there was a little disorder at home, but for us, it seemed too much. Of course, we don't have children. Living with one other in the same place makes the home messy and crowded. Then I talked to my husband, and he agreed to get a housekeeper to do the housework every two weeks. I didn't pay that woman's salary; it was my husband's duty. I made him realize that homework is hard and he should pay money. However, the house was still messy every 2 weeks, but it was better than before. Until we made some rules. For example, if there is a dirty dish in the dishwasher, anyone who sees it would be supposed

to wash it; this rule worked for a while, but not all the time. Another rule was that if I had to spend my time in the kitchen, my husband would sit in the kitchen and not do his personal duty so that somehow the two of us allocated equal time to housework. But you know? These were all small tasks, and I had to do the final work myself. But anyway, my husband understood that he had duties. For example, when we went shopping, especially during the Corona pandemic, he had to disinfect the equipment, and I had to wash the fruits. Do not think that he did everything automatically. I had to say to him step by step.

Sarah states:

My husband is a very religious person. At first, he did not do the housework at all, but step by step, he participated in the housework. I found a way. For example, when I heard a holy sentence(hadith) somewhere about Hazrat Ali and how much he helped Hazrat Fatimah with housework, I would read it to my husband. Sometimes I asked my sister, who is a religious teacher, to send me a religious clip or a movie about helping the wife with housework. I would play the clip loudly at home so he could hear it, and I think this solution greatly impacted my husband. In addition, I recently had my back operated on; when he saw that I could no longer work as before, he started to help me.

7.4.2   Men's Gradual Participation

In this model, the man mostly believes in the traditional division of labor, i.e., the man is a breadwinner and the woman is a housekeeper, but over time, due to economic factors, and influence from the group of friends, he gradually participates in household affairs. Gradual participation refers to the role of teaching domestic labor and getting men used to doing their duties at home. This point differs from the study of Huber and Spitze (1981), who believed that working outside the home increases cooperation and collaboration.[39] Moreover, research results indicate a cultural gap in the gender socialization of children. In other words, boys are not prepared in the stages of growth and upbringing in the Iranian family, and even in schools, to play cooperative roles with girls. Of course, this result regarding gender segregation in Islamic culture is justifiable. Gender segregation occurs from the age of puberty for girls (9 years old), and even earlier from the age of entering primary school, which is seven years old. Girls and boys, until the end of school education, and before

---

[39]   See Joan Huber, & Glenna Spitze, "Wives' Employment, Household Behaviors, and Sex-role Attitudes." *Social Forces,* 60(1) (1981): 150–169.

entering the university at the age of 18, are faced with gender segregation and lack of participation and cooperation in social roles.

In the best-case scenario, boys and girls after entering the university at 18, can continue gender socialization in public environments. In the worst case, considering the existence of single-sex universities in Iran and the lack of desire of boys to study in university compared to girls, until marriage, they do not reach the model of participation and understanding until marriage.

In Many Iranian families, male children continue to live with the family until the years after puberty and even adulthood. They have taught their boys that they should not work at home and that all the duties in the father's house should be with their mothers and sisters, and after marriage in their nuclear family, all the domestic labors are with their wives.

Nafiseh states:

> In the early days of my marriage, my husband believed that women were created to do housework, but husbands should not do housework. Of course, he had many parties with his friends at our house after a while. Step by step, my husband saw that his friends were cooking. He also became interested in cooking and even decided to cook one day. The words of his brother and his friends affected him.

Another concept that can be shown in hidden resistance is to play the role of an incompetent woman. In some cases, women, to make the men help them with housework, pretend to be incompetent and present the situation to the man as if only the man can solve their problem.

Shohreh states:

> I always have to do the housework myself. And my husband tells me that this is your duty and he doesn't help with the housework. But my mother has an exciting way. My mother always wanted to force my father to work at home. For example, she says my hands are painful, I cannot do the housework anymore, and I am tired. This girl—she points to me—also does not do the housework cleanly. She asks my father to help and do the housework. So, my father says that you two are useless, and then he cleans the floor himself.

Azam states:

> Actually, my husband never did the housework, even though he came from the village to the city as a teenager and had to do his own work, but

from the beginning of our life together, he went to work; and I started doing the housework so that everything would be ready and clean when he came back. At that time, I was a teacher and I was working part-time. Before school, I would wake up early and do the chores at home. When my first child was born, I became a full-time teacher and had to be in school more. Sometimes I would say to my husband, for example, Ahmed, I have a headache, please wash the dishes today, or, for example, my back is painful. Of course, I was exaggerating a little, so my husband helps me with the housework. Step by step, my husband understood his duty and learned to assist me in the housework.

In gradual participation, men do not do the domestic labor in the initial stages of their marriage, but over time, they were forced to participate with the gradual training of their wives or the circumstances that arose. For example, forcing women to work outside the home and participate as breadwinners, giving birth to children, and increasing domestic labor gradually forced men to learn and participate in domestic labor.

7.5   *Flaunting Power/ Economic Triangulation*
In the model of flaunting power, the gender roles of men and women are equal in terms of strength and power. In other words, women, like men, have relative resources and sound economic and cultural capital. In this model, to get rid of the position of subservience and gain more power, women take advantage of an economic partner, who may be their close relatives, such as their father or brother, or other relatives, such as their sister's husband, or even a stranger, such as their male colleague. In this pattern, women try to increase relative resources and make economic investments. As a result of increasing income and economic capital, a woman can be decisive in the family, determine the amount of domestic labor for herself and her husband, and even play a role in critical decision-making.

Mahbubeh states:

> In the beginning, we always fought about the division of labor. My husband always said that housework is not strenuous. But I have to work hard outside the house, and you have nothing to do at home. I was a housewife and had a three-year-old daughter. My husband owned a supermarket. I told him to let's change our places with each other. I went to his place for a week, and he did the housework at home. At first, he resisted, but gradually he accepted. He was annoyed and understood that the housework was not convenient anymore. I showed him in practice that housework is not as easy as he thought.

The term triangulation comes from psychology. A practical idea is used when a third person enters a marital relationship. Economic triangulation indicates a lack of complete trust between the couples, or a woman's lesser power in the relationship, who tries to bring a partner other than her husband into her economic relationship. This model shows a kind of economic model in the relationship between couples.

Shadi states:

> Thirteen years have passed since our marriage, although I was studying most of this time. Because I was not working, I did not know about my husband's savings, and he did not allow me to participate in economic decision-making. This was why I went to work to earn for myself. So, I bought a car with my brother and father. Of course, my husband knew all these issues, and somehow, because he didn't involve me in his money and decisions, he didn't mind me. I thought, now that after many years of our life, I have savings, my husband would help me, and we would have a joint account. But he didn't bother and said, "Did you face any shortage at home from the day we married until now?" I got help from my brother to give me the idea of economic investment. Honestly, when I went to work, I gave my husband a large amount, and he invested in the stock market, and then all my money was lost, and he also said that his money was also lost. But my brother told me to buy gold, and that's how I was able to save. The car was also his idea.

7.6   *The Model of Understanding or Extended Participation Model*

The extended participation model indicates a complete understanding between couples in the division of domestic labor. Of course, this understanding is not due to the powerlessness of couples or more power of one of them. It is based on the idea of equality which the couples believe in. The acceptance of equality between men and women has been widely discussed since the 1980s; however, especially in Iran and other developing countries, it has led to contradictions between the dos and don'ts and what is done practically. The word "participation" literally means being present in doing something. In sociology, participation means a state or condition that a person belongs to a specific group and performs a part of the tasks of that group. Participation in the family has different types: intellectual participation, emotional and psychological participation, behavioral participation[40] (Aghajani, 2002), and not to mention, participation in gender roles.

---

40   Nasrollah Aghajani, "Participation of Family Members." *Strategic Studies*, No. 16, (2000).

Touba states:

> For example, when my husband and I decide to go to the market, we write everything we need ... we don't spend much money. First, we buy the equipment we need. Then we plan what to buy for the next month and budget for the next month. My husband helps me with laundry, sweeping, and housework. My daughter does the same, does whatever she can, and almost both of my daughters try to contribute as much as they can. I cook more, and near the New Year, I bake sweets and bread.

In some cases, men know more about domestic labor due to their childhood conditions, socialization, or growing up in a female environment. Additionally, in the socialization process, gender stereotypes about domestic labor are less formed in them. Therefore, there is no need for them to train, or challenge and resist them. An account of such a case is presented below.

Asal states:

> I don't force my husband to do housework, but he does it automatically. Because he lived with his grandmother, who was old. So, he had to be an independent child. Later, he studied in Shiraz for 7 years. He studied and lived alone, so I don't have any problem with my husband in this regard, and he does even more housework than I do.

8   Discussion

Division of domestic labor refers to the distribution of necessary responsibilities and tasks and maintaining the home and family members. The division of domestic labor is sometimes defined as the sexual or gendered division of labor. Since industrialization, there has been a transformation in the division of domestic labor. In academic discussions since the 1970s, the concept of division of domestic labor became necessary. Nevertheless, despite the importance of this issue, no proper study has been conducted on it in Iran.

In this chapter, I have discussed the lived experience of Iranian women regarding the division of domestic labor. Therefore, after reviewing theoretical concepts such as power, gender division of labor, and relative resources and conducting 23 in-depth and semi-structured interviews with married housewives and working women with different levels of Education, the interviews were first coded by MAXQDA 2018 software. Moreover, we used the thematic analysis method and then extracted six categories and 228 concepts.

The extracted themes reflect the range of participation in household chores to the lack of division of domestic labor that 23 Iranian women have narrated about their relationships in the family. On one side, there is a complete division of domestic labor; on the other, full participation is dominated.

The first theme, hegemonic Masculinity, is the initial and customary current in the Iranian family, which has a long history in family relationships and is confirmed by religious norms and traditional social values. In contrast to the traditional gender division of the domestic labor model, various types of female resistance and agency have been formed, the degrees of which are different, ranging from hidden and passive resistance to explicit challenge and, finally, assertive femininity.

In the theme of assertive femininity, which is the opposite of hegemonic Masculinity, the power and dominance of women in the family are accepted. Assertive femininity is one step of feminism that is acceptable in the developed world, but in Iran, it has not yet fully emerged. In other words, it has not been legalized. In this model, bread-making and decision-making are the woman's responsibility, and the woman does not hesitate to let others know about this.

The second theme refers to explicit challenge, which includes two models of compulsory self-sufficiency (undesired) and persuasion (desirable). In the model of compulsory self-sufficiency, women have a kind of forced independence for reasons such as the absence of the family man at home, the family man's imprisonment, the family man's disability, or his death. It means that women are forced to be responsible for the family, take care of the children, and play the role of breadwinner.

The difference between persuasion and Assertive femininity is that although a man can be responsible for the economic role of breadwinner, he is no longer the decision maker. In Compulsory self-sufficiency, the man is not present in the family, but in the persuasion model, the family man may still be the breadwinner, but he is unable to make decisions and lead the family. Thus, the Persuasion pattern seems to be the turning point in the sense that women may come to the understanding of family relationships that they need to be only decision-makers. In this case, this model is somehow close to Assertive femininity. However, on the other side of this pattern, the woman may be convinced that the man is under much pressure, so doing household chores is difficult even for him. Furthermore, the woman takes over all the duties and accepts more responsibilities than the man at home, despite working outside the home. They step forward and take charge of the family with their desire. Persuasion is the opposite of assertive femininity. In the model of persuasion, the woman does not try to reveal that her responsibilities are more than her husband's and does not allow her husband's inability become revealed to

others. However, in assertive femininity, the woman openly fights and challenges her man and does not shy away from letting others know she bears all
the responsibilities.

The next theme refers to women's hidden and passive resistance, gradually
ending men's participation in domestic labor. In this model, the woman learns
to avoid domestic labor. It is not because of women's laziness. It is a way for
a woman to force her husband to cooperate in domestic labor. In the gradual
participation of men, they learn to participate in household chores through
socialization with a group of relatives and friends. Living in student dormito-
ries, living independently, and being in the military are some events that help
men become somewhat aware of the responsibilities of homemaking. These
events for men can be called re-socialization, which can convey fairer values
to men in the family. However, the most prominent mistake men make is that
they consider housework a woman's duty and run away from housework. Of
course, mothers and other family members should not separate household
issues between boys and girls with gender discrimination thoughts. Sometimes
it is necessary to ask the girl to do the shopping and the boy to wash the dishes.
This way parents can shift the gender roles between boys and girls, which takes
a long time after childhood.

Another theme refers to the economic triangulation of women, which usually appears when men and women are equal in terms of economic power and
have the same relative resources, such as economic and cultural capital. In this
model, women resort to an economic partner who can be their father, brother,
relative, or colleague to increase their power and get out of a position of powerlessness. Women try to increase their decision-making role in the family and
reach a balance with the men in dividing the volume of household chores with
increasing incomes and economic capital.

The last theme, the modern division of domestic labor between couples, is
the understanding or pattern of extensive participation of men and women in
household chores. In this model, men and women try to participate intellec-
tually, emotionally, and psychologically, behaviorally, and participate in gender roles as much as possible. In rethinking the division of labor, Garcia and
Tomlinson term this as "collaborative decision making."[41]

With the increase of their capabilities and changes in relative resources such
as education and jobs, women do not accept the traditional gender roles anymore and have challenged them. Of course, other factors influence women's
agency such as structural contexts in society and culture. Cultural contexts, for
example, ethnicity, can affect the presented models. It can consider women's
attitude to the division of labor as fair even when it is unequal. Nevertheless,

41   Garcia and Tomlinson, "Rethinking the Domestic Division of Labor."

due to the small number of study cases in this research result, it is impossible to give a complete opinion about the role of ethnicity in women's attitudes towards the division of labor. Therefore, we are only satisfied with the variety of models and their variety.

Another point is that the family has power relations, and like other areas of power, it contains different types of women's resistance. The amount and type of women's resistance to facing the patriarchal power structure in the family are diverse. Several factors can affect the types of women's resistance, such as the age at which women get married, women's jobs, and men's education. For example, the study of Enayat and Soroush (2018), indicated that if women marry at an older age, are employed, and live with a more educated husband, they enjoy more power in the family and show less resistance.[42] Women are looking for understanding and cooperation, and if men recognize them and have more persuasive power, they will not resist men, and the family will experience a more peaceful atmosphere. The final critical point is the importance of understanding that in the real world, there is no pure division of domestic labor, and women in the process of married life may experience various types of division of domestic labor. Therefore, the border between these identified types is very narrow, and it is not easy to recognize one from the other.

Bibliography

Aghajani, Nasrollah. (2002). "Participation of Family Members." *Strategic Studies*, No. 16.

Bales, R.F., & Parsons, T. (1956). *Family: Socialization and Interaction Process*. London: Routledge.

Blair, S.L., & Lichter, D.T. (1991). Measuring the Division of Household Labor: Gender Segregation of Housework Among American Couples. *Journal of Family Issues*, 12(1), 91–113.

Blood, R.O., Jr., & Wolfe, D.M. (1960). *Husbands and Wives: The Dynamics of Family Living*. Free Press Glencoe.

Bourdieu, P. (2001). *Masculine Domination*. Stanford: Stanford University Press.

Boyatzis, R.E. (1998). *Transforming Qualitative Information: Thematic Analysis and Code Development*. Sage Publications.

Bubeck, Diemut. (1995). *Care, Gender and Justice*. Oxford: Oxford University Press.

---

42   Halimeh Enayat & Maryam Soroush, "The Amount and Type of Women's Resistance in Facing the Power Structure in Everyday Life." *Women in Development and Politics*, 2 (25) (2018): 85–112.

Bulanda, R.E. (2004). Paternal Involvement with Children: The Influence of Gender Ideologies. *Journal of Marriage and Family*, 66(1), 40–45.

Burton, M., Brudner, L., & White, D. (1977). A Model of The Sexual Division of Labor. *American Ethnologist*, 4 (2), 227–251.

Chafetz, Janet Saltzman. (1988). The Gender Division of Labor and the Reproduction of Female Disadvantage: Toward an Integrated Theory. *Journal of Family Issues*, 9 (1), 108–131.

Collis, M. (1999). Marital Conflict and Men's Leisure: How Women Negotiate Male Power in a Small Mining Community. *Journal of Sociology*, 35(1), 60–76.

Crompton, R. (2006). *Employment and the Family: The Reconfiguration of Work and Family Life in Contemporary Societies*. New York: Cambridge University Press.

Deutsch, F.M. (1999). *Halving it All: How Equally Shared Parenting Works*. Cambridge, MA: Harvard University Press.

Deutsch, F.M. (2007). Undoing Gender. *Gender & Society*, 21(1), 106–127.

Dieckhoff, M., Gash, V., Mertens, A., & Gordo, L.R. (2016). A Stalled Revolution? What Can We Learn from Women's Drop-out to Part-time Jobs: A Comparative Analysis of Germany and the UK. *Research in Social Stratification and Mobility*, 46B, 129–140.

Duncan, S., Edwards, R., Reynolds, T., & Alldred, P. (2003). Motherhood, Paid Work and Partnering: Values and Theories. *Work, Employment and Society*, 17(2), 309–330.

Elgarte, J.M. (2008). Basic Income and the Gendered Division of Labour. *Basic Income Studies*, 3(3), 1–7.

Enayat, H. & Soroush, M. (2018). The Amount and Type of Women's Resistance in Facing the Power Structure in Everyday Life. *Women in Development and Politics*, 2(25), 85–112.

England, Paula. (2017). *Households, Employment, and Gender: A Social, Economic and Demographic View*. New York: Routledge.

England, P., & Farkas, G. (1986). *Households, Employment, and Gender: A Social, Economic and Demographic View*. New York: Aldine Publishing Company.

Evertsson, M., & Nermo, M. (2004). Dependence within Families and the Division of Labour: Comparing Sweden and the United States. *Journal of Marriage and the Family*, 66, (5), 1272–1286.

Finch, J., & Mason, J. (2003). *Negotiating Family Responsibilities*. London: Routledge.

Garcia, R. & Tomlinson, J. (2020). Rethinking the Domestic Division of Labor: Exploring Change and Continuity in the Context of Redundancy. *Sociology*, 55 (2), 300–318.

Fox, B. (2009). *When Couples Become Parents: The Creation of Gender in the Transition to Parenthood*. Toronto: University of Toronto Press.

Fraser, Nancy. (1996). *Gender Equity and the Welfare State: A Postindustrial Thought Experiment, Democracy and Difference*. Princeton: Princeton University Press.

Hochschild, Arlie. (1989). *The Second Shift*. London: Penguin Books.

Huber, J., & Spitze, G. (1981). Wives' Employment, Household Behaviors, and Sex-role Attitudes. *Social Forces*, 60(1), 150–169.

Komter, A. (1989). Hidden Power in Marriage. *Gender and Society*, 3 (2), 197–216.

Kulik, L. (2002). Marital Equality and the Quality of Long-term Marriage in Later Life. *Ageing & Society*, 22(4), 459–481.

Lee, C.K., & Beatty, S. E. (2002). Family Structure and Influence in Family Decision Making. *Journal of Consumer Marketing*, 19(1), 24–41.

Lukes, S. (2005). *Power: A Radical View*. Basingstoke: Palgrave Macmillan.

Mannino, C.A. & Deutsch, F. M. (2007). Changing the division of household labor: A negotiated process between partners. *Sex Roles*, 56(5–6), 309–324.

Maret, E., & Finlay, B. (1984). The Distribution of Household Labor Among Women in Dual-earner Families. *Journal of Marriage and the Family*, 46 (2), 357–364.

Meehan, T., Vermeer, C., & Windsor, C. (2000). Patients' Perceptions of Seclusion: A Qualitative Investigation. *Journal of Advanced Nursing*, 31(2), 370–377.

Mohanty, C.T., & Torres, L. (Eds.). (1991). *Third World Women and the Politics of Feminism*, (Vol. 632). Bloomington: Indiana University Press.

Okin, Susan Moller. (1989). *Justice, Gender and the Family*. New York: Basic Books.

O'Reilly, J., Nazio, T., & Roche, J.M. (2014). Compromising Conventions: Attitudes of Dissonance and Indifference Towards Full-time Maternal Employment in Denmark, Spain, Poland and the UK. *Work, Employment & Society*, 28(2), 168–188.

Parsons, T. & Bales, R.F. (1956). *Family Socialization and Interaction Process*. London: Routledge.

Presser, H.B. (1994). Employment Schedules Among Dual-earner Spouses and the Division of Household Labor by Gender. *American Sociological Review*, 59 (3), 348–364.

Quek, K.M.T., & Knudson-Martin, C. (2008). Reshaping Marital Power: How Dual-career Newlywed Couples Create Equality in Singapore. *Journal of Social and Personal Relationships*, 25(3), 511–532.

Strauss, A. (1978). *Negotiations: Varieties, Processes, Contexts, and Social Order*. San Francisco: Jossey-Bass.

Tomlinson, J., Olsen, W., & Purdam, K. (2009). Women Returners and Potential Returners: Employment Profiles and Labour Market Opportunities—A Case Study of the UK. *European Sociological Review*, 24(2), 1–15.

Wheelock, J. (1990). Capital Restructuring and the Domestic Economy: Family Self Respect and the Irrelevance of 'Rational Economic Man'. *Capital & Class*, 14(2), 103–141.

Zipp, J.F., Prohaska, A., & Bemiller, M. (2004). Wives, Husbands, and Hidden Power in Marriage. *Journal of Family Issues*, 25(7), 923–948.

CHAPTER 3

Structural Transformation of Women's Employment in Iran

Zahra Karimi

1 Introduction

The 1979 Islamic Revolution in Iran started a new and contradictory era for Iranian women. Due to Islamic rules and regulations, women are faced with new restrictions in society and workplaces. High ranking managerial jobs for women decreased considerably and public institutions encouraged women to retire much earlier than the formal retirement schemes. Men were prioritized for job vacancies and women's participation rate dropped in the 1980s. Yet at the same time, many religious and traditional families, especially in small towns and villages, were convinced that by the new Islamic regime, they could send their young daughters to high schools and universities to pursue their studies. This changing social attitude increased the number and proportion of women in higher education significantly.

By raising education levels, women's presence in the labor market, particularly in professional jobs started to change. As employment and earning independent income have a direct impact on women's status, most Iranian-educated women are interested in working. However, Iran's economic conditions create serious obstacles to the employment of women. Iran has experienced low and volatile economic growth during the past 4 decades and the country is not able to generate enough productive and stable jobs. In addition to the economic challenges, some cultural beliefs such as "male breadwinner" also created obstacles for women's employment; as state-owned institutions and semipublic firms prioritize men for job vacancies.[1] This policy is justified by the need to support men's income as the head of households that is beneficial for all family members.

Confronting economic and social barriers, many brilliant women started their own businesses despite the uncertainty and high risks in Iran's investment climate. The number and proportion of self-employed and entrepreneur

---

1 Maghsood Farasatkhah, "Higher Education and Labour Market." *Women Research*, 2(1) (2004): 147–163.

women have been rising in the past 3 decades; while the share of traditional employment, such as farm activities, and unpaid family work, has been decreasing. Furthermore, the growth of the number of professional women wage earners in public and private companies is much higher than their male counterparts. Therefore, women have transformed their role in Iran's labor market. If the economic situation of the country improves, women's presence in various economic sectors will increase more rapidly. This chapter investigates the causes of structural change in women's employment and its consequences on women's economic and social position in Iran.

2   Iranian Women's Education and Employment

Iranian women's share in education was relatively low before the 1979 Islamic Revolution. After the revolution, many traditional and religious families were convinced that girls must continue their studies in secondary schools and universities that are managed and run by Islamic rules.[2] So, the number and proportion of women in different educational levels increased considerably. During 1979–2019, the total number of male students in elementary and secondary schools raised by 51.6 percent (from 4.9 million to 7.4 million) while the number of female students increased by 128.6 percent (from 3 million to about 7 million) and the share of female students grew from 38.2 to 48.6 percent of the total students (Figure 3.1).

As Figure 3.1 shows, the number of students has decreased since the late 1990s, according to the change in the age structure of Iran's population. Yet during 1979–2019, the gap between male and female students was steadily decreasing. It is noteworthy that a higher level of women's education changed their attitude towards fewer children and reduced family size since the late 1980s. The family size dropped from 5 in 1980 to 3.2 in 2021.[3] Similar change was experienced in the tertiary level. The number of male university students increased from 121,000 in 1979 to 1,676,800 in 2019 but the number of their female counterparts rose from 54,000 to 1,523,200. So, the share of women among university students jumped from about 30 percent to more than 47 percent.[4]

---

2   Pooya Alaedini & Mohamad Reza Razavi, "Women's Participation and Employment in Iran: A Critical Examination." *Critique: Critical Middle Eastern Studies*, 14(1) (2005): 57–73.

3   Iran Statistics Centre, *Employment and Unemployment Surveys*, Tehran. (2022).

4   Ibid.

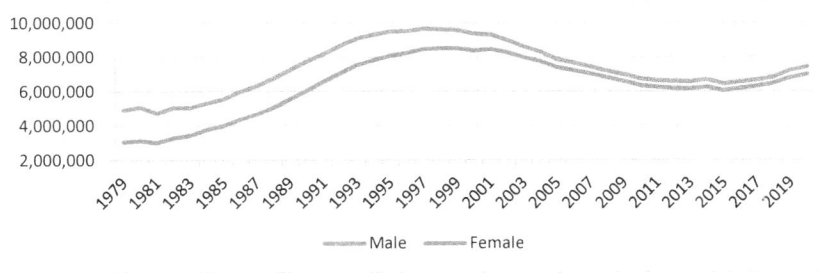

FIGURE 3.1   Elementary and secondary school students
        SOURCE: IRAN STATISTICS CENTRE 2022

The main reasons for such a huge change in female share among students were the support of the Islamic Republic for women's education and the decline in the number of children in middle and low-income families since the late 1980s.[5] Households with a few children can afford to support the education of their children, both boys and girls. Iranian parents are interested in their daughters' empowerment for securing good jobs and being financially independent when they are married. Education plays a crucial role in building women's capacity to capture economic opportunities and to establish competitive businesses.[6] Highly educated women enthusiastically enter the labor market after graduation. In addition to women's high education level and their tendency to enter the labor market and their demand for similar job opportunities with their male counterparts, inflation, economic hardship and declining family's real income, have forced many women to work to cover parts of the living costs. It is noteworthy that increasing women's presence in economic activities is an excellent opportunity to benefit from the huge investment in education.[7]

3   Structural Change in Women's Employment

Despite the rapid increase in women's education level, their presence in the labor market still is very weak. The female participation rate was about 13 percent in 1976. It increased to 17.44 in 2019, just before the Coronavirus pandemic,

---

5   Homa Hoodfar, "Devices and Desires, Population Policy and Gender Roles in the Islamic Republic." *Middle East Report*, 24(190) (1994): 11–17.

6   Hadi Salehi Esfahani & Parastoo Shajari, "Gender, Education, Family Structure, and the Allocation of Labor in Iran." *Middle East Development Journal*, 4(02) (2012): 1250008-1–1250008-40.

7   World Economic Forum, The Global Gender Gap Report. (2022).

and dropped to 13.84 in 2020. Women's economic activities have not changed considerably. However, there are great changes in employment structure and the combination of skilled and unskilled jobs for women. Investment in human capital by households for both sons and daughters has changed some of the features of Iran's labor market. The most important change in the structure of Iranian women's employment is the rise of women's entrepreneurship and professional jobs and the considerable decline in women's employment in low-value added and unpaid family works. Furthermore, as Allen et al. (2007) shows rising unemployment encourages many women to start their own businesses as self-employed or entrepreneurs to escape unemployment and poverty.[8] Sarfaraz (2017) finds that in Iran high unemployment rate among educated women inspires them to start their own businesses.[9] However, Bahramitash and Esfahani (2011) indicate, an increasing number of women entrepreneurs are interested to use their talents and skills to run successful businesses and the family financial needs have a minor role in their decision for starting economic activities.[10] Therefore, various reasons motivate women to enter into the labor market and fight for achieving success and financial independence.

3.1   *Women in High Skilled and Professional Jobs*

During the past 4 decades, many educated and talented women started their own businesses in various economic activities. From 1976 to 2019, the number of women entrepreneurs increased by 812 percent (from 5358 to 48889). Many women also started their own businesses as self-employed. In this period, the number of self-employed women increased by 737 percent (from 130,693 to 1,094,124 persons). In 2019, more than 26 percent of active Iranian women were entrepreneurs or self-employed. While in 1976, these rates were 2.9 and 4.7 percent, these rates increased to 5.5 and 12.2 percent respectively (Table 3.1). It indicates that from 1976 to 2019, despite social and legal restraints, the annual growth rates of women entrepreneurs (19.3 percent) and self-employed (17.6 percent) were much higher than their male counterparts (4.6 and 4.7 percent respectively). These great changes show that families support women's investment in economic activities. The share of women entrepreneurs and self-employed is rising rapidly in various sectors, such as clothing, toys and

8   I. Elaine Allen, Nan Langowitz, & Maria Minniti, *Global Entrepreneurship Monitor: 2006 Report on Women and Entrepreneurship*. The Center for Women's Leadership: Babson College, 2007.

9   Leyla Sarfaraz, *Women's Entrepreneurship in Iran: Role Models of Growth-Oriented Iranian Women Entrepreneurs*. Springer, 2017.

10   Roksana Bahramitash & Hadi Salehi Esfahani, *Veiled Employment*. New York: Syracuse University Press, 2011.

TABLE 3.1   Women's employment status in Iran (1976–2019)

	Total	Entrepreneurs	Self-employed	Private wage earners	Unpaid family workers	Public wage earners
1976						
Men & women	8,799,420	182,229	2,810,211	3,071,927	1,021,312	1,673,092
Men	57,587,400	176,871	2,679,518	2,749,781	525,589	1,427,174
Women	1,212,020	5,358	130,693	322,146	495,723	245,918
2019						
Men & women	24,273,517	889,963	8,939,097	9,658,590	1,195,951	3,589,916
Men	19,952,992	841,074	7,844,973	8,169,331	469,957	2,627,657
Women	4,320,525	48,889	1,094,124	1,489,259	725,994	962,259
1976–2019						
Men's increase	12,365,592	664,203	5,165,455	5,419,550	−55,632	1,200,483
Women's increase	3,108,505	43,531	963,431	1,167,113	230,271	716,341
Men's annual growth	3.9	8.9	4.6	4.7	−0.3	2.0
Women's annual growth	6.1	19.3	17.6	8.6	1.1	6.9

SOURCE: IRAN STATISTICS CENTRE 2022

foodstuffs. Personal satisfaction, the motive to gain more power, and economic needs are the main sources of motivation for women entrepreneurs.[11]

From 1976 to 2019, the number of self-employed women increased from 130 thousand to more than 1 million. A large part of women who could not find job were added to the group of self-employed (Table 3.1). For instance, in 2020, more than 17000 women taxi drivers were working in newly established

---

11   Roksana Bahramitash. *Women's Entrepreneurship: Contemporary Practice.* The Oxford Encyclopedia of Islam and Women, 2013.

E-Hailing services firms. Most of them work as self-employed. Many of these laborers are highly educated workforce but they cannot use their skills, and had to start this job as the last choice.

An increasing number of women enter into modern and growing sectors like information technology, electronics and transportation. Access to telecommunication in urban and rural areas and the use of electronic commerce facilitate their activities. Social media, such as Instagram and WhatsApp, have played a very important role in women's employment in the past 3 decades. Educated and skilled women use social media to introduce their own products or advertise the productions and services of other companies for their potential customers. Many women start online classes for sports, like Yuga, and education, such as English courses. Successful activities of women entrepreneurs in Iran inspire the young generation to follow suit to overcome all challenges and realize their own dreams.

Despite the high annual growth of women entrepreneurship during 1976–2019 (19.3 percent) which is much higher than the growth of their male counterparts (8.9 percent), the share of women among Iranian entrepreneurs is still low (5.5 percent). However, the share of women in self-employment in Iran is 12.2 percent. These differences show that it is much easier to start a business as self-employed, which generally needs lower capital and management skills and does not require many various permissions from different government offices. It must be mentioned that when the economic condition is more favorable, entrepreneurship will grow more rapidly. Many Iranian women entrepreneurs established their own businesses in the 2000s when the economic situation was relatively good and Iran had friendly relationships with most of the developing and developed countries, especially in the MENA region.[12]

There is a widespread concern that the rise in female participation rate will deteriorate the unemployment problem. Some of government policies, such as boosting birthrate, are designed to reward housework and discourage women's participation in the labor market. It is formally announced that being married and having children are high advantages in employment assessment in government entities. Therefore, it is no surprise that women professionals who are not married and do not have any children, have more difficulties being employed in government institutions. Such policies actually guarantee more jobs for men. In fact, many active women do not occupy men's positions in companies. Women entrepreneurs create new job opportunities in deprived regions or in special fields that are not attractive to men. As an example, Sara Shahverdi, started her motorcycle repair shop in Barzin village in Zanjan

---

12   Zahra Karimi, Women's Entrepreneurship and Political Situation. Unpublished.

province, 57 Kilometers away from the nearest city—Khodabandeh,[13] which is a traditional region in Iran. But she could convince her husband and her fellow villagers that a woman can do various jobs competently.[14] Haydeh Shirzadi is another excellent example of an Iranian social and economic entrepreneur who was born in a deprived village in the West of Iran. She continued her education in Germany and received her Ph.D. in Environment Protection. She returned to Iran, and after overcoming opposition from various institutions to gain the necessary permissions, she established the Kermanshah Recycling and Composting Company in 1998, during the reformist Government. The company processes and changes the harmful waste into useful fertilizers. At present, she continues her work in Kermanshah despite unfavorable business environment and difficulties of importing machinery and equipment because of US sanctions against Iran.[15]

The number of educated women working in professional jobs in public and private companies is rising. During 1976–2019, the number of women wage earners in private firms increased from 322 to 1489; and in the meantime, women employees in public institutions rose from 245 to 965,000. In sum, the number of women wage earners in public and private entities increased by 291 and 361 percent respectively (5 times more than in 1976). Among women wage earners, the highest rise was related to specialists and highly skilled workers; their share in women's employment rose from 15.5 percent in 1976 to 36.6 percent in 2020. The number of women in management jobs also increased significantly in this period (from 40,000 in 1976 to more than 704,000 in 2020). Thus, there is a structural change in women's position in Iran's labor market, from unskilled rural workers to skilled urban workers. Transformation in women's job positions strengthened their social and economic status. Yet Iranian competent women try hard to change traditional beliefs and encourage highly educated youths not to be afraid of various obstacles. It is noteworthy that while the share of women in low-value-added and unskilled jobs has declined from 52 to 30 percent, highly skilled and specialized jobs grew from 15.5 percent to more than 37.1 percent of women employment (Table 3.2).

Although Iranian women's share in professional jobs increased significantly in the past decades, their presence at the management level remained very low. Men generally have monopolized positions in high-ranking management of public and private entities. Although there are no rules and regulations to ban women's management in public and private firms, there is a glass ceiling for

---

13   A small city in Zanjan province.
14   Sarfaraz, Women's Entrepreneurship in Iran.
15   Karimi. Women's Entrepreneurship.

TABLE 3.2 Transformation in women's jobs (1976–2019)

	Total	Scientific & professional jobs	High ranking managers & staffs	Clerical & office jobs	Vendors & service providers	Farms & fishering jobs	Drivers & manufacturing workers	Unspecified
1976								
Men & women	8,799,420	555,745	40,557	437,682	1,029,000	2,983,603	3,308,676	444,157
Men	7,587,400	367,889	39,209	374,342	953,609	2,756,966	2,668,116	427,269
Women	1,212,020	187,856	1,348	63,340	75,391	226,637	640,560	16,888
2019								
Men & women	24,273,517	4,006,471	762,896	809,042	3,676,778	3,323,859	11,208,245	486,226
Men	19,952,992	2,547,328	619,200	585,497	3,156,649	2,666,138	9,899,728	478,453
Women	4,320,525	1,459,143	143,696	223,545	520,129	657,721	1,308,516	7,773
1976–2019								
Men's increase	12,365,592	2,179,439	579,991	211,155	2,203,040	-90,828	7,231,612	51,184
Women's increase	3,108,505	1,271,287	142,348	160,205	444,738	431,084	667,956	-9,115
Men's annual growth	3.9	14.1	35.2	1.3	5.5	-0.1	6.5	0.3
Women's annual growth	6.1	16.1	251.4	6.0	14.0	4.5	2.5	-1.3

SOURCE: IRAN STATISTICS CENTRE 2022

women's attendance in high-level management in Iran, similar to most other countries. Obvious and hidden measures are still applied to prevent women from getting high management positions. Yet, as Table 3.2 indicates, from 1976 to 2019, the growth rate of top management positions for women was much higher than for men. It shows that Iranian women are trying hard to break the glass ceiling too; as the share of women in high management jobs increased from 3.3 percent in 1976 to 18.8 percent in 2019.[16]

3.2   Women in Traditional and Low-Skilled Jobs

In the past 3 decades, the number of children in urban and rural families decreased rapidly. By declining the size of Iranian families, children became valuable assets even in middle- and low-income families and education for both girls and boys became more important for their parents. Traditionally all children in middle- and low-income families helped in field works and handicraft production, especially carpet weaving, since early childhood. But nowadays child labor has reduced considerably. Iranian families generally support the education of their children, yet unpaid family workers are still present among the poorest families. Anyhow, the share of unpaid family workers in total employment has dropped significantly. While in 1976, 11.6 percent of Iran's employed workforce was unpaid family workers, this rate dropped to 4.9 percent in 2019. This change was much larger for women. As Table 3.1 indicates, in 1976, 40.9 percent of employed women were unpaid family workers. This rate decreased to 16.8 percent (these rates for their male counterparts were 6.9 and 2.4 respectively). At present a great part of child labor is related to migrant Afghan families residing in Iran. Karimi (2011) shows that most children carpet weavers in Kashan—a city in the central part of Iran that is very famous for its beautiful and high-quality carpets—are Afghan migrant workers.[17]

During 1976–2019, the share of employed women in rural areas which are concentrated in farm works and handicrafts decreased from 62 percent to 28 percent of total women's employment; and the share of women employment in urban areas raised from 38 to 72 percent.[18] Therefore, the great transformation of Iran labor market was reflected in two aspects of women employment: significant increase in the share of women in high-value-added professional jobs in urban areas, and decline in the proportion of unpaid family workers

16   Iran Statistics Centre, Employment and Unemployment Surveys.
17   Zahra Karimi, "The Effects of Trade Liberalization on Gender Inequality in Iran: The Case of Women Carpet Weavers," in *Veiled Employment*, eds. Roksana Bahramitash and Hadi Salehi Esfahani, New York: Syracuse University Press, 2011.
18   Iran Statistics Centre, Employment and Unemployment Surveys.

and farm works in villages. Despite these important developments, women's traditional role in family and society is still one of the main barriers to their active presence in the labor market, especially in small towns and villages. Most women in villages and small towns cannot migrate to big cities to find jobs. Generally, women who leave their families and move to big cities in the hope of finding a better life end up in prostitution, and collaboration with criminals, especially in the illegal drug trade and drug addiction, as there are not many firms in big cities that are interested in employing women. But men who migrate from towns and villages can work in various industries and services in cities with the help of their friends and relatives.[19]

3.3   *Women's Vulnerability during the Coronavirus Pandemic*

The Coronavirus pandemic had a deleterious effect on women's employment in Iran, like many other countries around the world. During 2018–2019, Iranian women lost more than 660,000 job opportunities. More than 14,600 women entrepreneurs quit their businesses. 232,000 self-employed women and 247,000 women wage earners lost their jobs. It must be noted that a great number of women who lost their jobs, get out of the labor market. Therefore, during the worst stagflation, unemployment rates remained relatively low. Many women, especially in services, lost their jobs and returned to their jobs much later than their male counterparts. Between the years 2019 and 2020, 16.9 percent of women lost their jobs, while this rate for men was 2.3 percent. In the same period, the number of active women decreased by 18.7 percent; this rate for men was 2.8 percent.[20] This large difference clearly shows the volatility of women's activity. When there is a possibility to find jobs, many women enter into the labor market and when they lose their jobs, they get out of the labor market and become inactive again. The impact of the Coronavirus pandemic shows that despite the improvement of women's status in Iran's labor market, as entrepreneurs and professional employees, female workers are still more vulnerable at the time of external shocks compared to male workers.

4   Structural Change in Iranian Households

Iranian families experienced great changes during the past 3 decades. In addition to declining family size, there is also a significant change in the traditional model of the man as the breadwinner. At present, household members with

---

19   Karimi, Women's Entrepreneurship and Political Situation.
20   Iran Statistics Centre, Employment and Unemployment Surveys.

better jobs and higher education and income generally have deeper influence in family decision-making and have more power to guide the household. In many Iranian families, women's income is the main source for covering household expenses. In formal statistics, all these women are not named as the head of the household, because of social taboo against the families who do not have a male member as the family head. Therefore, many employed women who provide the main part of the family income, introduce their father, brother, or husband as the head of the household in census and surveys. So, the number of female-headed households in Iran is underestimated and must be much higher than formal statistics.

However, during 2006–2019, the number and proportion of female-headed households in Iran increased from 9.5 to 13.7 percent of the total households. So, the customary belief about men as the heads of households is no longer the general household structure in Iran. It is worth noting that a growing number of highly educated and employed women decide not to get married and remain single. During 2011–2019, the share of single persons among female-headed households rose from 37.3 to 41.5 percent. These highly educated women usually have professional jobs and earn good incomes. They usually decide not to get married or ask for divorce when face violence. Empirical studies also show that women who have independent income and higher education tolerate physical and mental violence much less than inactive women with lower education.[21] Therefore, education and employment changed the traditional household type in two ways: many ordinary families have actually female as the head of the family; and increasing number of educated women who have independent and sufficient income, live as a single person family. People, especially in big cities respect the new women's social and economic roles; as they can see women are successful in managing the family affairs and generally children of employed women are more successful in their education.

A growing number of Iranian women is working outside the house and caring for family members. Generally, family is the priority of active Iranian women. While they try their best to achieve their goals in their workplaces outside their houses, they allocate enough time and effort to family affairs to meet the needs of their husband, children, and parents. Many employed women have the full responsibility of their babies or teenage children, and their husband does not want or cannot help them. Anyhow, most active women are successful in managing housework and their business affairs, but they have to reduce their own leisure time. As they generally believe that they must prove to their family members that working outside the home does not harm their

---

21   Farasatkhah, "Higher Education and Labour Market."

family. Iranian women must be really powerful to implement several duties in the house to be recognized as good wife and mother, and also in the workplace where they have to prove that they are not weaker than men.[22]

Thus, many Iranian households faced a great cultural change, as educated women are not mere housewives, but they want to contribute to the family income and insist on equal rights in decision-making about important family affairs. Women's higher education and better jobs have intergenerational effects as well. Girls who have educated mothers generally have higher education levels, enjoy more freedom in choosing their husbands and marry later than girls with uneducated mothers.[23]

4.1   Iranian Women's Status in the Household and Society

In addition to the economic problems, there are social obstacles that prevent many women from working. According to the traditional belief, men are families' breadwinners. Many occupations are in the monopoly of men. Although some entrepreneurs emphasize that female employees are more careful in precise work, and are more patient and cooperative than their male counterparts, many public and private managers believe that women lack enough energy for hard work, and their technical knowledge and learning capability are low. They have various family responsibilities that have a negative impact on their job. Public entities, especially during economic crises, prioritize men for various occupations. New policies related to raising child birth created more pressure on educated women to get married and have more children to be able to get employed in public universities and research institutes. The Islamic Republic is interested in increasing its population growth to tackle the problem of an aging society in the near future. Such rules and regulations create tough conditions for women professionals to find jobs.[24]

Economic and social barriers for professional women encourage them to migrate to other countries. An increasing number of highly educated and skilled women, who cannot find suitable jobs and acceptable living conditions in Iran, migrate to other countries and become successful experts, even distinguished scientists, like Maryam Mirzakhani, and reputable entrepreneurs such as Anousheh Ansari, in their host countries and even all around the world. Yet

22   M. Farahmand & E.M. Pour, "Child Marriage and Helplessness," *Contemporary Sociology,* 9(17) (2020): 115–145.

23   Haleh Afshar, "Women, Marriage and the State in Iran," in *Women, State and Ideology: Studies from Africa and Asia,* ed. Haleh Afshar, (70–86). New York: New York University Press, 1987.

24   Haleh Esfandiari, "The Majles and Women's Issues in the Islamic Republic of Iran," *In the Eye of the Storm: Women in Post-Revolutionary Iran,* eds. Mahnaz Afkhami, Erika Friedl. New York: Syracuse University Press, 1994.

obstacles do not prevent motivated women from entering the labor market. Iranian women know that they must be very competent to overcome these barriers and be employed; and they must make more efforts in their work, compared to their male counterparts, to keep their jobs and try their best to show their ability in workplaces to gain self-satisfaction and in the meantime increase the family income and welfare.[25]

To explore the impact of women's education and employment on their status in households and society, I conducted a field survey among 174 educated men and women in Sept. 2021, to study the effects of economic changes on the women's position in their families, among their friends and society. 60 men participated in this survey which enabled me to compare the status of men and women in similar conditions. 64.4 percent of the respondents were between 20–30 years old, 25.9 percent were between 30 to 40 years old, and 9.8 percent were more than 40 years old. 16 percent of respondents had high school diploma and 84 percent had university degrees. 36.6 percent of respondent were married and 63.4 percent were single. 55 percent were employed and 45 percent were unemployed, mostly inactive, such as university students. The result of the survey shows that for 44.8 women and 42.9 percent of men in the sample, employment is important for their financial independence; and most women are really interested in getting a job to be financially independent. They also believed that employment increases their respect in their family; 27.8 percent of men and 22 percent of men stated that being employed has a positive impact on their position in the households (Figure 3.2). Only 3.4 percent of female respondents did not experience more respect in the family because of their employment.

Employment increases the respect of men and women among their friends. 83.4 percent of women and 78.8 percent of men in the sample stated that employment promoted their status among their friends and relatives. Only 3.3 percent of women did not experience any respect among their friends because of their employment. 87.7 percent of women and 86.1 percent of men believed that employment improved their self-esteem. The result of our survey shows that employment increases the power of 61.4 percent of women in decision-making affairs in the household. This rate is 71.4 percent for men. While employment has a great positive effect on women's status in the family, this impact for men is still bigger for men in the sample (Figure 3.3).

Employment increases social activities for both men and women. 61.4 percent of women in the sample stated that their social activities increased because of their employment. This rate for men is about 70 percent. Employed

25   Azadeh Kian "Gendered Occupation and Women's Status in Post-revolutionary Iran." *Middle Eastern Studies*, 31(3) (1995): 407–421.

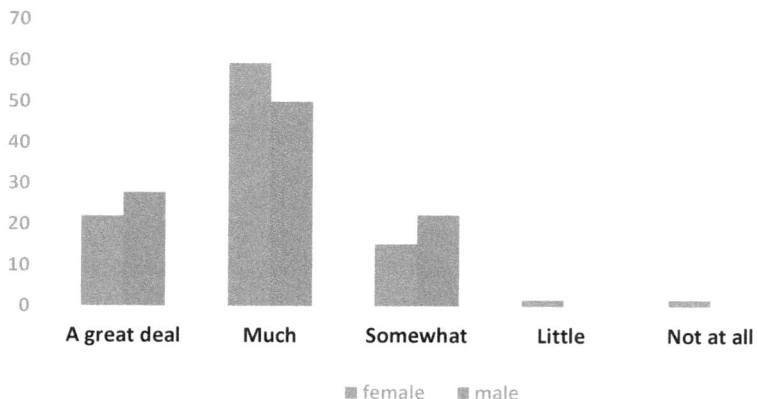

FIGURE 3.2 The impact of employment on respondent's status in the household
            SOURCE: THE SURVEY'S RESULT

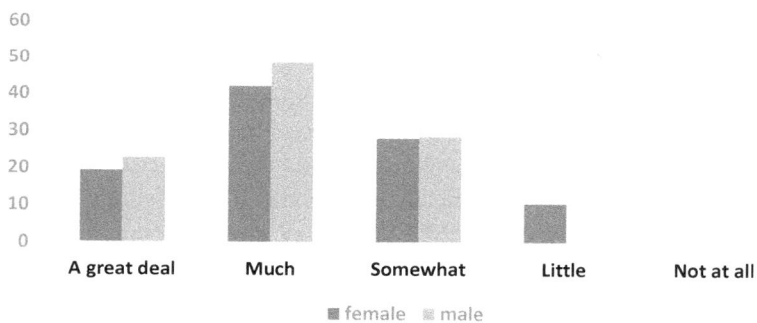

FIGURE 3.3 Employment impact on position in the household for decision-making about
            important family affairs
            SOURCE: THE SURVEY'S RESULT

women's participation in political activities is much more limited than men. The procedure for confirming the eligibility of candidates has also a negative impact. Many women are concerned about being rejected by the Guardian Council which may have negative consequences for their jobs. All respondents were interested in working. While 47.2 percent of female students believed that they could find a job in accordance with their education and skills, this rate for their male counterparts was 56 percent. Contrarily, 20.7 percent of women and 8 percent of men were very pessimistic about finding suitable jobs relevant to their education and skills. Optimism encourages educated women to keep looking for good jobs (Figure 3.4).

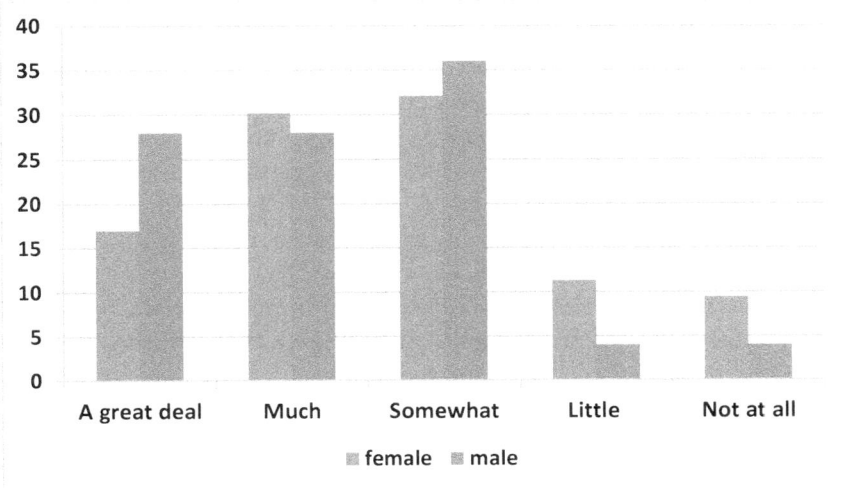

FIGURE 3.4 Optimism about finding a job in accordance to education and skills
SOURCE: THE SURVEY'S RESULT

The field survey confirms that an increasing number of Iranian-educated women are willing to be socially and economically active. Traditional beliefs, various obstacles of government policies, and economic hardship do not impede them from entering the labor market and try their best to secure suitable jobs.[26] Educated women fight against gender discrimination to improve women's status in the labor market. It is necessary to change the laws, rules and regulations that limit women's rights to move up the ladder of economic and social hierarchy and facilitate women's presence in various aspects of social life.

5   Conclusion

Since the 1979 Islamic Revolution, the number and proportion of women increased at various educational levels; as religious and traditional families were convinced that girls are safe in the Islamic environment of schools and

---

26   Other studies corroborate this sentiment. For instance, See Mehrangiz Kar, "Iranian Law and Women's Rights", *Muslim World Journal of Human Rights*, 4 (1) (2007): 1–13; Azadeh Kian, "Women and Politics in Post-Islamist Iran: The Gender Conscious Drive to Change." *British Journal of Middle Eastern Studies*, 24(1) (1997): 75–96; Valentine M. Moghadam, "Women's Employment Issues in Contemporary Iran: Problems and Prospects in the 1990s." *Iranian Studies*, 28 (3–4) (1995): 175–200.

universities. Declining family size accelerated this trend as a middle-income family, with one child or at most two children, afforded to finance studies of children at undergraduate and postgraduate levels. So, the number of female university students increased considerably. Iranian families support girls' education to guarantee their better life. A growing number of Iranian parents believe that employment is vital for women's economic and financial independence and social status.

An increasing number of university graduate women entered into the labor market; highly educated and skilled women were increasingly employed in public and private entities; and the proportion of professional jobs in total female employment increased significantly. Women have had such achievements despite serious economic and social difficulties. Iran's economy is not able to generate sufficient productive and stable job opportunities, as employment generation is closely related to investment growth.[27] During the last decade (2011–2021), investment declined especially due to harsh international sanctions. Competent and skilled women try their best to secure suitable jobs; and in many cases when they face barriers to work as wage earners, they start their own businesses as self-employed.

High investment risks could not stop women entrepreneurs who established their own firms in deprived regions. At present, there are many successful women entrepreneurs in various economic activities, such as recycling waste, clothing, animal husbandry and IT services. Thus, the Iranian labor market experienced significant changes related to women's employment in the past 4 decades. The number and proportion of women self-employed and entrepreneurs increased significantly which show family financial and emotional support of women's economic activities, because women generally cannot start their businesses without the help of their families. A growing number of educated and skilled women find professional jobs in public and private entities. At the same time, the share of unpaid family workers declined considerably among Iranian-employed women. In sum, the presence of women in high-value-added jobs in big cities has increased rapidly, while the share of low-value-added jobs in small towns and villages declined considerably among Iranian active women.

Although women's situation in Iran's labor market, especially in urban areas, has improved in past decades, they are still more vulnerable than their male counterparts during economic shocks. The Coronavirus pandemic destroyed

---

27   Zahra Arasti, "An Empirical Study on the Causes of Business Failure in Iranian Context." *African Journal of Business Management*, 5(17) (2011): 7488–7498.

many jobs in industries and services, yet its impact on women's jobs was worse than men. Iranian women who worked in the services sector suffered the most during the pandemic and its related economic recession.

Despite the dramatic increase, female participation is still low in Iran since when women's employment in high-value-added professional jobs in big cities increases, the low-value-added jobs in traditional sectors like carpet weaving and farm works declines in small towns and villages. Difficulties in getting jobs do not stop thousands of Iranian women to start their own businesses or find jobs to obtain financial independence and a stronger voice. Yet, if Iran's economy functions properly and generates enough jobs, a great part of "*inactive*" women will enter the labor market to use their capabilities and skills in various jobs and increase the income and welfare level of their families. The conducted survey shows that employment means a better position in the family and society for most Iranian women. The high self-esteem of competent Iranian women helps them to overcome various obstacles and motivates them to follow their goals with more power and energy.

If Iranian women are constrained from starting businesses or being employed, the country will be deprived of the competencies and creativity of half of the population. The necessary condition for accelerating women's presence in Iran's labor market is to vitalize the economy, by creating socio-economic stability and providing an encouraging business environment with low risks for private businesses. The sufficient condition is changing cultural attitudes about women's capabilities and skills, and improving social beliefs regarding equal rights for women and men in the labor market. In other words, investment and production growth are necessary prerequisites for a rapid increase in women's employment in high-value-added jobs. Solving international problems and lifting sanctions will pave the way for high growth of domestic and foreign investment in Iran. In addition, facilitating business activities for the private sector, and fighting corruption will motivate Iranian and foreign firms to generate stable and productive employment opportunities for educated and skilled men and women in Iran.

Bibliography

Afshar, H. (1987). Women, Marriage and the State in Iran. In H. Afshar (Ed.). *Women, State and Ideology: Studies from Africa and Asia* (pp. 70–86). New York: New York University Press.

Alaedini, P., & Razavi, M.R. (2005). Women's Participation and Employment in Iran: A Critical Examination. *Critique: Critical Middle Eastern Studies*, 14(1), 57–73.

Allen, I.E., Langowitz, N., & Minniti, M. (2007). *Global Entrepreneurship Monitor: 2006 Report on Women and Entrepreneurship*. The Center for Women's Leadership: Babson College.

Arasti, Z. (2011). An Empirical Study on the Causes of Business Failure in Iranian Context. *African Journal of Business Management*, 5(17), 7488–7498.

Bahramitash, R., & Esfahani, H.S. (2011). *Veiled Employment*. New York: Syracuse University Press.

Bahramitash, R. (2013). Women's Entrepreneurship: Contemporary Practice. *The Oxford Encyclopedia of Islam and Women*.

Bahramitash, R., & Esfahani, H.S. (2014). Gender and entrepreneurship in Iran. In N. Chamlou & M. Karshenas (Eds.) *Women, Work and Welfare in the Middle East and North Africa*. London: Imperial College Press.

Esfandiari, H. (1994). The Majles and Women's Issues in the Islamic Republic of Iran. In M. Afkhami and E. Friedl (Eds.) *In the Eye of the Storm: Women in Post-Revolutionary Iran*, New York: Syracuse University Press.

Esfahani, H. S., & Shajari, P. (2012). Gender, Education, Family Structure, and the Allocation of Labor in Iran. *Middle East Development Journal*, 4(02), 1250008-1–1250008-40.

Farasatkhah, M. (2004). Higher Education and Labour Market. *Women Research*, 2(1), 147–163.

Farahmand, M., & Pour E.M., (2020). Child Marriage and Helplessness. *Contemporary Sociology*, 9(17), 115–145.

Hoodfar, H. (1994). Devices and Desires: Population Policy and Gender Roles in the Islamic Republic. *Middle East Report*, 24(190), 11–17.

Iran Statistics Centre (2022). *Employment and Unemployment Surveys*. Tehran.

Kar, M. (2007). Iranian Law and Women's Rights, *Muslim World Journal of Human Rights*, 4 (1), 1–13.

Kar, M. (2000). *Women in Iran's Labour Market*. Roshangaran Publisher.

Karimi, Z. (2011). The Effects of Trade Liberalization on Gender Inequality in Iran: The Case of Women Carpet Weavers. In R. Bahramitash & H.S. Esfahani (Eds.). *Veiled Employment*. New York: Syracuse University Press.

Karimi, Z. (2022). Women's Entrepreneurship and Political Situation. Unpublished.

Kian, A. (1995). Gendered Occupation and Women's Status in Post-revolutionary Iran. *Middle Eastern Studies*, 31(3), 407–421.

Kian, A. (1997). Women and Politics in Post-Islamist Iran: The Gender Conscious Drive to Change. *British Journal of Middle Eastern Studies*, 24(1), 75–96.

Moghadam, V. (1995). Women's Employment Issues in Contemporary Iran: Problems and Prospects in the 1990s. *Iranian Studies*, 28 (3–4), pp. 175–200.

Sarfaraz, L. (2017). *Women's Entrepreneurship in Iran: Role Models of Growth-Oriented Iranian Women Entrepreneurs*. Springer.

World Economic Forum. (2022). *The Global Gender Gap Report*.

CHAPTER 4

The Socio-historical Process of Women's Scientific Progress in Iran

Afsaneh Tavassoli and Maliheh Abedi

1 Introduction

More than two centuries have passed since Mary Wolston Craft of England wrote a letter to the legislators of the French Revolution declaring that free education was not only the right of men but also the right of women as half of the human race. In her book, "A Vindication of the Rights of Women," she called for equal rights for women and men to be enshrined in post-revolutionary law.[1] Although this demand was not met at the time, the tireless struggle for humanity continues to this day, where women are equal to men with the right to free education in most countries of the world as a natural right. Women in Iran, like in other countries, are going through a tortuous path through patriarchy, and their success in the social institution of education is perhaps more remarkable than any other social institution. The number of women attending institutions of higher education in Iran has been steadily increasing since 1989. However, it should not be overlooked that there are obstacles and limitations left over from the historical period of agriculture with the reconstruction of gender stereotypes, even in education wherein we are still facing gender gaps. However, these gaps are at the level of global gaps. Studies show that women in Iran broke the barrier of educational patriarchy like other women in the world, and they will gradually overcome other obstacles along with women in the world.

Today, to determine the development status of countries, one of the important indicators is to measure the situation of women compared to men in four dimensions. Economic participation, political participation, education and health are the most important areas in which gender gaps are considered as indicators of development. Surveys show that men and women on the global average have experienced differences in achieving equality in health and education, but their level of economic and political participation continues to suffer from deep differences. The purpose of this chapter is to examine to what

---

1 Mary Wollstonecraft, *A Vindication of the Rights of Woman*, ed. Miriam Brody. Harmondsworth: Penguin, 2004.

extent society has been successful in making the gender parity of education. Iranian women, despite facing many restrictions, have been able to overcome many obstacles. In fact, in line with global changes, gender differences in health and education in Iran are disappearing. "Science and education" allow Iranian women to achieve dignity and pursue high-standard goals. By acquiring science and technology, women will gain awareness and knowledge on the one hand, and on the other hand, they will be able to secure the position they like while guaranteeing their independence and progress.

2   Women's Struggle to Acquire Knowledge throughout History

More than two centuries ago, Mary Wollstonecraft from England, wrote a letter to the legislators of the French Revolution declaring that free education was also the right of women as half of humanity.[2] She called for the establishment of equal rights for women and men in the laws after the French Revolution. She knew that if this equal-gender right is not achieved, the future of humanity will not revolve around equality and justice. Although this demand was not fulfilled at the time, the determined struggle for humanity has continued to this day, where women are equal to men with the right to free education in most countries of the world as a natural right. In her review of Jean-Jacques Rousseau's book "Emile," Craft admits that education is a must for women as well as for men, and raises an issue under the title of "Masculine Reason" through which she declares that women also have rational power.[3] This was a matter of doubt until then and women were considered to have feelings and men to have a reason, and this became the basis of inequality in the education of men and women.

In theological, philosophical, literary and scientific thought, and in popular beliefs, a "female" is shown to be mentally weaker and emotionally stronger, while a "male" is shown as mentally superior, strong, and mostly rational. As a result, the lack of success, leadership, and representation of women in fields that emphasize rationality, especially in the fields of science, technology, engineering, and mathematics, were considered simply as a consequence of the different natures and capacities of men and women.[4] Over the past 50 years, many of these beliefs have become obsolete with the progress of

---

2   Ibid.
3   Ibid.
4   Evelyn Fox Keller & Gertrude Scharff-Goldhaber, "Reflections on Gender and Science." *American Journal of Physics*, 55 (3) (1987): 284–286.

women in academia and workplaces, especially in Arts and Humanities.[5] However, a great number of thinkers in the field of feminism contend that science and sociology have a male basis and are male-dominated.[6] The rare presence of women in science throughout history is evidence of this male basis. For example, women's participation in medicine occurred in several early Western civilizations. The study of natural philosophy in ancient Greece was free for women. Women participated in the first alchemy in the 1st or 2nd centuries AD. During the Middle Ages, religious assemblies were important places for the education of women, and some of these societies provided women with opportunities to contribute to scientific research. Historians interested in gender and science have conducted studies on women's scientific efforts and achievements as well as their obstacles, and strategies used to get their work reviewed and accepted in major scientific journals and other publications. The historical, critical, and sociological examination of these issues has become an academic discipline.

Meanwhile, the 11th century which witnessed the emergence of the first universities, i.e., when formal academic education began, was an era when many women were deprived of university education.[7] The first well-known woman to hold a university chair in a scientific discipline was the 18th-century Italian scientist Laura Bassi. It can be argued that this Italian female physicist earned this official title since Botany, outside of the university, was the science that benefited most from the contributions of women in the early modern era. The attitude towards the education of women in medical fields in Italy has been more liberal than in other regions, and this facilitated the presence of women in the universities of that country as lecturers. Although gender roles were largely deterministic in the 18th century, women made significant advances in science. During the 19th century, women were excluded from most formal scientific education. However, during this period, they began to enter educated societies and intellectual circles. At the end of the 19th century, the emergence of colleges for women provided opportunities for their education. Polish-born Marie Curie, who conducted pioneering research on nuclear fission, was the first woman to receive the Nobel Prize twice in physics and chemistry.[8]

---

5 Lydia Saad, *A Sea Change in Support or Working Women*. Washington, D.C.: Gallup, 2017.

6 A. Geske Dijkstra & Lucia C. Hanmer, "Measuring Socio-Economic GENDER Inequality: Towards an Alternative to the UNDP Gender-Related Development Index." *Feminist Economics*, 6 (2) (2000): 41–75.

7 Leigh Ann Whaley, *Women's History as Scientists: A Guide to the Debates*. Santa Barbara, California: ABC-CLIO, INC., 2003.

8 Rutherford, "Marie Curie." *The Slavonic and East European Review*, 13(39) (1935): 673–676.

Although the presence of women in some fields such as medicine and surgery can be traced back to the early history of humans, historically, women
have less participation in medical fields compared to men, and their employment rate also varies by their race, economic, social, and geographic status.
Women informally worked in medicine as caregivers or paramedical professionals. Since the beginning of the 20th century, most countries in the world
have provided equal access to medical education for women, although not
guaranteeing equal job opportunities and gender equality in medical spe-
cialties worldwide. All these obstacles are observed even though the studies
show that female doctors may provide higher quality care than male ones[9]
(Tsugawa et al., 2017). In the history of Iran, there are also effective women
in the field of medicine. Taj al-Moluk Meshkat Hazrati, the first gynecological
surgeon, was one of the members of the first group of females who entered
medical school. She was able to get permission to study at medical school,
and in 1938, she studied medicine at Tehran University. At the same time, she
specialized in two fields: gynecological and general surgery. Marjan Jahangiri,
who graduated in Britain in 1988, continued her studies in the field of cardiol-
ogy as the first female cardiothoracic surgeon in Europe. Sakine Pari, the first
Iranian female surgeon, was born in the Soviet Union, her mother was from
the Armenians in Iran and her father was from Hamedan. She completed her
studies in the Soviet Union and specialized in surgery and oncology in 1933.
She returned to Iran a year later and received the license to practice medicine,
and started her practice in Iran at the age of 32.

Despite all the existing ups and downs for women, it is hard to overlook
their presence and efficiency in the fields of Mathematics and Engineering.
Comprising half of the population, women are important elements in the
development and progress of the whole society. Ignoring them in any field
leads to removing half of the effective forces. As the surveys suggest, since
women were accepted in different social, scientific, and educational fields,
and started their activities, different societies have experienced more progress
and improvement. Therefore, in the field of science and education, the presence of women is an integral part of progress and development. Today, women
have had a profound impact on the development of the technology. Their
achievements throughout history demonstrate their exquisite adaptability
and prove that their knowledge and skills are essential requirements in today's

---

9   Yusuke Tsugawa, Anupam B. Jena, Jose F. Figueroa, E. John Orav, Daniel M. Blumenthal,
    & Ashish K. Jha, "Comparison of Hospital Mortality and Readmission Rates for Medicare
    Patients Treated by Male vs Female Physicians." *JAMA Intern Med*, 177(2) (2017): 206–213.

world. Iranian universities have taken significant steps in the last few decades to improve and facilitate the presence of women in science, technology, engineering, and mathematics.

3   Inequality and Gender Gap in Science

Studies show that there is a general belief that literacy, scientific endeavor, and research lead to the professional development of academics in the scientific area and gender is not a deciding factor. For instance, if statistics show that, out of 1,000 men and 1,000 women who had earned doctorate degree in economics, more men than women become university professors, it is typically concluded that men must have engaged in more academic activities after earning their degree.[10]

Over the past century, gender inequality has been a salient feature of human social life. There is a broad, but not universal, consensus regarding the superiority of men over women in all societies. However, it is clear that there are major differences in the level and nature of gender inequality in different societies. Even in societies where gender equality is culturally valued, "male dominance" and "sexual hostility" can be detected. Women, in most patriarchal societies, may gain a lot of power, authority, independence, and prestige for themselves. Gender inequality or gender stratification in its sociological interpretation is the unequal distribution of wealth, power and benefits of society between men and women[11] (Sanderson, Heckert, & Dubrow, 2005). Research shows that a more equitable distribution of positions and resources between men and women leads to economic growth and greater productivity, and countries that invest in female education have higher economic growth rates. Therefore, eliminating the inequalities in various matters suggests paying attention to the differences between men and women and providing access to various economic, cultural, social, and political resources so that women have access to the same resources as men despite all the differences (see Figure 4.1). Chouari, Ghiss, and Zabaniotou (2021) noted in their research that although job opportunities, employment criteria, health insurance, and social welfare are equally

10   Ginther Donna K., "Economics of Gendered Distribution of Resources in Academe," in *Biological, Social, and Organizational Components of Success for Women in Science and Engineering: Workshop Report.* Washington, DC: The National Academies Press, 2006.

11   Stephen K. Sanderson, D. Alex Heckert & Joshua K. Dubrow, "Militarist, Marxian, and Non-Marxian Materialist Theories of Gender Inequality: A Cross-Cultural Test." *Social Forces*, 83(4) (2005): 1425–1441.

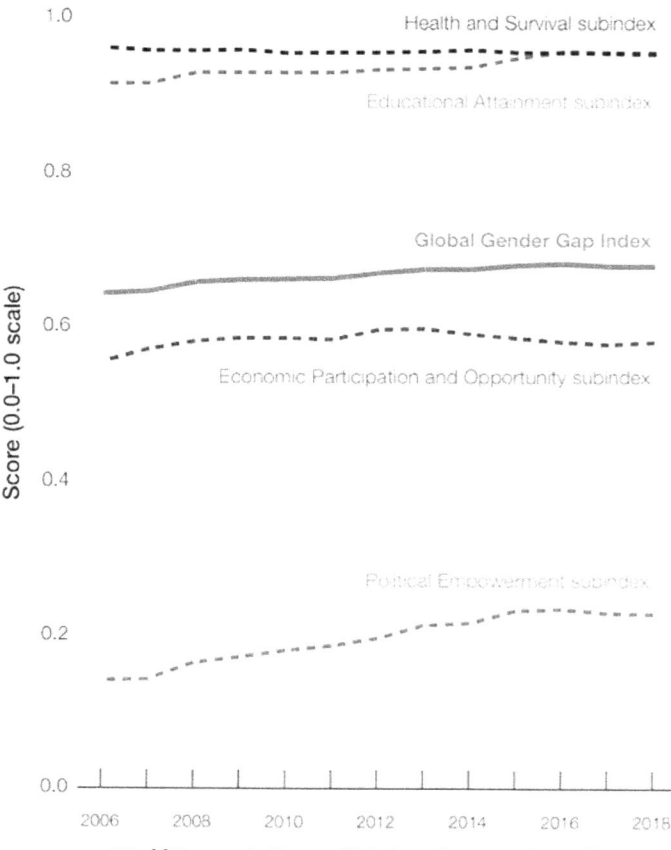

FIGURE 4.1   World Economic Forum, Global gender gap index and evolution
of sub-indices, 2006–2018
SCHWAB, 2018

available regardless of gender, career promotion is still one of the most challenging issues for women compared to men. The results of this research indicate that despite the belief in gender equality, achieving and adopting a culture of gender equality for progress is a challenge.[12]

Ignorance of such differences has shown itself in the field of science. Women have faced limitations throughout history in different eras, i.e., science has also been gendered and has witnessed gender segregation. The recent years'

---

12   Monia Chouari, Moncef Ghiss, & Anastasia Zabaniotou, "Academic Promotion and Leadership: 'Moving the Needle' for the Enhancement of Gender Equality in Tunisian Higher Education Institutional Members of the RMEI Network Following the TARGET Framework." *Open Research Europe*, 1(14) (2021): 1–18.

various equality movements and the elimination of gender, racial, economic, social, etc. inequalities gave birth to an increasing presence of women in the field of science and education worldwide. However, there are still inequalities in some societies with specific cultures. The existence of a gap in educational equality means that gender equality is a requirement in education. Many studies have concluded that the gender gap is shallower today, giving the impression that there will soon be an equal number of male and female researchers. It also shows that the current initiatives to attract and retain women are working adequately.[13]

4   Equality and Elimination of Gender Gap in Science

Today, gender gaps in the economic, political, educational, and health arenas are measured as indicators of the development of countries. Surveys show that men and women have experienced differences in achieving equality in health and education on a global average, while their levels of economic and political participation continue to suffer from striking differences. Meanwhile, education is an important indicator that shows the level of development of society at the macro level.[14] Educational equality can be defined as providing people with the same academic talent with equal opportunities to grow and succeed in the educational system, regardless of their family background. The inequality or equality of opportunity means inequality between the male and female in benefitting from education, inequality between religious minorities or inequality in the access to educational facilities in different regions of the country. According to Rawls, the three principles of equality of opportunity in the field of educational systems include: 1) providing educational facilities for qualified people, 2) providing minimum education for each person, and 3) creating special facilities and supplies for disadvantaged groups.[15]

A quick look at the global efforts shows that, so far, many declarations, treaties, and conventions have been issued in the field of education to emphasize the right of people to free and compulsory education and to protect them against all forms of neglect and injustice. However, the evidence indicates that gender justice has not yet been achieved in access to education. Hence, in 2000, at the World Summit on Education in Dakar, Senegal, the member

13   Luke Holman, & Devi Stuart-Fox, Cindy E. Hauser, "The Gender Gap in Science: How Long Until Women Are Equally Represented?" *PLOS Biology*, 16(4) (2018).

14   Gholam Abbas Tavassoli, *Sociology and Education: Yesterday, Today, Tomorrow*. Tehran: Science, 2009.

15   John Rawls, *A Theory of Justice*. Cambridge: Harvard University Press, 1971.

countries including Iran committed to implementing the plan of "education for all" to achieve gender justice in access to education. Equal opportunity is a key goal of the political agenda in many countries, and as a result, political leaders iterate the importance of reducing the gap in educational achievement between young people from different social origins, i.e. reducing the inequality of educational opportunities is usually understood as the relationship between the students' social origins—for example, parental class, status, education or income—and their education level when they leave school for the labor market.[16]

Ensuring women's rights and allowing them to reach their full potential is critical for achieving gender equality and a range of international development goals. Empowered women and girls contribute to the health and productivity of their families, communities, and countries, and create a ripple effect that benefits everyone.[17] Education is a key area to focus on. Although the world is making progress in achieving gender equality in education, girls still have a higher percentage of children out of school compared to boys. It is typical for, families with limited means who cannot afford to pay for school fees, uniforms, and supplies for all their children, to prioritize education for their sons. Families may also rely on girls' labor for housework, carrying water, and childcare, leaving limited time for school. However, prioritizing girls' education may provide the highest return on investment in developing countries. An educated girl will have healthier children and can send her children to school although she is likely to postpone marriage and start a smaller family. She has more opportunities to earn money and participate in political processes. Promoting women's education is known to reduce the level of child mortality and promote the education of the next generation, each of which has a positive effect on economic growth. In general, the change in the status of women in today's society also affects their status in the family and causes the power relations in the family to move towards greater equality.[18]

The increase in the presence of women in higher education can also be explained based on Merton's theory of goals and means. According to this theory, women can achieve their goals—securing a position, dignity and social status, independence and using the charms of student life—through using a

16   Raymond Boudon, *Education, Opportunity, and Social Inequality: Changing Prospects in Western Society*. New York: Wiley, 1974.

17   Afsaneh Tavassoli & Lee Ken Teo, "Islamic Feminist Political Narratives, Reformist Islamic Thought, and Its Discursive Challenges in Contemporary Iran." *Inter-Asia Cultural Studies*, 22(1) (2021): 49–66.

18   Afsaneh Tavassoli & Vahideh Saeidi, "The Impact of Women's Employment on Power Structure in Eyvankey Families." *Woman in Development & Politics*, 9(3) (2011): 133–149.

tool called pursuing education at higher levels. In addition, due to the specialization of jobs and the importance of expertise in securing a position, increasing the level of education provides women with more opportunities for participation in the economic environment.[19]

5   Gender Gap in Higher Levels of Education

Higher education and research are key tools for empowerment and social change. Universities can be powerful institutions for promoting gender equality, diversity and inclusion in higher education and society. Nevertheless, universities remain gendered organizations.[20] The existing inequality in the education system can be examined and studied from three perspectives: a) in terms of access to education, b) in terms of the resources that have been provided to the educational system as system inputs, and c) in terms of the system performance.[21] Enrollment of women in higher education has tripled globally between 1995 and 2018. However, recent research has provided evidence that the gender gap in higher education has narrowed significantly in recent decades, consistent with continuing gender inequality in the labor market. Furthermore, the "equal access" to education and academic careers that women have enjoyed in the past years has not yet led to "equal outcomes" in terms of leadership and academic positions, payment, research and publications in a higher education setting.[22]

Women are overrepresented among teaching staff at lower educational levels, but their presence decreases in higher education. In 2018, 43% of teachers in higher education were women, while 66% and 54% of them were teaching in primary and secondary education, respectively. In 2020, only 30% of the world's university researchers were women. Women are still underrepresented in senior faculty boards and higher education decision-making bodies in many countries. This fact can be explained by women's lower access to education as a symptom of institutional cultures that are neither inclusive nor conducive to

---

19   Leila Falahati, (2020). *Higher Education and Cultural-Social Developments of Women.* Tehran: Institute for Social and Cultural Studies, 2020.

20   Rodrigo Rosa, Eieen Drew, & Sioban Canavan, "An Overview of Gender Inequality in EU Universities" in *The Gender-Sensitive University: A Contradiction in Terms?* eds. Eileen Drew and Siobhan Canavan. (Routledge, 2020), 1–15.

21   M. Mahmoud & A. Mohammad Reza, Economic of Education. Organization for Studying and Compiling Humanities Books of Universities, 2013.

22   Maria Elena Hurtado, "Gender Inequality in Higher Education Persists." *University World News*, 12 March, 2021.

broader social and cultural change for greater gender equality. Conventional faculty recruitment processes that reward in a linear way and full-time uninterrupted academic pathways contribute to the underrepresentation of women in senior academic positions. However, there are signs that women are making progress. For example, the number of top universities led by women is increasing, though they still make up less than one-fifth of the leading institutions.[23] The problem of gender imbalance in educational positions has been a topic of many studies that sought ways to resolve this problem. They point to the statistics of the gender difference in the power structure in higher education and also acknowledge that in the United States and Europe, men predominantly occupied senior management positions such as President, Vice president, or full professor.

6   Women Facing the Gender Gap in Science in Iran

Archaeological excavations in Shahr Sokhte, an ancient prehistoric city near Zabul in Sistan and Baluchestan Province in Southeastern Iran reveal that women in this region enjoyed a high social status during the fourth to third millennium BC. 90% of the seals discovered in the existing graves were owned by women, who constituted more than 60% of the population. The distribution of these seals-trade and government tools that represent economic and administrative control shows that these women were a powerful group in prehistoric society. Prior to the constitutional revolution, there were no centers or organizations established by the government or individuals regarding the education of girls. Educational centers were limited within the framework of home schools and private tutoring in homes, and their educational contents had not changed either. However, on the threshold of the Constitutional Revolution, due to the influence of modernist ideas and the expansion of the idea of education to eliminate deficiencies, the idea of establishing girls' schools in a new style gained momentum. In this period, the limited opportunities provided and the support of the government and legal protections, helped women establish girls' schools first in a national form, and then in a state form, and the educational program of these schools was different according to their national status.[24] In Iran, formal education for women began with the opening of the first primary school for females. When Iran started its modernization phase in

---

23   Ibid.
24   Nasim Farahmand, *Education and Educational Institutions for Girls in the Qajar Period.* Yas Bakhshayesh Publications, 2019.

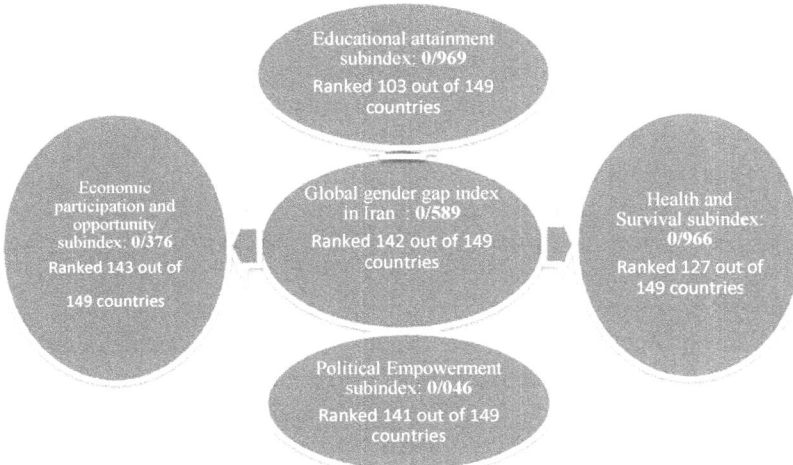

FIGURE 4.2 Global gender gap index in Iran

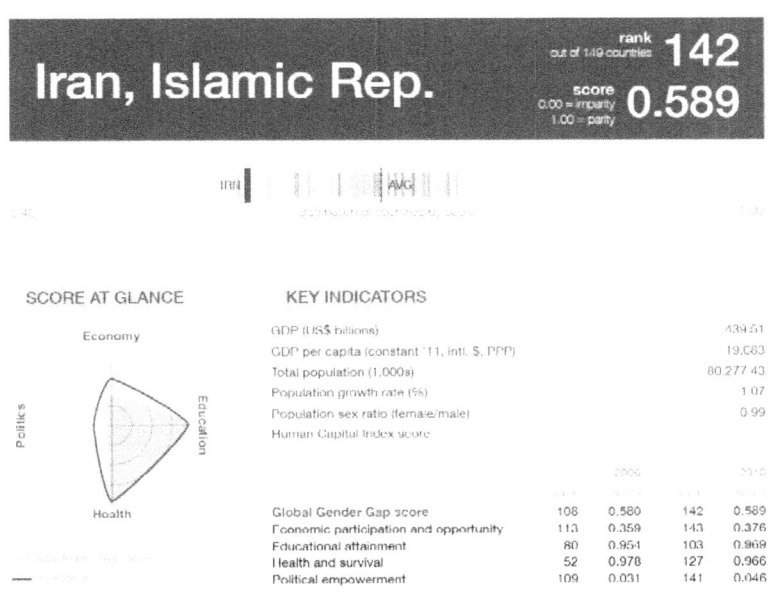

FIGURE 4.3 Comparison of gender gaps in Iran and the world
SOURCE: GLOBAL GENDER GAP REPORT, 2022, P. 198

the early 20th century with the expansion of women's schools under the rule of Reza Shah Pahlavi, education played a significant part in Iranian society.[25] Women took entrance exams for universities up until 1989.

Iranian women went through the winding path of patriarchy, and their success in the social institution of education was perhaps more significant and conspicuous than any other social institution.

Since 1990, the number of women attending higher education institutions in Iran has been steadily increasing. Yet, it should be noted that with the reconstruction of gender stereotypes even in education, there have been obstacles and limitations remaining from the historical era of agriculture. When estimating research indicators and the gender of research leaders such as the first authors of articles, corresponding authors of the articles, and project managers, we are still facing a gender gap at the global level (see Figure 4.2). Research shows that women in Iran have been able to overcome what is called the barrier of patriarchy in education, like other women in the world, and gradually overcome other obstacles alongside other women of the world. Figure 4.3 shows that Iranian women have made significant progress compared to other countries. Iranian women have had an effective and impressive presence in various fields both in Iran and at the international level. In science and technology, for example, Maryam Mirzakhani, an Iranian mathematician and Professor at Stanford University won the Fields Medal in 2014 for her work in the field of "Dynamics and Geometry of Riemannian Surfaces and their Metric Spaces", which is the highest award in mathematics. She was the only woman and the first Iranian to win the Fields Medal. This also applies to Muslim women and Asian women. In recent years, there have been many advances in the field of women's education and acquisition of science. As Table 4.1 shows, the number of female researchers in Asian and African countries (with more Muslim populations) is not significantly different from the world ratio (10% less). Even in Central Asia, the percentage of female researchers is more than in the world (10% more).

TABLE 4.1   The statistics of the number of female researchers in the world

Countries	Percentage of researchers who are female
Central Asia	46%
World	30%
South and West Asia	20%
East Asia and the Pacific	20%

25   Golnar Mehran, "The Paradox of Tradition and Modernity in Female Education in the Islamic Republic of Iran." *Comparative Education Review*, 47(3) (2003): 269–286.

6.1 The History of Women's Education in Iran

Women in Iran have gone through numerous ups and downs on their journey to equality of opportunities culminating in the freedoms that have been
established for human beings around the world. Learning and conquering
the peaks of knowledge were highly prized achievements in ancient Iran,
which is why scientists enjoyed a spiritual reputation among society members. Iranian women, like men, value the effort to grow and improve knowledge and have given a special place to intellectuals. Since education was
not all-inclusive and from a social point of view it was limited to a certain
class, or from an individual point of view only men with talent and motivation were able to achieve it, the effort and seriousness were not observed
among men and especially women in achieving it. However, with the rise of
industrialization, societies started changing, stepping into the process of civilization and urbanization. This transition from traditional to modern concepts altered many aspects of social life, and made knowledge acquisition,
like many other aspects, an obvious and necessary matter. This rule applied
equally to Iranian men and women. Literacy in the old schools, which meant
the ability to read the holy texts, including the Quran, or recite poems by
famous poets like Ferdowsi, Saadi, Hafez, etc., flourished and developed into
the semi-formal study of science. Little boys and girls at the age of five began
to enroll in co-ed Arabic alphabet classes. Many of these teachers, though
unofficially, were women and in some areas, they were known as Atto. After
learning literacy for several years and acquiring knowledge that was often
limited to reading and writing in some situations, children were pushed
away from old school to traditional employment areas, and boys were taught
men's occupations while girls were taught housekeeping and some feminine
skills such as carpet weaving to prepare for married life, which started very
early compared to the current era. The beginning of formal education and
the establishment of the first schools met with resistance from the supporters of traditional education in old schools.[26]

Although there is historical evidence of the emergence of schools during
the time of the Khwarazmshahs, authentic documents that can be more accurately cited suggest that official schools in Iran were established around 1838 AD
in Urmia and then in Tabriz, and introduced Iranian men of all ethnicities and
religions to the new sciences. After that, Dar al-Funun school was opened in
1851 AD and then we see the reopening of schools in different cities of Iran.
Girls' schools were established much later despite serious opposition. The first
girls' school named "Parvaresh" was opened by Ms. Azmoudeh in 1903, but the
opposition and pressure from the opponents of culture ended in the closure of

---

26   Abdullah Mostofi, *My Life History or the Social and Administrative History of the Qajar
      Period,* (2nd ed.). Tehran: Zova, 1942.

this school four days after its establishment. The government officials closed the school with threats and obscenities, but after a while, the founder of this school established another school in a different place called "Namous." What should be kept in mind is that education for girls in Iran of that era was not considered appropriate, hence, setting up a school for girls was an important and difficult step. Families who were concerned about the education of their daughters would help them become literate by hiring a private teacher. Toubi Azmodeh was born in one of these families.[27] Even though some girls' schools had already been established in Iran, the more serious establishment of girls' schools was put into practice following the Constitutional Revolution owing to some representatives' perception that educated mothers could bring about more successful men. Once the development of contemporary formal schools for men and then for women became the norm having experienced many ups and downs, many traditional families nevertheless resisted enrolling the female members of the family in new schools and viewed literacy in a modern style as a sign of immorality.

6.2   *Iranian Women's Orientation to Science-Based Education*

According to Norbert Elias, the network of actions is so complex that trying to perform appropriate behaviors within this network is so important that in addition to the conscious form of self-control, another type of self-control such as an automatic mechanism is formed in a person, which works unconsciously.[28] He believes that the process of civilization or the changes that took place to curb violence in the social structure possess functional importance in the relations of power and dignity. In recent times, along with the complexity of social existence, a person learns how to restrain and control himself regularly. In fact, Elias expanded the interpretation framework that may be described as the concept of a single civilization. His goal was to provide a more general and adequate paradigm for studying long-term processes instead of reductionist and incomplete models of classical sociology. An important complementary principle here is that the study of the process of social development and transformation that Elias calls "social development" is essentially related to the analysis of "psychological development," that is, the process of psychological development and transformation and change in personality structure. The social status of women, originating from changes in society, has always

---

27   Eliz Sanasarian, *The Women's Rights Movement in Iran: Mutiny, Appeasement, and Repression From 1900 To Khomeini, 1982*. Tehran: Akhtaran, 2014.

28   Norbert Elias, *The Civilizing Process: The History of Manners and State Formation and Civilization*. Oxford: Blackwell, 1997.

undergone changes in various historical periods with many concomitant ups and downs.[29] Perhaps the arrival of Islam in Iran can be considered the most important changing factor among Iranians, which led to the acceptance of Islamic values and introduced direct changes in the status of Iranian women.

Elias' approach makes it possible for us to analyze the historical evolution of Iranian women's educational and scientific training in order to gain a deeper understanding of Iranian women's scientific education. The majority of the works and documents from ancient history are accounts of male conquests. These same documents also suggest that conditions for education were more favorable for aristocrats, elders, and particularly men. In addition, the majority of science students were men. In history, including the history of Iran, women have been mentioned in passing, and the limited information obtained from these sources does not provide us with accurate knowledge about women. However, through the study of the historical development of women's positions, one can see that women have a lot to say in science and culture despite all the prejudice and unfair treatment they face today.

Since the dawn of the Achaemenid civilization, science, literature, and the arts have held a prominent place among Iranians. The ancient works and written documents show that science has always held a special place in Iranian culture, yet it has always been dominated by men. In fact, science used to be under the control of aristocrats and elders, and those from lower social classes could only study it if they aspired to be a part of the court and the nobility, but males continued to dominate it. Numerous men from different walks of life who showed interest in science have left behind their works at various points in history. Even Iran's mythological and oral literature paid attention to science, but it was primarily controlled by men.[30]

There are many sources of information from the Qajar period about the status of women. From this period when the scientific recording of history began, more detailed information about the status of women is also available. Women in the Qajar era were generally illiterate. The then-patriarchal society believed that women should not know and understand anything, and there was no need for women to learn calligraphy and literacy. It goes without saying that due to cultural and financial constraints, girls from lower social levels were not permitted to attend school, and the majority of literate women were nobles and princes. These historical documents suggest that the education of noble and court women was quite common, and was used to distinguish the superior from the inferior women. Before the Constitutional Revolution, few

29   Ibid.
30   Iiya Gershevitch, "Old Iranian Literature." *Iranian Studies*, 1 (1976).

women had the possibility of becoming literate. When nobles hired private tutors to educate their sons, they occasionally permitted the female members of the family to take classes from those tutors as well. Some middle-class families enrolled their daughters in public schools.[31]

After the Constitutional era and the establishment of girls' schools, the women who graduated from these schools founded other schools. Their cultural acts were motivated by the fact that in addition to learning textbooks, they grew more conscious of their conditions as a result of comparisons made between Iranian and European women in the classrooms. It was even conceivable that news about European women was passed from schoolgirls to their mothers and then discussed in public settings such as mosques and public baths. In fact, from this time onward, Iranian women took a more serious step towards acquiring knowledge and eliminating existing inequalities. Since acquiring knowledge in Iranian society was one of the important indicators of distinguishing people, Iranian women also pursued the acquisition of science and knowledge seriously.[32] Publications were a key source of information on females' education throughout the Qajar era. Newspapers and periodicals stressed the role of literate women in the development of society in addition to the materials they published about the significance of mastering science. In certain cases, they also discussed how women's education was handled in other Muslim nations, including the Ottoman Empire. In order to persuade the opponents of the education of women and girls through a new way, women published articles advocating women's education in numerous periodicals and sent numerous letters to the parliament.

Abdul Hossein Nahid, in his book entitled *"Iranian Women in the Constitutional Movement,"* states that women relied on the verses of the Qur'an and hadiths in praise of science.[33] One such woman was Esmat Tehrani, a noble-minded woman who wrote interesting articles in *Iran-e Now* newspaper. She tried to make men believe that educated wives are valuable.[34] In this era, the exclusiveness of court education is being broken down. Education which was once exclusive to the privileged class was now being used for the lower level. Women also sought to gain more awareness. To eliminate class and gender discrimination, they considered studying and education as a way to escape from the dominant patriarchal culture. The number of new schools,

31   Ervand Abrahamian, *Iran Between Two Revolutions.* Trans. A. Gol-Mohammadi & M.E. Fatahi. Tehran: Ney Publications, 2017.

32   Abdul Hossein Naheed, *Iranian Women in the Constitutional Movement.* Tabriz: Ahya, 1981.

33   Ibid.

34   Janet Afary, *The Iranian Constitutional Revolution, 1906–1911: Grassroots Democracy, Social Democracy, and the Origins of Feminism.* New York: Columbia University Press, 1996.

including girls' schools at the end of the Qajar Era despite political and social disturbances and economic problems increased. In 1913, *Shokoofeh* magazine published a list of 63 girls' schools in Tehran with about 2500 students and announced that girls make up one-seventh of students in Tehran's schools.

Although educational policies and women's performance in education in the middle of the Qajar period had a great impact on many people, and slowly changed the traditional view that considered women to be weak and without creativity, livelihood gaps, traditional beliefs, and central government's weakness in establishing security still prevented the significant progress of women's education.[35] One of the important aspects of women's efforts to achieve their desires in the new era of Iran's history was to achieve literacy, education and awareness of various branches of science and knowledge. To achieve these objectives, and to pave the way for further and future achievements, they endured pressures and experienced hardships. Therefore, one can argue that women began to learn science in a new way in the Qajar period, while they were still facing social obstacles. In fact, with Elias' process approach, one can contend that the Qajar period is the beginning of the process of psychological development of Iranian women in terms of their ability to learn and learning.

6.3   *Beyond Discrimination and Reaching Knowledge*

During the Qajar era, even though more economic, educational and career opportunities were created for Iranian women under the autocratic royal regime, the gender norms and traditions of the society did not allow women to participate in the development process. During the first Pahlavi era, Reza Shah's main objective was westernization and development which made him support the education and presence of women in the society. The development of the quasi-capitalist system and economic development, in conjunction with modernization policies, helped the growth of women's employment in the 1950s. Besides, the uniform and secular education required government intervention in girls' schools. Women's education started in the 1930s and some 70 women were admitted to Tehran University during those years. Most women's schools back then were private and were set up by the women themselves without any assistance from the government.

During the second Pahlavi period, the six-point reform program, also known as the White Revolution was launched in 1963. Following the implementation of the Knowledge Corps in 1963, several leading Iranian women proposed educational programs for rural girls. This proposal was put forward at the time the Minister of Education revealed the ratio of 500 to 1 illiteracy for village

---

35   Sanasarian, *The Women's Rights*.

girls in relation to men in Iran. The right to education for women during the time of Mohammad Reza Pahlavi, was regarded as a method to achieve modernization.[36] Specialized and professional training for women was not only a means to secure a suitable job, but also to eliminate the socio-cultural problems caused by extensive imports of foreign labor.

Iran has always paid special attention to religion and religiosity throughout history. After the arrival of Islam, the teachings of Islam attracted the attention of a large portion of Iranian people. The existence of Islamic teachings about the role of women in the success of men and the presence of women in history shows that proper and comprehensive education for women is necessary for societies to move from stagnation to scientific and social progress. Women are actually the main foundation of the family system and the main motivators for their children to acquire science and knowledge. Pursuing the educational demands of women in a new way in the history of Iran has always been faced with many problems and obstacles. History shows that great men and women have never failed to rise above the barriers of blind prejudice, and their efforts brought the educational status of women to the point where there is now a mass presence of women in Muslim society as we see in various scientific and cultural fields.

After the Islamic Revolution and the changes that occurred due to ideological thinking, women's issues were approached differently. In the first and second development plans, the Iran-Iraq war did not allow much attention to women's issues. However, after the war, governments' attention was drawn to women's issues, especially women's education. At the beginning of the victory of the revolution, universities were closed for two years causing the decline of girls' education in the early years of the revolution. After ten years, one of the important policies of governments was to expand education and eradicate illiteracy. Once the conditions became more favorable, training and empowerment of women were put on the agenda of the governments. For instance, in 1999, women's studies courses were added to the university curriculum. In the 6th parliament, a plan was presented to eliminate discrimination, according to which women had no restrictions whatsoever to go and study abroad on their own. Women who were marginalized during the past years and previous eras used the current status to raise themselves, and increased their awareness by augmenting the level of literacy, and looking for equal social rights as those of men. What can be inferred regarding the status of science and knowledge among Iranian women is that Iranian women consider the study of science and

---

36   Ibid.

knowledge as a way to reach resources that used to be in the hands of men. In fact, in different ages, we have witnessed the support of different governments for women's education. However, since a large number of community members in Iran have had a traditional and religious approach, and have not been able to adapt themselves to the teachings that are compatible with Western and anti-Islamic thinking, many women did not enter the flow of educational progress and literacy. The revolution and the Islamic approach governing various educational institutions made the half-silenced religious strata of society also enter the field of learning.

In a sense, science and literacy were among the key determinants of individual differentiation in Iranian society, according to Elias's perspective, and they were viewed by lower-class individuals as a path to the upper class. Iranian women also had less access to economic, political and social resources. They pursued learning more seriously in order to have access to power sources. It is safe to argue that during the Qajar era, the support for women's education was mostly aimed at the nobles, and during the Pahlavi era, anti-religious approaches prevented half of the religious people from achieving literacy in a modern way. Thus, the government's exclusive support slackens the progress of the women's science education movement. After the 1979 Revolution, however, one can argue that despite all the existing discrimination, the discrimination between men and women in education has remained very insignificant. Eliminating this discrimination provided women with access to equal opportunities in education and educational literacy. In addition to the government support for the presence of women, women from different walks of Iranian society would also like to be present in scientific fields.

6.4   *The Role of Women's Movements in the Tendency to Learn Science*

The development process in Iran has passed a winding historical path. The formation of theories of women or gender and development was associated with the history of political interventions in developing countries as well as the women's movement around the world. It has been confirmed that the experiences of policymakers have had a significant impact in revising the concerns of this field. The education of women is supported by all the feminist movements. However, these movements approach this problem differently, and they have distinct strategies, defenses, and proposals. When the 19th-century women's movement took women's issues more seriously and eventually succeeded in creating the Charter for the defense of women's rights in America under feminism, more focus was placed on the rights of women in connection to education. The Convention on the Elimination of All Forms of Discrimination

Against Women, which was signed in 1979 marked the pinnacle of feminist defense of women's education, and is the 20th century movement's greatest triumph.[37]

One of the most significant periods in Iran's history is the Qajar era. Iran's struggle between tradition and modernity began during this time. One of the concerns of intellectual communities has always been the question of women's education, both during constitutionalism and after the movement's success. These women's demands appear to have been made out of a desire for knowledge and science rather than to conceal their Iranian and Islamic heritage. The majority of the founders of girls' schools in the Qajar period considered the religious beliefs of the community; the reaction to separate the problem of education and learning from the process of Westernization was quite an astute reaction, which was mostly ignored during the early Pahlavi period.[38] In the traditional Islamic viewpoint, learning and gaining knowledge from anybody and in any locales is beneficial and praiseworthy. Women employed all the available means to accomplish their objectives. They quoted religious texts that urged equal treatment for men and women and utilized the senses of honor and shame of constitutional men, spent their dowries and inheritance, and even took advantage of their relationships with the royal women. In fact, some of the women's aspirations and ideals came true. Although the parliament was closed in November 1916, the achievements of women in this short period of the revolution were preserved and increased significantly in the following years. It should be noted that the early supporters of women's rights often believed that more educational and social opportunities for women would strengthen family relationships and the progress of the country. Therefore, proponents of Iranian women's rights in the first place attempted to persuade men that an educated woman better understands the traditional values and customs of the family and helps their nation to step on the path of civilization by highlighting the motherly and wifely duties of women.[39]

The women's movement improved access to education during the Pahlavi era but ignored the crucial subject of women's political engagement. Few women advocated the right of women to vote in politics since they mostly believed that until they had successfully defeated discrimination in work and

---

37   M.S. Directly, "A Comparative Approach to the Philosophical Origins of Women's Social Issues in Islam and Feminism (part two): Islam's View of Women's Education." *Strategic studies of women*, 11(1) (2001): 48–69.

38   Solmaz Qolizade Mehdi Khan, "A Look at the Education Status of Iranian Girls and Women during the Constitutional Period." Shahrvand Newspaper, (2016).

39   Afary, *The Iranian Constitutional Revolution.*

education, they would not be able to truly participate in politics. Thus, the fight for political equality against the role of motherhood became the focal point of women's efforts starting in 1925 as the number of educated Iranian women increased.[40] During Reza Shah's era, with the support of some women, adult classes in secondary schools for girls were opened in Tehran, Tabriz and Rasht. According to available reports, women's interest in education was so much so that more than a thousand illiterates registered. In addition, there were classes for training in foreign languages in the women's club in Tehran. Many of the leaders of the women's movement succeeded in convincing the government for women's scholarships. Therefore, long-term plans to enhance women's engagement in the job market and the provision of training and scholarships, as well as the involvement of more female teachers, were taken into consideration. During the time of Reza Shah, active women were from the elite class, they were more involved in charity work. On the other hand, the new generation that worked under the supervision of Mohammad Reza Shah consisted of almost unknown figures who served in the Iranian Women's Organization. During this period, the organization of women's affairs was formed, which complemented the Shah's gender policies, i.e. completing the transformation of women's initiatives and actions into loyal organization. To consolidate and mobilize the larger members of the community, the Shah completed his father's goal by delegating the task of organizing women to a state-sponsored, and multipurpose organization.[41]

Under the patronage of Ashraf Pahlavi, the Organization of Women's Affairs mobilized women and prepared them as much as possible for the progress of Iran, although the voices of dissident women were ignored. Through its research department, this organization studied issues related to family welfare, women's work and literacy, and various gender laws. At this time, the process of reforms was slow for women due to the following reasons: to begin with, the women's movement was under the supervision of the regime and consisted of several hundred aristocratic females around the Shah's sister who were trying to stabilize their own position or improve it. Therefore, the women's movement did not have to fight at this time, and women of the middle class and lower classes of society did not participate in it either. Secondly, the Iranian

---

40   M. Shiyani & H. Zare, "Women and Development: Iranian Women's Roles under the Qajar and Pahlavi Dynasties." *Sociological Review*, 29(2) (2023): 49–78.

41   Daniel Béland & Rezvan Ostadalidehaghi, "Women without Guardians" in Iran: Gender, Cultural Assumptions, and Social Policy. *Journal of International and Comparative Social Policy*, 29(1) (2013): 48–63.

women's movement lacked the national ideals and idealism of the most successful Asian movements. Thirdly, the government's fear of opposition and conservative forces did not allow them to implement some reforms. The government of Iran brought forward the issue of women's rights to be on the same page with some international currents and attract foreign aid.[42]

With the change of power after the Islamic Revolution, many cultural changes were created among different classes and the ruling class. The revolution was based on the slogan of supporting the oppressed and weaker sections and eliminating discrimination and inequality. Hence from the very beginning, they sought to show that there is no inequality among different classes in terms of access to facilities. The Islamic Revolution pays attention to the fact that Islam has a distinct view towards women in such a way that from the perspective of the verses of the Qur'an as the holy book of Muslims, men and women are presented as having human commonalities, honored by God (Surah *Isra*, verse 40), having a single purpose in creation (Surah *Dhariyat*, verse 56) and having the same possibility of happiness and closeness (Surah *Hadid*, verse 12). Despite these shared values, their developmental and functional differences turned them into two distinct but complementary entities. This view can be analyzed and explained in the wise system of creation, although historically and especially after the death of the Prophet the diminution of the role and presence of Muslim women in various fields, including learning is quite obvious. Muslim women have not played a very bright role, neither in the field of producing thought and knowledge nor in the realm of writing, historiography, and narration until the last century although they were never completely removed.

In fact, the ruling power has somehow tried to spread inequality and exclude women throughout the history of science, but Iranian women always tried to maintain their presence in the acquisition of knowledge and awareness. The influence of cultural factors cannot be ignored. The cultural conditions of Iran and the ruling patriarchal power have slowed down the growth and scientific process of Iranian women. On the other hand, the type of Iranian culture and women's approach has caused Iranian women's movements to be often in line with awareness. The emphasis on literacy and increasing women's awareness is something that distinguishes Iranian women's movements. In fact, they hold that ignorance is at the root of injustices and the acceptance of oppression. Iranian women had, indeed, behaved differently from conventional global movements based on their own culture and did not equate women's

---

42   Shiyani & Zare, "Women and Development."

freedom to certain superficial freedoms, placing knowledge acquisition and the improvement of the conditions for women's education as their top priorities. Iranian feminist movements have manifested in two currents. The initial movement, which is almost from the beginning of the formation of Iranian feminism, sought to transform Iranian women into Western women, trying to empower women without considering Iran's cultural and traditional values.[43] In fact, during the modernization of Iranian women, they tried to assimilate to western culture before trying to localize the feminist version. The same lack of attention to the traditional and cultural background of Iranian women and families caused half of the Iranian women population to be ignored. The Islamic feminist movement, which tries to rewrite its rules and regulations according to religious principles, was developed following the Islamic Revolution. In fact, they think it is essential to update Islamic laws and decrees pertaining to women to reflect contemporary ideas and take into account the requirements of modern women.

6.5   *Cultural-Religious Variables Affecting Women's Education in Iran*

As women sought education, they encountered numerous cultural and religious challenges. In the historical and cultural context of Iran, these variables can be categorized as follows, with some acting as obstacles and others as facilitators:

1.   Traditional culture and religion: the creation of this culture emerged as an obstacle in the era before and after the Constitutional Revolution. Traditional religion was a serious obstacle to the presence of women in education in two ways. This type of religion, whose pioneers were religious or traditional influential men at the local, national or political level, did not consider women's entry into the field of science Islamic and they believed that women's presence in new schools would lead them to leave their chastity. The reasons for these objections cannot be solely religious rituals and laws. The patriarchal system, which serves as the foundation for numerous initiatives aimed at preventing women from advancing, is founded on an agricultural way of life and traditional employment that prioritizes gender division of labor. Women were reserved for the private sector, housekeeping, childbearing, raising children, and possibly home-based jobs. Sexually, women were also part of the man's property or, with a more balanced definition, under the control of the man and

---

43   Cheraghi Kootiyan, "Iranian's Encounter with Feminism: from Iranian Feminism to Islamic Feminism." *Marifat*, 23(4) (2014): 31.

therefore any demands from women are excessive and can make them unchaste. With such conceptions, the presence of women in new schools, leaving the house, getting acquainted with different forms of family life, different clothing styles, and different types of social relations can destroy the institutionalized structure of women's life and provide another definition of woman which is not acceptable to customs and norms of the society. From the point of view of this group, religion and culture are tied to each other and one cannot be considered without the other. From this perspective, in this historical period, if the culture emphasizes women's staying indoors, it is emphasized by the religion as well.

2. Modern culture: This culture is the result of political-economic attitudes that historically brought many social changes in the Pahlavi era and is based on the fundamental transformation of the way women are viewed. Wide interactions with Western societies and freedom formed based on liberalism in Iranian society, led women to study and to work outside the home. Many women were still not officially employed, but since the 1950s education and training expanded and with the establishment of teacher training university a large number of women began to work as teachers at girls' schools. With the growth of women's presence in organizational jobs that necessitated higher education for women, significant changes occurred in society's thinking towards women's education. With the modern approach, there was no obstacle to the presence of women in the field of education, either in school education or higher education. However, education as a modern and Western-based concept was mixed with non-religious tendencies, and the presence of women in the field of employment and its precursor, i.e. acquiring knowledge, was tied to a different type of clothing and lifestyle. Although this issue was not official and women with any type of dress or style of behavior, whether religious or non-religious, attended scientific or professional gatherings without prohibition, women with religious or traditional clothing did feel shame. This feeling which was caused by the culture of modernity that equated type of clothing with modern lifestyle, created a discriminatory approach not in opportunities but in attitudes. However, religious women could also achieve the highest educational levels.

3. Intellectual culture and religion: This culture, which is more visible historically in the era after the Islamic Revolution emphasizes the presence of women in society based on religion and shows symbols of women in Islamic history such as Hajar, Asia, and Fatima. As an influential religious intellectual, Ali Shariati's emphasis on and juxtaposition of women

who destroy the structure of the bourgeoisie, with women who destroy anti-feminine norms in the beginning of Islam and changing a woman's position as an inherited commodity into heirs, indicate the growth and progress of women by being in the public domain. A woman as a woman and not as a being who only has the role of wife, mother, child and sister is one of the concepts that flow to the society in his literature.

Along with these abstract concepts, it is also clear that women who wear religious attire, whether out of choice or because it is required by law, have more presence in public. Anchored within such discourse, the proponents of traditional and religious-traditional culture, despite their prior objections about the presence of women in society and because of the relatively safe environment they feel for the presence of women, consent to women's participation in scientific fields and not only do not view learning science as a barrier to women's chastity, but there is also a sense of competition among these families for the enrollment of female children in higher education. As a result, a society is created where not only families respect modernity as the guiding principle but intelligent religious families and traditional religious families place an emphasis on girls' and women's formal education and view it as having a high social status.

6.6   Gender Division of Household Work as an Obstacle to Women's Education

One of the most significant factors that affect the presence of women in the public sphere including learning knowledge is the gender division of labor at home. Even though families with different lifestyles have no objections against girls' education which is by itself a major facilitator in females acquiring knowledge, the foundations of patriarchal thinking in society emphasize the priority of men in the public sphere of employment and learning. Thus, social reconstructions still define women's affairs for women in priority, and the pressure of different roles is an obstacle to the advancement of women's knowledge. The pressure of roles can identify three types of conflict, including conflict based on time, conflict based on tension or pressure, and conflict based on behavior.[44] In this regard, the proponents of the deficiency hypothesis also believe that playing important and diverse roles such as motherhood, wife, and career roles have caused burnout and pressure in working women,

---

44   Seyed Mohammad Mirkamali & Frank Mukhtarian, "A Comparative Study of Job Pressures and Coping Methods Among Male and Female Principals of Public Secondary Schools in Tehran." *Psychology and Educational Sciences*, 37(2) (2008).

and threatens their mental health. Moreover, based on this hypothesis, any additional role leads to an increased pressure on one's time and energy. Major roles such as job, mother, and wife require basic facilities, effort and time, and a person cannot fulfill all the demands of different roles, therefore he/she feels that in just one of the areas they can have a strong sense of commitment. A woman, according to cultural gender segregation, should spend more of her time on housework and in case of being married, on raising children rather than on education, and a man, from a cultural point of view, does not help the woman in the household affairs, which makes the woman bear the pressure of the role that is caused by the multiple and contradictory roles.

6.7   *The Law and Its Complications*

Numerous laws encourage women's learning and education at all levels in line with their right to education. As a result, the law effectively and explicitly supports women's education and does not create barriers for women. But on the sidelines of the law, it should be noted that there are laws that could prevent women's education. For instance, permission for women to leave the country must be given by their husbands or the right to housing and other conditions during marriage can indirectly create an obstacle to a woman's education. For example, when a married woman is accepted at a university other than the city where she lives, in addition to obstacles such as her defined domestic roles, being a wife and perhaps a mother, she can also face the problem of not being able to change her place of residence without the permission of her husband.

6.8   *Women's Progress in Knowledge and Science*

Educational justice is underscored in the Constitution of the Islamic Republic of Iran as well as in international declarations. Paragraphs 1, 14, and 15 of the third article and the nineteenth and twentieth articles of the constitution have it that all members of the country should have the right to equal access to education and training opportunities regardless of their individual, family, and social limitations. Undoubtedly, the educational system plays an essential role in the training of human resources and the development of society, and efficient human resources will be achieved as a consequence of equal educational opportunities. The main mission of education is to empower individuals to fully develop their talents and recognize their creative capabilities, and this goal bears more significance than the others. Although achieving this goal is difficult and far-fetched, it is considered necessary in the search for a fairer and better world to live in. Currently, educational inequalities are one of the most important categories in the field of educational planning which have a decisive role in expanding and improving education.

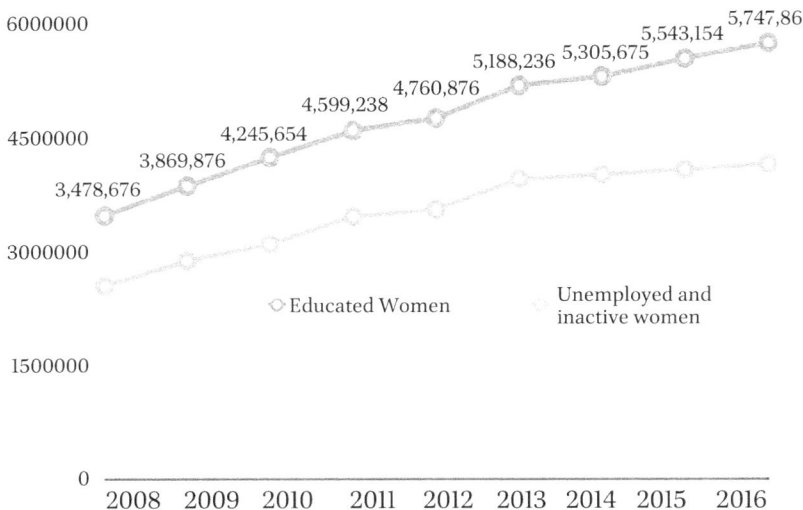

FIGURE 4.4 Increasing trend of educated women and their employment

Similar to the higher education of other countries, Iran has witnessed an increase in the presence of women in the last decade. The presence of women in universities since the late 90s and the increase in the number of girls in the 2000s corroborate this sentiment. For instance, the academic year 2003–2004, for the first time ever, witnessed 141,000 (53.94%) women out of a total of 261,000 students admitted to the country's universities and higher education institutions (full-time and part-time).[45] This increasing trend continued until the end of the 2000s. From 2010 onwards, the number of female students decreased, and in 2015, the contribution of women reached 47% of the total student population while the contribution of men reached 53%. However, it should be noted that this decrease occurred in the student population of the entire country (government and non-government) and the share of female students in public universities is still around 57%. The important point to bear in mind is that female students outnumber male students in public universities, where a higher level of talent and academic performance is required for admission. Moreover, women over the past two decades, in public universities, continuously had a share of at least 55%, and currently, they constitute 57% of the students of public universities.[46] The balance between education and employment is also important. This process is shown in Figure 4.4.

---

45   Institute of Research and Higher Education Planning, 2013.
46   Falahati, (2020). *Higher Education.*

In general, the evidence indicates that, despite historical, cultural, religious, and economic limitations based on patriarchy, Iranian young educated women appreciate education more than other members of Iranian society.[47] Despite all the obstacles in their path, women have made every effort and have nearly equaled men in their quest to reach the highest points of knowledge.

7   Conclusion

It is now fair to conclude that women do not seek a university degree in the hope of finding an affluent life today. Rather, they are adopting a practical approach to make their voices being heard and take leadership, especially in terms of participation at the individual and community levels. One of the important indicators for measuring the development of any country is the presence of women in society because the level of a country's development is measured by the participation of all people, especially women's presence in the political, social, and economic arenas. Therefore, how society deals with women is one of the important indicators of political and social development in a country. In fact, societies' dealing with women provides the conditions for the active presence and effective participation of women. According to the conducted studies, it can be argued that women's willingness to participate in the field of science and knowledge is one aspect of the matter, and the provision of conditions for the presence of women is another aspect. Perhaps there were female scientists who remained silent in the shadow of the limited rules of society. Men can have access to science and knowledge due to their dominance over society's resources, while the inequalities ruling society, the gender stereotypes, and biased policies are all obstacles to women's progress. Finally, it should be acknowledged that the growth of women in the field of science and knowledge is improving in Iran; and the gender gap in this field is getting closed leading to a future full of justice and equality.

From the historical study and process of Iranian women's education, one can see that governments, besides tradition and religion, play a very important role in this direction. In different eras, the intensity of the influence of government has controlled women's movements. The dominance of patriarchal culture and authoritarian male governments had a dramatic impact on the condition of Iranian women. In the periods before the Islamic Revolution, most governments paid attention to the expansion of the public sphere of women, while in the period after the Revolution, the government tried to have

---

47   Charles Kurzman, "A Feminist Generation in Iran?" *Iranian Studies*, 41 (3) (2008): 297–321.

more control over the private sphere of women. In the course of Iranian women's education, in addition to paying attention to the empowerment of women and being in the currents of globalization, the cultural and religious structures of Iranians and Iranian women must also be taken into consideration. In fact, governments' support and women's own desire in terms of psychological development led to the fact that Iranian women are now leading figures in knowledge and education despite all the discriminations.

Bibliography

Abrahamian, E. (2014). *Iran Between Two Revolutions*. Tehran: Ney.

Afary, J. (1996). *The Iranian Constitutional Revolution, 1906–1911: Grassroots Democracy, Social Democracy, and the Origins of Feminism*. New York: Columbia University Press.

Béland, D., & Ostadalidehaghi, R. (2013). "Women without Guardians" in Iran: Gender, Cultural Assumptions, and Social Policy. *Journal of International and Comparative Social Policy*, *29(1)*, 48–63. doi:10.1080/21699763.2013.803997.

Boudon, R. (1974). Education, Opportunity, and Social Inequality: Changing Prospects in Western Society. New York: Wiley.

Cheraghi Kootiyan, I. (2014). Iranian's Encounter with Feminism: from Iranian Feminism to Islamic Feminism. *Marifat*, *23(4)*, 31.

Chouari, M., Ghiss, M., & Zabaniotou, A. (2021). Academic Promotion and Leadership: 'Moving the Needle' for the Enhancement of Gender Equality in Tunisian Higher Education Institutional Members of the RMEI Network Following the TARGET Framework. *Open Research Europe*, *1(14)*. doi:10.12688/openreseurope.13217.2.

Dijkstra, G., & Hanmer, L.C. (2000). Measuring Socio-Economic Gender Inequality: Towards an Alternative to the UNDP Gender Related Development Index. *Feminist Economics*, *6 (2)*, 41–75.

Donna K.G. (2006). Economics of Gendered Distribution of Resources in Academe. In *Biological, Social, and Organizational Components of Success for Women in Science and Engineering: Workshop Report*. Washington, DC: The National Academies Press.

Directly, M.S. (2001). A Comparative Approach to the Philosophical Origins of Women's Social Issues in Islam and Feminism (part two): Islam's View of Women's Education. *Strategic studies of women*, *11(1)*, 48–69.

Elias, N. (1997). *The Civilizing Process: The History of Manners and State formation and Civilization* (Repr ed.). Oxford: Blackwell.

Falahati, L. (2020). *Higher Education and Cultural-Social Developments of Women* (M. Ahmadi ed., Vol. 0). Institute for Social and Cultural Studies.

Farahmand, N. (2019). *Education and Educational Institutions for Girls in the Qajar period*. Yas Bakhshayesh Publications.

Gershevitch, I. (1976). *Old Iranian Literature*, Iranian Studies.

Holman, L., & Stuart-Fox, D.H., Cindy E. (2018). The Gender Gap in Science: How Long Until Women Are Equally Represented?, *PLOS Biology*, *16*(4), e2004956. doi:10.1371/journal.pbio.2004956.

Keller, E.F., & Scharff-Goldhaber, G. (1987). Reflections on Gender and Science. *American Journal of Physics*, 55 (3), 284–286.

Kurzman, C. (2008). A Feminist Generation in Iran? *Iranian Studies*, *41 (3)*, 297–321. doi:10.1080/00210860801981260.

Mahmoud, M., & Mohammad Reza, A. (2013). *Economic of education* (Vol. 0), Organization for Studying and Compiling Humanities Books of Universities.

Hurtado Maria, E. (2021). Gender Inequality in Higher Education Persists. University World News, 12 March.

Mehran, G. (2003). The Paradox of Tradition and Modernity in Female Education in the Islamic Republic of Iran. *Comparative Education Review*, 47(3): 269–286.

Mirkamali, S.M., & Mukhtarian, F. (2008). A Comparative Study of Job Pressures and Coping Methods Among Male and Female Principals of Public Secondary Schools in Tehran. *Psychology and Educational Sciences*, *37*(2)(1).

Mostofi, A. (1942). *My Life History or the Social and Administrative History of the Qajar Period* (2nd ed.). Tehran: Zovar.

Naheed, A.H. (1981). *Iranian Women in the Constitutional Movement*. Tabriz: Ahya.

Qolizade Mehdi Khan, S. (2016). A Look at the Education Status of Iranian Girls and Women during the Constitutional Period, *1995*.

Rawls, J. (1971). *A Theory Of Justice Cambridge*, Harvard University Press.

Rosa, R., Drew, E., & Canavan, S. (2020). An Overview of Gender Inequality in EU Universities. *The Gender-Sensitive University*, 1–15.

Rutherford. (1935). Marie Curie. *The Slavonic and East European Review*, *13*(39), 673–676.

Saad, L. (2017). *A Sea Change In Support For Working Women*. Washington, D.C.: Gallup.

Sanasarian, E. (2014). The *Women's Rights Movement In Iran: Mutiny, Appeasement, And Repression From 1900 To Khomeini, 1982*. Tehran: Akhtaran.

Sanderson, S.K., Heckert, D.A., & Dubrow, J. K. (2005). Militarist, Marxian, and Non-Marxian Materialist Theories of Gender Inequality: A Cross-Cultural Test. *Social Forces*, *83*(4), 1425–1441.

Schwab, K. (2018). The Global Gender Gap Report 2018.

Shiyani, M., & Zare, H. (2023). Women and Development: Iranian Women's Roles under the Qajar and Pahlavi Dynasties. *Sociological Review*, *29*(2), 49–78. doi:10.22059/jsr.2023.91519.

Tavassoli, A., & Saeidi, V. (2011). The Impact of Women's Employment on Power Structure in Eyvankey Families. *Woman in Development & Politics*, *9*(3), 133–149.

Tavassoli, A., & Teo, L.K. (2021). Islamic Feminist Political Narratives, Reformist Islamic Thought, and its Discursive Challenges in Contemporary Iran. *Inter-Asia Cultural Studies*, 22(1), 49–66. doi:10.1080/14649373.2021.1886481.

Tavassoli, G.A. (2009). *Sociology and Education: Yesterday, Today, Tomorrow*. Tehran: Science.

Tsugawa, Y., Jena, A.B., Figueroa, J.F., Orav, E.J., Blumenthal, D.M., & Jha, A.K. (2017). Comparison of Hospital Mortality and Readmission Rates for Medicare Patients Treated by Male vs Female Physicians. *JAMA Intern Med*, 177(2), 206–213. doi:10.1001/jamainternmed.2016.7875.

Whaley, L.A. (2003). *Women's History as Scientists: A Guide to the Debates*. Santa Barbara, California: ABC-CLIO, INC.

Wollstonecraft, M. (2004). *A Vindication of the Rights of Woman*, edited by Miriam Brody. Harmondsworth: Penguin.

CHAPTER 5

Women and Politics in Post-Revolution Iran: An Overview

Zahra Nejadbahram

1 Introduction

Political developments in a society introduce momentous changes to the lifestyle and identity of citizens. These changes manifest themselves in their needs, demands and approaches. Throughout history, women were viewed as second-class citizens. With the development of human society and formation of democratic political establishments and the acceptance of suffrage as an underlying principle of such systems, the stage was set for women's voices to be heard in society. The struggles of Iranian women on social and familial fronts over the past 150 years have painted a once unimaginable picture of them on the world stage. One can trace the history of political movements and the contribution of women to the day-to-day affairs of society back to the 18th century. Initially, women acted individually and sporadically. As time passed by, women were turned into a growing chorus and made their mostly conservative movement more palpable.[1] Toward the end of the 20th century when globalization was on the march and the popular move toward democracy was gathering momentum, women in different countries acted to get involved in politics and to contribute to the process of decision-making.

The approach of society to these developments has always been tinged with doubt. In Iran, the ripples emerging on the road to political participation—which started before the revolution—turned into a seismic wave after the revolution. In a country where jobs in the education and healthcare system used to provide the best platform for women's presence in society, the formation of a new political establishment coincided with calls for their serious contribution, and women tapped into their potential to take giant steps toward such contribution. A look at actual turnout figures in proportion to eligible voters and election participants in 12 rounds of presidential elections would reflect the momentum with which women entered politics. When as many as

---

1 Shirin Ahmadnia, The Proceedings of a Conference on Women's Political Participation in Islamic Countries, Tehran, Allameh Tabataba'i University, 2004.

20 million were eligible to vote in the first presidential election, 70 percent turned out to cast a ballot. In the 12th presidential election, the number of eligible voters jumped to more than 56 million and turnout stood at over 73 percent. In the intervening elections, turnout averaged 50-plus percent, with some election years registering 80 percent turnout.

What is interesting is that women accounted for 49 percent of voters against the 51 percent figure for men.[2] Statistics also show that the number of female representatives in the legislature rose from four in the First Assembly to 17 in the 10th and 11th parliaments. As much as that trend has been progressive, it needs to be seriously boosted. A similar pattern can be seen in the number of female students and educated women who participated in different presidential elections. That is why developments in women's participation during and after the revolution warrant review and assessment. This chapter tries to look at the context of these developments and find an answer to the following question: What are the biggest internal and external obstacles standing in the way of women's political participation?

2   Political Participation

The word "participation" means involvement in and contribution to an activity. Strictly speaking, it is the voluntary involvement of some members of the public in sociopolitical programs and initiatives that play a key role in national development. Participation is the result of measures to render the public more sensitive, boost the level of their understanding and bolster their capability to respond to economic, political and social development programs.[3] Just like other political concepts, political participation is a much-debated type of contribution whose definitions and interpretations have changed in the wake of World War II. According to Michael Rush, political participation covers all voluntary behaviors of citizens that leave a direct or indirect impact on public policies of a society.[4] Some link political participation to civil rights which impact or seek to impact collective affairs.[5] A similar definition of political participation has been put forth by Lester W. Milbrath, who describes it as

---

2   Interior Ministry figures.
3   G. Ja'farinia, "A Review of Socioeconomic Factors Affecting Political Participation of Citizens in Khormoj." *Research Letter of Political Science*, 7(2) (2012): 87–122.
4   Michael Rush, *Politics and Society: An Introduction to Political Sociology*. London: Routledge. 1992.
5   Hans Kelin, "The Right to Political Participation and the Information Society." Montreal, Global Democracy Conference, 2005.

"actions of private citizens by which they seek to influence or to support government and politics."[6] Levels of participation are of the essence here. Since
every action that sees a person get involved in an activity is participation, the
type of participation should be looked at through the prism of its levels.

3   Levels of Participation

Researchers liken the levels of political participation to a hierarchy that reveals
the depth of involvement. Milbrath and Rush have presented models that cover
all types of political participation along the spectrum in any political establishment. These models view holding political and executive office as the highest level of political participation and casting votes in elections as the lowest.
The most important levels of political participation, in ascending order, are as
follows: 1. Casting ballot, thus playing a role in political and social selection,
2. Freedom of expression and membership in active political institutions and
critiquing the performance of institutions, officials and the state, 3. Running
for political office and getting involved in free electoral campaigns, 4. Getting
involved in structural reforms, and 5. Taking action to introduce fundamental changes in state institutions as well as state structure. Based on the levels
mentioned above, the most important components or variables playing a role
in participation fall into two categories: individual and social. Sociopolitical
system, and age, gender, occupation and family are pillars of political participation which create two types of stimulants: external and internal. The former
is rooted in the sociopolitical system, while the latter is driven by aspects of
people's personal lives which in turn help form their perceptions and views.
Interaction between these two variables leads to decision-making and eventually to participation.

4   Sociopolitical Approach to Women's Political Participation

Common approaches to women's political participation can be defined in the
context of socialization, a process during which individuals identify and internalize common values on which a social system relies. Political socialization
leads to political participation in society. In the process, individuals learn that
they need to exercise the right to self-determination through participation in

---

6   Lester W. Milbrath, *Political Participation: How and Why People Get Involved in Politics?*
    Chicago: Rand McNally, 1977.

sociopolitical decision-making. Primary and secondary factors are involved in political socialization.[7] Likewise, sexual socialization is a process in which people develop sexual orientation and learn how to behave as a man or woman.[8] According to this theoretical paradigm, depending on mainstream culture, one of the variables most effective in political participation is gender and sexual socialization. Thus, political socialization, which is based on primary factors such as age, family and peers together with secondary factors including political system, parties, and trade associations paints a different gender-based picture of women's political participation. In light of political participation, women's political action manifests itself in taking on traditions and traditional views on the one hand and being part of the power structure on the other.

5   Women's Political Participation

Women's political participation is defined as their involvement in political affairs such as casting and winning votes. Although such involvement goes back quite a while, it is fairly new in the history of human civilization. That is why this kind of participation requires analysis. Research suggests that women show apathy toward politics even though they are constantly faced with political issues. Although humans are political beings, they do not seem to have a sense of belonging to two manifestations of politics: state and government. The reasons why women are far from interested in politics fall into two categories: 1. General factors impacting political participation, including that of men and women. In women's case though, the deterrence is more intense. 2. Women's-specific factors, including characteristics, which are in turn influenced by issues such as culture and political socialization.[9] Political pundits believe that socioeconomic and cultural position, religion, ethnicity, race, a society's political structure and age are among factors that directly influence political participation. Gender belongs to the same category too.[10]

In a traditional way of thinking, whenever the question of female gender is brought up, a set of predetermined responsibilities in comparison with men

7   Azam Ravadad, "Iran's Political Cinema and Female Film Directors." The Proceedings of a Conference on Women's Political Participation in Islamic Countries. Tehran, Allameh Tabataba'i University, 2004.

8   K. Safiri, *Sociology of Gender*. Tehran: Jamehshenasan Publications, 2009.

9   O. Chaboki, "The Role of Psychological Factors in Women's Political Participation." The Proceedings of a Conference on Women's Political Participation in Islamic Countries. Tehran, Allameh Tabataba'i University, 2004.

10   Ibid., 286.

quickly jumps to the foreground. That is immediately followed by a standard conclusion: Women are made to learn that politics is the realm of men, a concept they should internalize and consider normal. In conditions as such, the cultural norms individuals come to learn in the course of socialization define politics as masculine and boost expectations that women should be solely committed to household and social services. This approach is rooted in functionalism.[11] Although women's political participation is a fairly new concept in the social literature of the world, Iran included, it is defined in the context of wider social participation. So, women's political participation, either en masse or in the form of individual elites, covers all activities that stem from the realm of power. Despite the active, effective presence of Iranian women during the course of the revolution, the level of their post-revolution political participation requires a closer look.

6   Women's Political Participation after the Revolution

During and after the 1979 revolution, women's participation emerged on three fronts. Public participation saw women take part en masse in national rallies and demonstrations, alongside their families or independently, to air their views on national issues.[12] Electoral participation saw women turn out to cast ballots. Given the voter population, women accounted for 45 to 49 percent of the electorate and political participation in which women served as political representatives in the national assembly and councils as well as in managerial positions. The ratio of women's participation on the third front was limited and progressed slowly despite their massive presence on the first two fronts.

---

11   This is also the viewpoint of Talcott Parsons and Robert Bales on gender differences and socialization. For this viewpoint, see Z. Shojaei, *An Anthology for Tomorrow's Women.* Tehran: Sureh-Mehr Publications, 2004; and M. Movahed, "Women's Political Participation and Social Factors: A Case Study in Bandar Abbas." *Women's Studies Journal,* 1(3) (2003): 3–28.

12   Political/public involvement refers to involvement in decision-making and in setting the stage for political activities such as participation in elections, rallies and demonstrations, etc. (sociology.blogfa.com Qom). Political/intellectual involvement: As a member of a multitude, each person tries their best, individually or in collaboration with others, to find their way into lawmaking bodies and to assume managerial positions at the highest level in order to be able to contribute to decisions to implement laws to the letter and/or make revisions that are necessary for social growth and development at a local or national level. See N. Mosaffa, *Women's Political Participation in Iran.* (Tehran: The Institute for Political and International Studies, 1997), 666–67.

The advances made in the post-Islamic revolution era should not be over-looked, especially in the fields of health and literacy. In these two areas, Iran enjoys a good position in the region in terms of global indexes. On the political front, though, relative success has been scored along the difficult path. That calls for closer attention to obstacles standing in the way and to the necessity of measures to promote such participation.

According to the Global Gender Gap Report, Iran ranks 150th among 156 countries in the global gender gap index, down two notches over last year.[13] In the economic participation and equal opportunity index, Iran's best performance comes in wage equality for similar work where it ranks 110th, having covered more than half of the path toward closing the gender gap (scoring 0.579). The lowest rank (152nd) is in workforce participation rate (scoring 0.246).

As for educational attainment, Iran ranks 119th, with the best performance as far as the gender gap is concerned belonging to enrollment (95 percent). This index covers four areas, namely literacy rate, primary education, secondary education and tertiary education. A look at Iran's status in all four sub-indexes suggests that the country has covered more than 85 percent of the gender gap in these fields. The widest gender gap can be seen in tertiary education where the female-to-male ratio is the lowest. Sex ratio at birth and life expectancy are the pillars of the health and survival index where Iran somewhat filled the gap by scoring 0.994 and 1.008 respectively. Although Iran's rank in the health and survival index (129th) is worse than its rank in educational attainment (119th), in the health index the gender gap status—with a score of 0.963—is slightly better than in educational attainment (0.953).

According to the same report, when it comes to political empowerment the country's status is different. Iran's 151st rank (with a score of 0.036) is barely any indication of the gender gap being filled. Women in parliament, women in ministerial positions and years with a female head of state (in the last 50 years) are the sub-indexes of political empowerment. Iran fares best in the sub-index involving women in ministerial positions. Under the seventh government, a woman took the helm of a ministry. Overall, the report suggests policy-making in Iran is geared toward filling the gender gap when it comes to educational attainment and health. In these two fields, not much gender gap remains to be filled. On the political empowerment front, the rate of running for office and the voter population should be examined. In the latest election for the Islamic Consultative Assembly, 17 women found their way into the chamber.

---

13   World Economic Forum: The Global Gender Gap Report 2020.

According to figures released by the Interparliamentary Union in 2022, some 26.2 percent of MPs in parliaments of 178-member states are women. In Iran, that figure is closer to 5 percent. It comes as women's turnout for the last parliamentary election (that of the 11th parliament) stood at 48 percent, with men constituting the remaining 52 percent of the electorate. A similar trend can be seen in various presidential and parliamentary as well as council elections. The status of women in managerial positions warrants scrutiny too. Due to the country's managerial structure, which has developed a not-required approach to women's management, Iranian women have failed to secure a remarkable place in the ranks of state managers. However, that has not come against the backdrop of growth in women's desire for socioeconomic and political participation. A study released in 2016 showed that women's share of managerial positions has grown from 1.9 percent under the fifth government to 17.4 percent when the 12th government was in office.[14] Of course, the growth in question is mostly related to low- and mid-level management and not to senior management.

The same study suggests that women's share of senior managerial positions under the fifth government stood at 1.1 percent and rose to 5.2 percent when the 11th government was in office.[15] This means that there has been a slow growth in women's assumption of senior managerial positions. The Sixth National Development Plan required the allocation of 30 percent of senior managerial positions to women. As far as women's management was concerned, that is the apex of lawmaking, a huge improvement was made over the course of the pre-revolution era. As it has been mentioned earlier, women's participation either came in multitudes or in the form of elites. Their participation en masse was considerable and came in different forms: 1. Involvement in the revolutionary process, 2. Turnout for periodic elections, 3. Turnout for rallies and demonstrations, 4. Membership of groups and associations, and 5. Participation in volunteer programs and contribution to the war effort during the imposed war. Political participation at an elite level, which meant rising to ministerial positions, winning seats in parliament and councils, gaining membership of political parties and/or assumption of top managerial posts, has shown slow yet progressive progress. The same holds true for political parties and institutions.

An important index in the structure of political parties is the number of female members having seats on their central councils. It should be noted that the Islamic Iran Republicanism Party has yet to name members of its central

---

14   Saeedeh Amini, "A Comparative Study of Women's Social Condition in the Last Two Decades." *The Journal of Social Science*, 26 (75) (2017).

15   Ibid.

council.[16] The percentage of female members of Principlist parties is smaller than reformist parties. A recent congress of the Islamic Iran Solidarity Party, a major reformist party, has named a woman as its secretary general.

When the ninth and tenth governments were in office, vice presidents for legal affairs were women. Under the seventh, eighth and ninth governments, the heads of the Department of the Environment, who served as vice-president, were women. In the eighth, ninth and tenth governments, there were five women deputy ministers. For the first time under the seventh government, a woman was named Minister of Health and Medical Education and that ushered in new opportunities for women. Despite the nature of the Islamic revolution and the viewpoints of its leader on the large-scale presence of women in all revolutionary matters, the country is a long way off its ideals but a progressive path has been created for women. Removal of mental obstacles to women's sociopolitical participation within families on the one hand, and the academic growth of Iranian women on the other should be credited for such progression. The political participation index that focuses on electoral turnout and political designations requires a closer look at women's political participation from social and individual perspectives. On the individual front, women's apathy toward political participation should be discussed.

7   Women's Reluctance to Politics

The highest level of women's political participation—running for elected office and political organizations—seems to show that they are less than willing to make their presence felt in political arenas. A study in the Middle East has revealed that women's presence in the workforce in oil-rich countries such as Iran, Algeria, Iraq, Syria and Yemen is slightly lower than their peers in countries with low oil reserves like Egypt, Jordan, Lebanon, Morocco and Tunisia. The West Bank and Gaza Strip are exceptions, though.

---

16   There are 40 reformist institutions in the country. But only 23 of them can be labeled parties. Others are institutions, guilds, foundations and exclusive clubs. Iranian Productivism Society; Reform Progression Party; Islamic Iran Solidarity Party; Will of the Iranian Nation Party; Assembly of Reformist Sacrifice-Makers Party; Assembly of Forces Following Imam's Line; Freedom Party; National Cooperation and Unity Party; Nedaye Iranian Party; Assembly of Islamic Iran Graduates; National Trust Party; Islamic Iran National Development Party; Mardomsalari (Democracy) Party; Islamic Labor Party; Party for Unity of Iranian Nation; Islamic Iran Freedom and Justice Party; Party for Solidarity of Iranian Graduates; Nation's Path Party; Executives of Construction of Iran Party; Islamic Iran Youth Party; Society of Intellectual Muslim Women; Assembly of Reformist Women.

In oil-rich countries, people earn a huge amount of money through means other than gainful employment, including privileges they are granted thanks to natural resources. This has lessened the need for them to rely on gainful employment and this in turn has shrunk the ranks of female employees. Besides, massive investment in education as a result of higher income as well as social conventions on the distribution of wealth has increased the rate of women's education, but women's actual presence in the workforce in the region has nothing to do with their potential presence in the job market. Conversely, countries with low natural reserves have inevitably relied more heavily on the development of labor-intensive activities and on a stronger presence of women in the workforce. That is why the rate of women's labor force participation in these countries has come closer to their capacity.

An analysis of labor market discriminatory practices such as the gender wage gap and occupational segregation shows women are treated differently in the labor market. However, this unequal treatment typically conforms to the experience of other countries in the world where women have a stronger presence in the workforce. Discrimination as such explains why the labor force participation rate for women differs in different parts of the world, especially in the Middle East and North Africa. Surveys of households in the Middle East and North Africa suggest that married women are most likely not to enter the workforce and that motherhood diminishes the odds even further. A reverse trend is seen elsewhere in the world where women are more likely to join the ranks of employees when they get married and bear children. Given research results, internal factors—apart from job discrimination which undoubtedly has a strong impact—are at play when it comes to the smaller numbers of Iranian women in the workforce. Women in Iran do not display a passionate interest in being employed.

By and large, a traditional gender model determines the roles and dynamism of individuals in households in the Middle East and North Africa. This model has three components: 1. Centrality of family, instead of individuals, as the main building block of society where men and women are given complementary—and not equal—roles. Men and women view the institution of family as a cultural blessing. 2. Confirmation of men's role as the only breadwinners of the family 3. And, a fundamental law of decency that ties the family's honor and dignity to women's honor and calls for restricted relations between men and women.

The small number of female candidates who have run for city and village councils shown in the table below can have statistical significance, although it is showing a progressive trend. The table shows women candidates are outnumbered by male contestants; we can closely scrutinize the minimum representation of women against the maximum representation of men. Public attitude toward politics at large and people's view of women's presence in the workforce are partly to blame for women's reluctance. Nonetheless, the Islamic revolution has gone the extra mile to improve women's participation in different sectors, an involvement that lays the groundwork for their political participation down the road.

According to a 2020 report by the Office of Vice-President for Women and Family Affairs, the number of women managers is expected to rise to 30 percent by the end of the Sixth National Development Plan.[17] The growing number of women in managerial posts will pave the way for their increased political participation; an achievement post-revolution Iran gained in its Sixth

TABLE 5.1   Candidates of different rounds of Islamic city and village councils by gender

	Female candidates	Male candidates	Overall no. of candidates	Women's share	Men's share
1st election (1998)	7,267	328,862	336,138	2.1%	97.8%
2nd election (2002)	5,867	213,090	218,957	2.6%	97.3%
3rd election (2006)	7,131	240,628	247,759	2.8%	97.1%
4th election (2013)	12,095	247,568	259,664	4.6%	95.3%
5th election (2017)	17,885	269,450	278,452	6.3%	93.6%
6th election (2021)			+298,000	+8.0%	−92.0%

17   When the 12th government was in office, a 179th session of the Supreme Administrative Council on July 18, 2017 acted on a proposal by the Administrative and Recruitment Affairs Organization of Iran to tap into the capabilities of talented youth and women, designate them to professional managerial posts and increased their share of executive management in the country. The council revised and approved an executive directive on how to pick and designate professional managers, subject to Decision No. 579095 dated June 21, 2016, as follows: Note 2. Women's share of managerial posts should rise to 30 percent by the end of the Sixth National Development Plan. The share of each executive body as far as such designations are concerned shall be determined and announced by the Administrative and Recruitment Affairs Organization in coordination with related institutions based on each organization's conditions.

National Development Plan. An increase in the number of female candidates who have run for city councils speaks of a forward movement of women as far as political participation is concerned. The designation of female managers at all levels rose to 22.6 percent in 2020 from 12.7 percent in 2017. As many as 8,488 women were added to the list of country's managers; with one percent at top-level positions, 15 percent at mid-level posts and 84 percent at lower-level posts. Overall, the number of female managers grew to 19,597 in 2020 from 11,109 in 2017, posting a total increase of 76.4 percent in three years. The percentage of top-level female managers climbed to 8.7 in 2020 from 6.1 in 2017; the figure was 3.14 percent for mid-level managers (up from a previous 1.8%) and 24.5 percent for lower-level managers (up from a previous 14.5%).

The number of female managers in provincial governors' offices which stood at 292 (3.8 percent) in 2017 rose to 554 (9.15 percent) in 2020; this amounts to a 7.89 percent increase in the designation of female managers in provincial governors' offices, governors' offices and district governors' offices over the past three years. It should be noted that 16 female managers were designated deputy governors-general in this period. Setting the stage for women's political participation requires a solid foundation which in turn needs managerial experiences, facilitated participation and education.

A gap has seemingly emerged between Iranian women's educational attainment and their political-economic participation after the revolution. Although efforts have been made in this regard, other than the level of women's willingness to join the workforce and get involved in politics—despite obstacles standing in the way[18]—there are additional issues that need to be dealt with. A survey of female students in different universities in 2013 revealed that more than 50 percent of respondents participated in elections, over 35 percent expressed willingness for effective political participation and about 54 percent either had no interest in political participation or had a neutral attitude towards it. This commands more attention when it comes to educated women in the country. Interestingly, only 13 percent of respondents said they were interested in getting involved in political activities. The survey also revealed that around 39 percent of students believed that men were more suitable for political office. A similar percentage thought otherwise, and about 23 percent of participants in the survey had no idea. It is worth mentioning that politics usually comes with restrictions as well as the price those involved in it should pay. The fact that female students are less interested in politics is understandable given that the number of people interested in politics in the world is small.

18   Zahra Nejadbahram, *Barriers to Women's Political Participation*. (Tehran: Rasanesh Publishers, 2009), 187.

However, countries have tried to educate their people politically by encouraging citizens to get involved in political affairs and by tapping into the potential of political parties and institutions. The condition is different in Iran because Iranian women have constantly had a strong presence in politics and in the developments leading to the revolution. Since the victory of the Islamic revolution, women participated with men in all political arenas, not to mention the times they were in leading positions. History has compelling evidence to bear this out. But the fact remains that women's involvement has taken the form of mass participation. In studying the main components of political participation such as knowledge, experience, economic participation and personal capabilities, one has to take into account the fact that Iranian women's slight interest in becoming elite politicians is more deep-rooted.

The literacy rate among women which increased substantially after the revolution and the number of university entrants which passed the 60 percent mark in the 1980s indicate that women could quickly catch up with men in terms of higher education and compete on an almost equal footing with them. The literacy rate among women now stands at 84 percent. Women have also taken giant strides in managerial posts but they still need to do more when it comes to economic and political participation.

8   Conclusion

In light of women's presence in academic circles where they obtain university degrees, an analytical gap seems to have emerged in discussions over their political participation. While women's employment rate stands at around 15%, their presence in the workforce is affected by their upbringings and their personal decision to be active in their households, except for a small number of women who seek to enter the workforce. As for women's political participation in which they face no serious obstacles, such as running for city and village councils as well as parliament, female candidates are smaller in number than women who go out and cast votes. The question that arises here is: If education and up-to-date knowledge as well as self-confidence are the main components of political participation, what causes women to have restricted access to political arenas?

In answering this question, two points command special attention: First, throughout the world, politics is a special arena that attracts special groups of people, with women maintaining a limited presence. Women are heads of state or government in ten countries, but compared with the number of world nations, which is 184, the figure is by no means considerable. Second, in addition to the existence of laws and facilitation, political participation calls for self-actualization, which is somewhat different from self-confidence. Individual self-actualization is a concept based on which an individual demonstrates a willingness to assume power and regards politics as an area different from others to get involved.[19] Self-actualization, which comes from teachings, skills and values that begin in childhood, flourishes in society.

The education women receive in family and society, together with their exclusive social roles which stem from the same education, brings into focus their desire for individual self-actualization in political affairs, especially in post-revolution Iran. Despite the fact that the stage has been set for women to have a strong presence in politics thanks to their educational potential and social opportunities such as the formation of political parties and institutions which prepare them for running for parliament and city councils, they display a scant willingness to make it a reality. The government's failure to lay the groundwork for women's political participation is also noteworthy. The creation of managerial opportunities for and showing examples of successful managers to girls are among the efforts that deserve careful attention. In the meantime, goal setting when it comes to women's political participation is a serious issue that should be driven through textbooks, formal and informal education, and what family and other social institutions such as media have to offer in this regard. A 2014 study revealed that women view politics as an

---

19   Individual self-actualization leads to a connection with political affairs. According to Nancy Schmidt, since politics is a human domain, individual self-actualization allows women to get connected to political affairs. Politics determines "what" humans are in the modern world, and humanity is reduced by those who reduce politics. The fundamental issue here is our willingness to shoulder the responsibility of our own lives. See Nancy Schmidt & V. Sermat, (1983). Measuring Loneliness in Different Relationships. *Journal of Personality and Social Psychology*, 44 (1983): 1038–1047; Maslow, the main founder of studies on self-actualization, believes that all humans have a proclivity for maximal application of their potential talents and capabilities. Such proclivity is called self-actualization. Maslow defined self-actualization as the process of growth and development of talents in order to reach perfection. To put it simply, individuals can fulfill their own potential capabilities and secure personal development only after effectively satisfying their social and emotional needs and confronting life efficiently. Maslow has identified a hierarchy of needs in a pyramid. There are five levels in Maslow's pyramid: physiological (food and clothing), safety (job security), love and belonging needs (friendship), esteem, and self-actualization. For Maslow's concept of self-actualization, see M. Farahmand & S. Mombini, & Y. Khorrampour, "A Review of the Relation between Self-actualization and People's View of Democracy: A Case Study of Students in Yazd University." *Journal of Sociological Studies of Youth*, 4(13) (2014): 89–110; A. Yar-Mohammadia, & F. Kamali, (2007). "A Review of the Relation between Emotional Intelligence and Self-Actualization of High School Freshman." *Journal of Social Sciences and Humanities of Shiraz University*, 26(3) (2007): 211–226; and D. Schultz, *Growth Psychology: Models of the Healthy Personality*. Trans. Giti Khoshdel. Tehran: Paykan Press, 2011.

all-male field and display deep reluctance to get actively involved in it, especially when it comes to holding influence in corridors of power. The main culprits in women's reluctance, the study found, were different socialization and sexual clichés women are indoctrinated with in the socialization process by institutions such as family, media, schools and educational circles. In other words, women's reluctance to get involved in power has more to do with the influence of socialization than the ruling system of government. To increase women's presence in politics, the first thing to do is to prevent the reproduction of sexual identities and clichés, a process which emanates from a society's culture in the context of the socialization process.[20]

As far as women's participation is concerned, socialization seems to be a major issue which is accessible through tapping into the already-mentioned potential in the context of individual and social empowerment. One important point comes to the fore here: giant steps have been taken as far as women's political participation is concerned, before and after the revolution. Formation of all-female parties, women's membership of political parties, the fact that a woman is leading a major party in the country, the growing tendency among women to run for political office and their interest in voting are perfect examples of the steps taken toward women's political participation. Compared with other countries, political participation has had different twists and turns in Iran. We should bear in mind that Iran's neighbors have seen increased female representation in parliaments thanks to positive discrimination, but Iranian women have adopted a spontaneous approach to politics with no positive discrimination in effect. Women's presence in educational circles, managerial posts and political office has been progressive even though it still has a long way ahead before becoming ideal.

Bibliography

Ahmadnia, S. (2004). The Proceedings of a Conference on Women's Political Participation in Islamic Countries. Tehran, Allameh Tabataba'i University.

Amini, S. (2017). A Comparative Study of Women's Social Condition in the Last Two Decades. *The Journal of Social Science*, 26 (75).

Chaboki, O. (2004). The Role of Psychological Factors in Women's Political Participation. The Proceedings of a Conference on Women's Political Participation in Islamic Countries. Tehran, Allameh Tabataba'i University.

---

20   See Mina Nazari, Ali Hosseini, Seyed Javad Emamzadeh, Mahdieh Pourranjbar, "A Study of the Relationship between Sociability and Women's Political Participation." *Women's Journal*, 1 (2014): 161–185.

Farahmand, M., & Mombini, S., & Khorrampour, Y. (2014). A Review of the Relation between Self-actualization and People's View of Democracy: A Case Study of Students in Yazd University. *Journal of Sociological Studies of Youth*, 4(13), 89–110.

Ja'farinia, G. (2012). A Review of Socioeconomic Factors Affecting Political Participation of Citizens in Khormoj. *Research Letter of Political Science*. 7(2), 87–122.

Kelin, H. (2005). The Right to Political Participation and the Information Society. Montreal, Global Democracy Conference.

Milbrath, L. W. (1977). *Political Participation: How and Why People Get Involved in Politics?* Chicago: Rand McNally.

Mosaffa, N. (1997). *Women's Political Participation in Iran. Tehran*: The Institute for Political and International Studies.

Movahed, M. (2003). Women's Political Participation and Social Factors: A Case Study in Bandar Abbas. *Women's Studies Journal*, 1(3), 3–28.

Nazari, M., Hosseini, A., Emamzadeh, S.J. & Pourranjbar, M. (2014). A Study of the Relationship between Sociability and Women's Political Participation. *Women's Journal*, 1, 161–185.

Nejadbahram, Z. (2009). *A Review of Barriers to Women's Political Participation in Iran.* Tehran: Rasanesh Publishers.

Ravadrad, A. (2004). Iran's Political Cinema and Female Film Directors. The Proceedings of a Conference on Women's Political Participation in Islamic Countries. Tehran, Allameh Tabataba'i University.

Rush, M. (1992). *Politics and Society: An Introduction to Political* Sociology. London: Routledge.

Safiri, K. (2009). *Sociology of Gender*. Tehran: Jamehshenasan Publications, 1, 7–28.

Schmidt, N. & Sermat, V. (1983). Measuring loneliness in different relationships. *Journal of Personality and Social Psychology*, 44, 1038–1047.

Schultz, D. (2011). *Growth Psychology: Models of the Healthy Personality*. (Giti Khoshdel, Trans.). Tehran: Paykan Press.

Shojaei, Z. (2004). *An Anthology for Tomorrow's Women*. 1, Tehran: Sureh-Mehr Publications.

Yar-Mohammadian, A., & Kamali, F. (2007). A Review of the Relation between Emotional Intelligence and Self-Actualization of High School Freshman. *Journal of Social Sciences and Humanities of Shiraz University*, 26(3), 211–226.

CHAPTER 6

Producing Space, Displacing Power through Political Discourse: Ali Shariati and the Discourse of Women in Iran

Afsaneh Tavassoli and Teo Lee Ken

1   Introduction

The study of intellectual history or political history develops from significant moments that arise in a society. Such occurrences give spirit and form
the lifeblood of historical-sociological enquiries on thinkers, ideologies, and
far-reaching social transformation. The 1979 Iranian Revolution is one such
moment. Michel Foucault, in emphasizing the distinctive and non-traditional
nature of the Iranian revolution and the struggles that would unfold thereafter,
noted presciently the revolutionary strength of religion, though at the same
time underestimating its durability.[1] Similarly, De Groot in reference to the
revolutionary movement wrote "such a movement had truly 'historic' significance, profoundly changing politics and culture in Iran, the political map of
the Middle East, and the character of international interests and involvements
in the region."[2] The significance of this pivotal event and process is timeless.
Its study is essential for the research field of political discourse and change in
Asia. In addition to the study of moments, the role and ideas of individuals
and social groups constitute another core element of such historical enquiries.
Thus, the discussion of this moment necessitates the reference to "the teacher,
preacher, rebel", Ali Shariati.[3]

Those who joined the Iranian revolution were affected by Shariati's innova-
tory theories and thus Shariati can be regarded as the forerunner of the Islamic
revolution.[4] Shariati synthesized Iranian literary culture, philosophies derived
from Europe and Shi'i Islamic thought. In his writings and social thought,

---

1   Janet Afary & Kevin B. Anderson, *Foucault and the Iranian Revolution: Gender and the
    Seductions of Islamism*. Chicago: University of Chicago Press, 2005.
2   Joanna De Groot, Religion, *Culture and Politics in Iran: From the Qajars to Khomeini*. London
    & New York: I. B. Taurus, 2007.
3   Ali Rāhnamā, *Pioneers of Islamic Revival*. Zed Books, 1994.
4   Muhammad Amin & Neelam Bano, "Implications of Ali Sharīatī's Political Thought for
    Iranian Revolution." *Journal of Islamic Thought and Civilization*, 5 (2) (2015): 56–67.

politics and religion converged. The role of Shariati as an ideologue of revolution has been discussed extensively.[5] Offering a distinguishing and contemporary discussion on Shariati, we argue that he did not merely ideologize and politicize Islam,[6] but distinctively constructed the *political*, and the space, that had not existed in narratives of the order and vision of Iranian society. In this novel space, the discourse of the women's question was renewed and expanded. Thus, despite the many criticisms and dismissal of Ali Shariati, his importance still stands out for his ideas have been the starting point and still frame the parameters for, firstly, the discussion of political ideas and religio-political discourse, and secondly the representation of the progressive, revolutionary and modern woman, in Iranian society.

In this chapter, we first highlight the social origins of Ali Shariati's social thought and political ideas. Next, it discusses how narratives of women and social change constitute a key component of his political ideas. In doing so, this chapter explains the nature and characteristics of Shariati's perspectives on politics and women. Thirdly, we examine how the articulation of Shariati shaped a distinctive space of political discourse and practice previously absent in Iranian society.[7] This chapter, simultaneously, discusses the subsequent critiques on, Shariati's perspectives on women, and the implications arising from those perspectives. Lastly, it concludes by considering the implications of Shariati's perspective of politics and women, and the contestations that occur within narratives of women, politics and society in the discourse on the women question, and Iranian public and national life generally.

The 1940s and 1950s to the mid-1960s of Iran was a period of intellectual ferment and political stirring. Distinct political discourses competed against one another. Among the three most dominant doctrines were the monarchical

---

5 See Dustin J. Byrd & Seyed Javad Miri, *Ali Shariati and the Future of Social Theory: Religion, Revolution and the Role of the Intellectual*, 2017; Robert D. Lee, *Overcoming Tradition and Modernity: The Search for Islamic Authenticity*. Westview Press, 1997; Ali Mirsepassi, *Intellectual Discourse and the Politics of Modernization: Negotiating Modernity in Iran*. Cambridge: Cambridge University Press, 2000; Rāhnamā, *Pioneers of Islamic Revival*; and Farhang Rajaee, *Islamism and Modernism: The Changing Discourse in Iran*. Austin: University of Texas Press, 2007.

6 Hamid Dabashi, *Theology of Discontent: Ideological Foundations of the Islamic Revolution in Iran*. New York: Routledge, 2017.

7 Stuart Elden, "There is a Politics of Space because Space is Political: Henri Lefebvre and the Production of Space." *Radical Philosophy Review*, 10 (2007): 101–116; Henri Lefebvre, *The Production of Space*. Trans. D. Nicholson-Smith. Cambridge: Blackwell, 1991; and Henri Lefebvre, *Dialectical Materialism*. Minnesota: University of Minnesota Press, 2009.

developmentalist, liberal nationalist and communist discourses.[8] The westernization drive of the royalist state, its autocratic nature and economic inequity also formed the social conditions that were the source and outcome of these intellectual-political protests and battles. At this point, Shi'i Islamic thought had not acquired a social dimension or radical perspective. After the mid-1960s, political discourses that incorporated narratives of Shi'i theology and tradition emerged in Iran. A religious intellectual current that sought the radical and social transformation of Iranian society congealed, pioneered and represented through the ideas of Ali Shariati.

2   **Ali Shariati and the Discourse on the Women Question:**
     Nature and Characteristics

Before Shariati and the 1979 Revolution, narratives on women, political and ethical-moral ideas had existed early in Iran. Women's consciousness and movement developed beginning in the late 19th century during the Qajar dynasty to the Constitutional Revolution of 1905–1911 to the 1950s. The establishment of the *Majlis* and a Constitution in 1906 during the Constitutional Revolution under Muzaffar al-Din Shah led to the formation of *anjumans* or places of gathering. Accompanying their establishment, women's *anjumans* advocating women's issues and welfare emerged. These *anjumans*, including *Anjuman-e Azadi Zanan* (Anjuman for Freedom of Women) and *Anjuman-e Mukhaddarat-e Vatan* (Anjuman of Ladies of the Nation), contributed to women taking part in the broader nationalist movement in the struggle for economic independence and national freedom. The women's movement fought also for female education and political participation in social life.[9]

In January 1907, the demand for access to education for girls was made, and 50 girl's schools were formed by 1910 in Tehran. That year saw the publishing of a newspaper dedicated to issues of women called *Danish* or Knowledge, and another publication *Shikufah* or Blossom in 1913. Women figures such as Taj al-Saltanah, Mahrukh Gawharshinas, Sadiqaya Dawlatabadi and Zaynab Amin occupied prominent positions in the educational, social and political spheres. Other figures such as Hasan Taqizadeh and Iraj Mirza also advocated for women's liberation, and for women to organize associations and form

---

8   Forough Jahanbakhsh, "The Emergence and Development of Religious Intellectualism in Iran." *Historical Reflections-reflexions Historiques*, 30 (2004): 469–489.

9   Janet Afary, "On the Origins of Feminism in Early 20th-Century Iran." *Journal of Women's History*, 1(2) (1989): 65–87.

institutions.[10] Thus, the women's question composes a fundamental subject within this trajectory. And the awareness women's welfare and rights, and their role in Iranian society was posed and has continuously been advocated by numerous political thinkers, writers, and activists from the early 20th century to the 1960s and 70s, to after the 1979 Iranian Revolution.[11]

2.1   The Political and Space

Two theoretical insights can be derived from these narratives and the processes of intellectual-political development accompanying them. First is the construction of the *political*,[12] where political ideas were articulated in society. Such ideas included justice, freedom, society, and equality, all of which were ethical-moral principles that intended to shape and imagine the social order and vision of Iranian society.[13] Complementing this construction of the *political* was also the formation and conceptualization of space. This was a space previously not existing in Iranian society.

Such space cultivated and harbored the concepts of women's justice and dignity, and the ideological and material conflicts regarding the nature, meaning and implications of those notions. Such struggles in this newly formed space took place not only in the mental and intellectual sense, but in the physical sense of mass action and movement. In this space, recently created and agitated by various political thinkers and writers, the ideal and knowledge merged with practice and action.[14] Those principles adopted and adapted by these thinkers and writers were European derived, and were in secular nationalist and leftist perspective. As Jahanbakhsh mentioned, these perspectives formed prevailing ideologies of the period.[15]

The emergence of Ali Shariati enacted a whole new space. His social thought and writings, speeches and activism, contributed to the expansion of the *political*. Shariati articulated an intellectual-political perspective that synergized European philosophies and social theory, and Shi'i Islamic religious

---

10   Ibid.
11   Farideh Farhi, "Religious Intellectuals, the 'Woman Question', and the Struggle for the Creation of a Democratic Public Sphere in Iran." *International Journal of Politics, Culture, and Society*, 15(2) (2001): 315–339; Valentine M. Moghadam, "Islamic Feminism and Its Discontents: Toward a Resolution of the Debate." *Signs: Journal of Women in Culture and Society*, 27(4) (2002b): 1135–1171; and Afsaneh Najmabadi, *Feminism in an Islamic Republic: Years of Hardship, Years of Growth*. Oxford University Press, New York, 1997.
12   See Claude Lefort & David Macey, *Democracy and Political Theory*. Trans. D. Macey. Cambridge: Polity Press, 1988; Pierre Rosanvallon, Dario Castiglione, & Iain Hampsher-Monk, *Towards a Philosophical History of the Political*. Cambridge University Press, 2001.
13   Rosanvallon, Castiglione, & Hampsher-Monk, *Towards a Philosophical History*.
14   Elden, "There is a Politics of Space."
15   Jahanbakhsh, "The Emergence and Development."

thought. A distinctive space emerged in Iranian society, one that embraced and contained narratives of Shi'i traditions, symbols, doctrines and convictions. Through Shariati's contemporaries and agendas, a novel "social space" was pushed into Iranian society,[16] challenging existing discourses and spaces, the Shah's government and the State. As part of the religio-political discourse, Shariati's articulation of the union between politics, Shi'i Islam and women formed a central constituent of this space.[17]

2.2   *Shariati's Perspective of Women in Iran: Three Ideas*

Among some of Shariati's most important works discussing the relation between women, politics, Shi'ism, and social change, are *Fatima is Fatima* and *Expectations from the Muslim Woman*. In the former, Shariati highlights several key principles. First, refers to the idea of equality for women. Women possess civil and religious equality with men. Shariati evokes the hierarchical nature of society and relations of power that exist and support these social structures. Such relations cause discrimination and exploitation, both political and economic. In this context, society should resist "power" and the "rulers:" "Instead of seeking history in rotted bones and fallen gravestones and rulers of the sword who hold the gold, seek history in the blood, life and motions of the people!"[18]

Shariati calls for "the people" to revolt and make history. In this process, Shariati advocates the pursuit of the values of "freedom, equality, justice, spiritual struggle" in the struggle. He utilizes the notion of equality and makes reference to the "people" in his call for resistance and change. It is one of the instances where he articulates and emphasizes the principle of equality, and relegates or rejects the use of gender categories or identities of difference.

In another passage, Shariati emphasizes the need to pursue the ideal of equality. Shariati discusses the narrative of the daughter of Prophet Mohammad, Fatima, and those who follow and emulate her in this pursuit. Shariati explains how Fatima continued the spiritual and political legacy of the prophet to spread and uphold "Truth, freedom, justice, piety, equality." Fatima embodies these values. She becomes the symbolic persona of equality, and the pursuit of this ideal corresponds to the remembrance of Fatima and continuing her legacy and struggle.[19]

---

16   Elden, "There is a Politics of Space."
17   Firoozeh Kashani-Sabet, "Who Is Fatima? Gender, Culture, and Representation in Islam." *Journal of Middle East Women's Studies*, 1(2) (2005): 1–24.
18   Ali Shariati, *Fatima is Fatima*. Tehran: Shariati Foundation, 1981.
19   Shariati, *Fatima is Fatima*.

The second idea that Shariati espouses is the principle of freedom. In *Expectations*, Shariati argues that the women's question has always been an intellectual problem. The discourses on women have been shaped by the engagement against modern thought and developments. Choosing one of two approaches, societies have either opposed tradition or initiated an ambiguous project of progress. For him, the ignorance of Western ideas and values is the cause, and Shariati critiques both traditional scholars and modern intellectuals. In *Fatima*, Shariati illustrates the position and role of a woman in the conventional family and Iranian society.[20] He depicts how the person of the woman is represented through tradition and religion. Both treat and identify women as incomplete, lacking control and subservient. He critiques the prevailing view of woman dominant. For Shariati, this is how "her mother, father, uncle and other members of her family" treats her through "religion, ethics, character, chastity and strength". Such existing customs are static and inhibiting.[21]

On the other hand, there is the modern woman. For such a woman, there are "dancing parties, surprises, bars, night clubs and dirty cafeterias" that she attends.[22] In contrast to the traditional woman, the latter possesses freedom in her choice of actions and places she attends. Shariati adds, for "she has money and no problems and no reason for living." Then "out of boredom, she leaves the house to go shopping and then, under a veil, she tries to compensate for her losses with amusement, exaggeration in jewelry, makeup, the multiple changes in decorations that it can bring about and expensive purchases of strange things so that she can induce wonder and amazement in others."[23] In *Expectations*, Shariati reproaches the West for the fixation on wealth and consumerism produced by modern life. He emphasizes the discourse of sex constructed by Freud as the driving ideology of modernity. Its domination and the preoccupation with excessive consumption degraded the value and dignity of women, Shariati argues. The West not only colonizes the East, but also the West itself, albeit in different ways.[24]

In these discussions, a certain perspective of the modern is employed by Shariati through a polarizing dichotomy to depict intentionally the other exact opposite of the traditional. He portrays the modern world and hence woman as representing cultural inauthenticity, lack of meaning and purpose, alienation

---

20   Ali Shariati, *Zanan dar cheshm-e va del-e Shariati*, 2018.
21   Ibid.
22   Shariati, *Fatima is Fatima*.
23   Ibid.
24   Shariati, *Zanan dar cheshm-e va del-e Shariati*.

and consumerism. We are aware that the modern represents various meanings, values and ideals, not necessarily highlighted by Shariati. However, Shariati is not ignorant of them, for he employs such categories and ideas throughout his works and speeches. In this context, Shariati adopts this depiction to deliver a critique of the negative aspects of the modern condition, thinking and culture. He, therefore, poses the problem of values and thought, and of the persona of the woman who is caught between two opposing yet problematic and digressive worldviews.[25]

Shariati argues the authentic modern, progressive and enlightened woman must take a different path. Or Shariati attempts to argue, a third path. She is distinct from the traditional and modern woman.[26] Such a woman can choose to cultivate new values and is prepared to resist old customs and culture that hinder change and the attaining of these values. Shariati offers a radical departure from the conventional notion of the woman persona. It is necessary to acquire knowledge and to partake in the "formation of a culture" and to develop and possess a "clear-sighted vision" for a society to become the new woman and to be free. She defends, and brings others to uphold "the human reverence of women."[27]

Similar to the person and symbol of Fatima who represents the ideal and principle of equality, Fatima is also the complete and exemplary personification of the ideal of freedom. Fatima chose a life of hardship, struggle and responsibility, exemplifying consciousness and autonomy through her commitment to the Prophet and Ali. Building on the personas of Fatima as well as Zeinab, Shariati argues that the real Muslim woman is one that chooses.[28] Fatima and Zeinab are the epitome, and link that ties together and represents Shariati's perspective of the relation between politics or political ideas, Shi'i Islamic thought and women. This is related, and leads to the third overriding theme in *Fatima is Fatima*, and that is a key feature of Shariati's social thought more generally in terms of his discussion and focus on women. This theme refers to the notion of identity.

The notion of identity forms arguably the most crucial and significant aspect of Shariati's social thought, and his attempt to articulate a progressive and modern perspective of women. In *Fatima*, the modern conception of a

---

25   Dabashi, *Theology of Discontent*; Shariati, *Fatima is Fatima*.
26   Ibid.
27   Ibid.
28   Shariati, *Zanan dar cheshm-e va del-e Shariati*.

woman poses and is concerned with the question of "Who am I?"[29] Shariati identifies three models for the modern woman, consisting of Hajar, Zeinab and Fatima. Hajar occupies a significant role in one of the most important events of *hajj*, the *sa'y*, and "is the first and distinguished character." Shariati calls for Muslims to play the role of Hajar in *sa'y*.[30] In the face of hardship and struggle, Hajar continues to persevere against the odds with conviction to pursue her purpose and realize her objective. She is therefore an exemplary role model for others to follow. Shariati explains that in the human social system and system of polytheism, as a woman, she is "a poor, belittled Ethiopian slave and maid." However, she is none of these "in the system of monotheism." Emphasizing Hajar's value and primacy as "the addresser of Allah," Shariati suggests that "in the house of Allah, she is the only woman, a mother."[31] Shariati, in rhetorical fashion, asks who is Hajar, and expresses that she has neither any support nor resources and is steeped in dire conditions. In oratorical, overelaborate and dramatic form, he unearths Hajar as an unwanted, lost and wretched being by employing the Islamic narrative of Hajar.[32]

Hajar also represents knowledge, and the unity of the temporal, for instance philosophy, and the divine or hereafter such as the will of God. Not only is Hajar a symbol of resolve and struggle, but also of faith. Shariati invokes the practices of *sa'y* and *tawaf* that occur during *hajj*, where the former represents effort, and the latter illustrates love and belief or spirituality, and its relation to Hajar. Therefore, Hajar symbolizes struggle and belief, and the union of reason and faith. It is the "woman, a black Ethiopian slave and a mother" Hajar, as the exemplar of a human that "all the worldly philosophers, scientists and great thinkers who are searching for faith and facts are to learn the great lesson of Allah."[33]

It is Fatima, who, Shariati discusses with the highest regards. Shariati reveals how prophet Mohammad called her among the four of "the best women in the world," the others being Mary, Assiyeh and Khadijah.[34] He traces the meaning of social commitment and responsibility as represented by Fatima's position and actions in the event and rendering of *Fadak*. Invoking the Shi'i narrative of *Fadak*, Shariati states how Fatima insisted on her claims to *Fadak* and persisted

---

29   Ibid.
30   Ali Shariati, *Hajj.* Trans. A. Behzadnia & N Denny. Evecina Cultural and Education Foundation, 1977.
31   Ibid.
32   Ibid.
33   Ibid.
34   Shariati, *Fatima is Fatima.*

in asserting her rights despite existing opposing views and individuals who rejected her requests and claims. This affirms the importance of struggle and for standing firm and pursuing one's rights and the truth. For Fatima, *Fadak* was passed down and an inheritance to her from Prophet Mohammad.[35] Fatima personifies rebellion, struggle and conviction.

Even after death, Fatima remains the figure for the conflict and struggle of goodness against evil, justice against injustice and the oppressed against the oppressors. In time and history, she becomes the inspiration and touchstone for all after her, and the new generations.[36] Fatima answered the question of how to be a woman with her profound childhood and adulthood. She was constant in her struggle and resistance on two fronts. Externally, Fatima upheld truth and ethics, and commitment and struggle in the home of her father, in the home of her husband and society. Internally, she refined her beliefs and ideals, and held steadfast to her convictions in her thoughts and behavior, and life as a whole.

Third and finally, Shariati discusses Zeinab. He explains the significance of Zeinab in Islamic history and in the struggle for Islam. He presents a heroic and revolutionary portrayal of Zeinab through the narrative of Karbala.[37] Zeinab was always with Husayn, her brother, in all the struggles against oppression and revolution of Karbala.[38] After the martyrdom of Husayn in Karbala, Zeinab persevered in carrying the message of truth and justice. If Husayn expressed and symbolized the ideal of justice through blood and sacrifice, Zeinab expressed the struggle for and truth of justice through words and the message.[39] Zeinab represents the leadership and radical qualities of women. As Islam is "a collection of living thoughts and ideas," Zeinab as well as Fatima, Shariati argues in *Expectations*, are the symbols of Islam for the liberated woman. The task of conscious and committed individuals, Shariati adds, is to convey the meaning of these personas for the generation at present, and for women.[40]

---

35   Ibid.

36   Ibid.

37   Shariati, *Zanan dar cheshm-e va del-e Shariati*.

38   Ali Shariati, *Shariati on Shariati and the Muslim Woman*. Trans. L. Bakhtiar. ABC International Group, 1996.

39   Shariati, *on Shariati and the Muslim Woman*; Shariati, *Zanan dar cheshm-e va del-e Shariati*.

40   Shariati, *Zanan dar cheshm-e va del-e Shariati*.

In all three portrayals of Hajar, Fatima and Zeinab, Shariati highlights their identity and personhood. He emphasizes their social and ethical being, and their autonomy. At the same time, Shariati invokes each status and role as a woman. Shariati employs, therefore, these two sides in two ways and manifestations, but for a reconciled single purpose. On one hand, he highlights their identity as a woman and their history, and role and responsibilities. On the other, Shariati goes beyond and elevates their status, not merely as a woman, but as a person with ethical and moral, and social and political commitment. They are part of the universal humanity. Possessing these characteristics, they struggle with conviction to attain the Islamic and humanitarian values and ideals of truth, justice and freedom. They are therefore, Shariati conveys, woman as woman, and also woman as social-ethical beings. For Shariati "the proper understanding of Fatima is the key to our salvation"[41] and in a notable passage expounds that "Fatima is Fatima."[42]

3 Politics and Space: Religio-political Discourse, Ali Shariati and Islamic Feminist Critique

The religio-political discourse that emerged in the mid1960s and of which Ali Shariati was a pioneer and conceived and articulated this discourse, led to the expansion of the *political* and more importantly constructed a novel space of political discourse in Iranian society. Such a space had not existed in the modern Iranian political landscape and narrative. With Shariati, the space of the religio-political emerged. It was a "conceived space"[43] that contained and amalgamated European-derived philosophy and social and political thought, Shi'i Islamic thought and Iranian literary culture and traditions. It was precisely the combination of idealism and materialism, and the linking of social conditions and troubles to the transcendental and utopian, which exposed Shariati to sharp and unforgiving critique, both then and now. However, theoretically and socially, this constituted a profound and radical moment, and intellectual-political move.

Such a move proved influential for it not only opened and constructed space in mental terms or in the abstract, but also in public and on the streets. This religio-political discourse and its articulation through the speeches and rhetoric of Shariati brought thousands and the masses onto the roads, parks, buildings and monuments to protest against the Shah and his government, and the

---

41   Shariati, *Zanan dar cheshm-e va del-e Shariati.*
42   Shariati, *Fatima is Fatima.*
43   Elden, "There is a Politics of Space."

State. A physical space emerged and expanded, arising from and linked to the "conceived space." The former, we can identify as "perceived space" and it is this space where rebels, revolutionaries and protestors acted and demanded social change. It is this interaction between the mental and physical, and the conceived and perceived, and its outcome, that led Foucault to observe the power and dynamism of an Islamic movement.[44]

These two spaces, *conceived* and *perceived*, are however not the only facets that form the essence and basis of the religio-political discourse. In addition to the link between the *conceived* and *perceived* spaces, there is a third facet and space that connects both the *conceived* and *perceived*. One of the vital places preceding the Iranian revolution was the *Hosseiniyeh Ershad*.[45] Founded initially and supported by Mohammad Homayun, Abdol-Hossein Aliabadi and Nasser Minachi Moqaddam, and led by the cleric and philosopher Murtada Mutahhari,[46] it was in *Ershad* where Shariati delivered his most forceful speeches.

Hosseiniyeh Ershad was distinct from other traditional Hosseiniyeh in terms of function and landscape. As a *place*, it combined the remembrance of Husayn through rituals and the cultivation of modern Shi'i political thought. While modern in form and equipped with modern technology, the Ershad also had traditional elements including ornamental designs, sayings of the Prophet's family and Persian poetic verses.[47] By combining traditional symbolisms and internal modern spatial design, the Ershad provided the space for intellectual debates, discourses on Islamic thought and the development of women's discourse. It held sessions encompassing Quranic lessons to sociology to language learning such as English. Events in Ershad also had artistic and aesthetic flair as it hosted theaters, talks on architecture and art shows. The rich eclecticism and diversity found in its events and discourses marked the unique characteristic of the Ershad.

The radical ideas and eloquent language Shariati expressed made his lectures popular. Those attracted young people, university students and activists in enormous numbers. In *Ershad*, these talks cultivated revolutionaries and militant agitators in their resistance and revolt against the Shah and his government. Here, woman activists and revolutionaries developed the ideas of, and were inspired to take up, radical and militant protest and action against

---

44   Afary & Kevin, *Foucault and the Iranian Revolution.*

45   Pamela Karimi & Saba Madani, *Monument to an Alternate Islamist Movement: Hosseiniyeh Ershad and its Legacy,* in *Cities and Islamisms: On the Politics and Production of the Build Environment,* ed. B. Batuman. Abingdon, Oxon: Routledge, 2020.

46   Ibid; Also see Rāhnamā, *Pioneers of Islamic Revival.*

47   Karimi & Madani, *Monument to an Alternate Islamist Movement.*

the State.[48] Shariati's extolling of intellectual-political perspective fusing political ideas, Shi'i Islamic narratives and liberation and struggle through the religio-political discourse shaped the activities and ideas of those revolutionaries. Such a form of engagement also followed and operationalized the symbolisms and meanings that Shariati attached to Fatima, Imam Ali and Husayn, the ideals they embodied, and the struggle and sacrifice they represented. It constituted a place for "political mobilization and cultural change."[49]

The instance of the *Hosseiniyeh Ershad*, thus, constitutes the third space of the triumvirate. As the "lived space," Elden argues it connects both the *conceived* and the *perceived*, and interacts with them.[50] This space is social in nature. It is the site and discursive field where the ideal and material interact and influence one another through and resulting in the social. De Groot notes that Shi'i revivalist perspectives and practices of politics are linked to "ideas, images and movements" and consequently have consequences on relations and structures of religion.[51] The dual architectural nature of tradition and modernity of the *Hosseiniyeh Ershad* and its spaces that infused commitment and action followed Shariati's social philosophy and views on art and society, where art served a social purpose.[52] The embodiment of the religious and secular in the design of the Ershad also epitomizes Shariati's intellectual project of reconciling tradition and modernity, and the divine and profane.[53] For Shariati and the religio-political discourse, it is this unified space of ideas, the public, action and practice, and the cultivation of conviction and agitation and militancy, which constituted, shaped and contained the perspective of the modern, progressive, and revolutionary Iranian woman persona or subject.

3.1   *Iranian Islamic Feminism and the Critique of Shariati*

However, the religio-political discourse and Shariati's perspective had its shortcomings and dangers. The implications in terms of the Shi'i Islamic theological narrative or perspective and Islamic government, as Afary had noted in her discussion of the revolution and its processes including gender relations and the social status of Iranian women, had been severe and far-reaching.[54]

---

48   Janet Afary, "Portraits of Two Islamist women: Escape from Freedom or from Tradition?" *Critique: Critical Middle Eastern Studies*, 10(19) (2001): 47–77; Rāhnamā, *Pioneers of Islamic Revival*.

49   Karimi & Madani, *Monument to an Alternate Islamist Movement*.

50   Elden, "There is a Politics of Space."

51   Elden, "There is a Politics of Space."

52   Karimi & Madani, *Monument to an Alternate Islamist Movement*.

53   Ibid., 130–132.

54   Afary & Kevin, *Foucault and the Iranian Revolution;* Moghadam, "Islamic Feminism and Its Discontents."

The legacy of Shariati's social thought and perspective, as has been mentioned above, incited many discussions, reflections and critique.

Najmabadi wrote of how the views of Shariati and the idea of "Islamic womanhood" had influenced the women protestors and factions of the Islamic tendency during the revolution.[55] Furthermore, the political perspective of Shariati and the political discourse against the Shah was also tied to third worldist ideology and discourse. In the contestations and conflicts of political ideas and discourses, the oppositional Shi'i Islamic political and the leftist socialist discourses were identified as representing and epitomizing Iranian nationalism and authentic cultural identity, against the Westernized Shah and his government and policies.

The attempt to focus on and change the position of women and their identity was an act and project to remove and eliminate Western influences and Westernization or *gharbzadegi*.[56] The results of this process and social change were varied, depending on the intellectual-political or political theological discourse or paradigm one belonged or subscribed to. In one Islamist paradigm, women who engaged Western perspectives of political ideas and gender were known as "*gharbzadeh*" or materialistic degenerate betrayers.[57] In the context of Shariati, the relation between his ideas, or at least the implications of his perspective, and the developments after the revolution and the religio-political Shi'i Islamic political and theological project contributed to the envisioning and realization of the symbol of the enlightened and revolutionary Fatemeh as the ideal archetype for the "new Iranian womanhood."[58]

Thus, after the revolution, women's identity, body, and role in Iranian society became the site of contestations, conflicts, and power and control. The theme and subject of woman and gender, or the "women question" became the centerpiece of the Iranian political Islamic discourse.[59] The person of the Iranian woman had come to be seen as encompassing sacredness and sanctity, and the representation of Islam, Iranian culture and the Iranian nation. Still, the many ideals and principles that were promised and pursued through the revolutionary uprising and social change as conceived by Shariati, for instance and among others, ceased to materialize fully. Additionally, as Najmabadi had observed and analyzed the post-revolution period, the prevailing political

55   Kashani-Sabet, "Who Is Fatima?" and Valentine M. Moghadam, *Modernizing Women: Gender and Social Change in the Middle East*. Lynne Rienner Publishers, 1993.

56   Moghadam, *Modernizing Women*.

57   Ibid., 142.

58   Kashani-Sabet, "Who Is Fatima?" and Moghadam, *Modernizing Women*.

59   Najmabadi, *Feminism in an Islamic Republic*; Arzoo Osanloo, "Khomeini's Legacy on Women's Rights and Roles in the Islamic Republic of Iran," in *A Critical Introduction to Khomeini*, ed. Arshin Adib-Moghaddam. Cambridge University Press, 2014.

discourse and paradigm identified a woman's body as the arena of "social sickness." Hence, rules on proper appearance and behavior including the veil were enforced and women without the veil were condemned in order to rid "authentic Iranian Islamic culture" of "Western diseases."[60]

The move to change the legal principles and laws that influenced the status of women in Iranian society and regulate their behavior and outlook, such as the removal of the Family Protection Law[61] and also the rules and ethics for veiling, seemed to have and for many countered and contradicted for instance the value and principle of equality among women and men so fervently and passionately articulated by Shariati. These changes also constructed limitations on the notion and degree of autonomy that women possessed in their capacity as moral, and social beings and persons to determine their ways of life. This extended to the spheres and acts in choosing the values and norms they sought to adhere to, including the absence and being dispossessed of alternatives in choosing their identity.[62] Similar gaps and weaknesses prevailed also in the economic and labor, education and social spheres. Shariati's revolutionary rhetoric and idealism, and the discourse on women failed its ideals and vision.

A different discourse of women therefore emerged in the subsequent post-revolutionary years. The political and intellectual narratives seeking to highlight the issues and problems of Iranian women arose and were propagated by the social class that partook in the Iranian revolution.[63] These narratives and their discourse emerged from the current of women's activism and writing, and feminism, which renewed and sought to address the "women's question" in different, contemporary and progressive and modern terms.[64]

One of these discourses would come to be known, as "Iranian Islamic feminism".[65] The term "Islamic feminism" remains a critical and contested theme. The women's movement occupies a considerable presence in the Iranian political and intellectual, and social landscape. There are groups or factions within this movement that advocate for women's rights and welfare within an Islamic paradigm or framework. These women activists and writers seek and argue that only a progressive and modern interpretation of the Quran

---

60   Najmabadi, *Feminism in an Islamic Republic.*

61   Osanloo, "Khomeini's Legacy on Women's Rights."

62   Moghadam, *Modernizing Women.*

63   Shahra Razavi, "Islamic Politics, Human Rights and Women's Claims for Equality in Iran." *Third World Quarterly*, 27(7), (2006): 1223–1237.

64   Najmabadi, *Feminism in an Islamic Republic.*

65   Fereshteh Ahmadi, "Islamic Feminism in Iran: Feminism in a New Islamic Context." *Journal of Feminist Studies in Religion*, 22(2) (2006): 33–53; Moghadam, *Modernizing Women*; Najmabadi, *Feminism in an Islamic Republic*; Nayereh Tohidi, "Islamic Feminism:" Negotiating Patriarchy and Modernity in Iran, in *The Blackwell Companion to Contemporary Islamic Thought*, ed. Ibrahim M. AbuRabiÊ. (Malden, MA: Blackwell Pub., 2006), 624–44.

and its principles, as opposed to its understanding and interpretation through a traditional and patriarchal lens, can maintain and safeguard the moral rights and being of women.

However, it is noted that many of these activists and writers refrain from using the term "Islamic feminism" or "feminism." Despite this abstaining, there is a critical, rich and extensive corpus of academic writings and scholarship that nevertheless has tried to capture and explain this social movement, or current at least, of women and Islamic reform in Iran. In these studies and discussions, "Islamic feminism" is used as a conceptual, descriptive and elaborative concept and term.[66]

Although the Shi'i Islamic theological and political discourse affected and reshaped the status and issues of Iranian women in reactionary ways, these had the effect also of empowering them and giving women more presence and roles in the public sphere. For instance, in the years succeeding the revolution although veiling was seen as a form of social control, Moghadam in citing Tohidi notes that some women have argued for recognizing and improving the social roles of women on the basis that the implementation of veiling will safeguard and has ensured the Islamic nature and order of Iranian society.[67]

Thus, while the perspective and ideas of Shariati have affected the status of women in conflicting and troubling ways,[68] they have also been used and rearticulated again in progressive and reformist ways to argue for the rights and welfare of women.[69] These programs and developments, has been driven among others by Islamic feminism, but also by other currents such as the broader narrative of feminism in Iran, including secular and liberal feminism. Many of the earlier pioneers and first generation, and proponents of Islamic feminism originate from those linked to or involved in the revolutionary movements. Some of them included Azam Taleghani, Zahra Rahnavard, Monireh Gorji and Maryam Behrouzi.[70]

---

66   See Ahmadi, "Islamic Feminism;" Farhi, "Religious Intellectuals;" Roja Fazaeli, "Contemporary Iranian Feminism: Identity, Rights and Interpretations." *Muslim World Journal of Human Rights*, 4(1) (2007); Paria Gashtili, "Is an 'Islamic Feminism' Possible? Gender Politics in the Contemporary Islamic Republic of Iran." *Philosophical Topics*, 41(2) (2013): 121–140; Moghadam, "Islamic Feminism;" Najmabadi, *Feminism in an Islamic Republic*; Razavi, "Islamic Politics;" Nayereh Tohidi, "Islamic Feminism: Perils and Promises." *Middle Eastern Women on The Move*, (2003); Nayereh Tohidi, "Women's Rights and Feminist Movements in Iran." *Sur International Journal on Human Rights*, 13(24) (2016): 75–89.

67   Moghadam, *Modernizing Women*.

68   Moghadam, "Islamic Feminism."

69   Tara Povey, *Social Movements in Egypt and Iran*. Basingstoke: Palgrave Macmillan, 2015.

70   Moghadam, *Modernizing Women*; Moghadam, "Islamic Feminism;" Najmabadi, *Feminism in an Islamic Republic*.

Subsequently, the development and expansion of writings and publications that engaged themes and issues of women and gender further consolidated the discourse on women or the women question, if not feminism, both Islamic and secular. The circulation of this discourse also derived from a collective movement active in the critical period of the 1990s. It consisted an inclusive reformist movement led by women's activists, youths, thinkers and writers that campaigned for the reform of government in accordance with political-ethical principles of social justice, freedom and right.[71] The proliferation and popularity of women's magazines, journals and newspapers in the 1990s in Iran, pushed the subject of women back to the Iranian political and intellectual, and social and cultural center stage.[72]

These journals and publications consisted of, among others, *Payam-e Hajar* (Hajar's Message), *Zan-e Rouz* (Today's Woman), *Farzaneh* (Sage), *Zan* (Woman) and *Zanan* (Women). *Zanan* for instance, founded by Shahla Sherkat in 1991, presented views and writings that addressed and challenged traditional and conservative interpretations of Islam, and the patriarchal understandings and practices sustaining the relation between women and men in Iranian society. In *Zanan*, several key narratives underpin the advocacy of women's welfare and status, and gender justice in Iranian society. The first pertains to the idea and perspective that gender inequality derives neither from divine nor natural origins, but arises from a social basis and social processes in society.[73]

Another critical narrative proffered is the reinterpretation of Quranic texts and Islamic law.[74] To confront the contemporary issues and problems of Iranian women in a modern and changing world requires the understanding and application of those sources in ways capable of addressing the present social, economic and political challenges of women in society. Last but not least, the perspective that not only Islamic sources and principles but also other fields and theories of knowledge can complement and support the uplifting of the social status of women and the improvement of their welfare and dignity in society constitutes the third crucial narrative cultivated by *Zana*.[75]

As a result, in addition to Islamic theological thought and jurisprudence, other branches of study such as philosophy, sociology, history and political science, among others, are necessary and can contribute to analyzing the social issues and conditions that affect women in contemporary Iranian society. The

71   Moghadam, "Islamic Feminism."
72   Janet Afary, *Sexual Politics in Modern Iran*. Cambridge University Press, 2009.
73   See Moghadam, "Islamic Feminism;" Najmabadi, *Feminism in an Islamic Republic*.
74   Ibid.
75   Ibid.

merging of the religious and humanities is a hallmark of *Zanan* for it allowed both the "secular and religious thought" to engage and debate. In the process *Zanan* thus contributed to the development and expansion of a meaningful critical and radical discourse of women, and in particular the discourse of Islamic feminism.

Another different though related perspective or response is that of post-Islamist discourse associated to those of Susan Shariati, Reza Alijani, Ehsan Shariati, Sara Shariati and Hassan Yousefi Eshkevari. This has also been identified as the neo-Shariati discourse.[76] Saffari notes that two competing legacies have resulted from Ali Shariati's political thought.[77] The first identifies the Iranian Revolution and subsequent formation of the Islamic Republic as the outcome of his ideas. The other understands and articulates Shariati's ideas as an ongoing incomplete discourse and vision, constituting an alternative to Islamic modernism and Islamism.[78] This includes Shariati's views on women, which require renewal and critical reinterpretation in light of contemporary conditions. Saffari argues that this is possible by focusing on the egalitarian principles found in Shariati's thought, and his emphasis on human agency to pursue change.[79] He also suggests, citing Mahdavi that the reflection of the past and the responsibility to be actors of reform constitute the two main elements of Shariati's thought.[80] Khanlarzadeh has also elaborated on this reengagement of the past in her discussion of Shariati and Walter Benjamin. She suggests that the former combined theology and political ideas to magnify theology's relation to the past to construct a revolutionary discourse to affect change in the present.[81]

Susan Shariati, among others, highlights the limitations of Shariati's perspectives on women and society. She opines that the women's question did not constitute a central thematic, but part of Shariati's larger political discourse.[82] Still, Shariati was a pioneer in articulating the equality of women and men, and the role of women to participate actively in political action and change.[83]

76   Mojtaba Mahdavi, "One Bed and Two Dreams? Contentious Public Religion in the Discourses of Ayatollah Khomeini and Ali Shariati." *Studies in Religion/Sciences Religieuses*, 43(1) (2013): 25–52.

77   Siavash Saffari, *Beyond Shariati: Modernity, Cosmopolitanism, and Islam in Iranian Political Thought*. Cambridge: Cambridge University Press, 2017.

78   Ibid.

79   Ibid.

80   Mahdavi, "One Bed and Two Dreams?;" Saffari, *Beyond Shariati*.

81   Mina Khanlarzadeh, "Theology of Revolution: In Ali Shari'ati and Walter Benjamin's Political Thought." *Religions*, 11(10) (2020): 504.

82   Saffari, *Beyond Shariati*.

83   Ibid., see also Shariati, *Zanan dar cheshm-e va del-e Shariati*.

Susan Shariati (2021) notes that during the 1940s and 50s when Shariati articulated his perspective of women, social movements were still developing[84] and the concern of the period was for constructing broader narratives and projects. In doing so, Shariati provided an intellectual framework for the critical analysis of women in society.[85] She maintains that Shariati was able to construct a discourse of women, and of awareness and change in society. And through the development of this political discourse, women are able to engage in public life and social movements, and to also question religious interpretations.[86]

Reza Alijani also offers a critical reinterpretation of Shariati's political thought and perspectives on women. Alijani argues that the basic principles of Shariati's discourse expressed criticism of Islamic ideology.[87] In advocating for a different understanding of relations between women and men, Alijani calls for the reforming of Islamic teachings to reflect changing and existing social realities. Thus, he distinguishes between the general inclination of Islam and rulings that are context-bound.[88] Alijani develops this social perspective by building on Shariati's socio-historical approach to understanding Islam.[89] Alijani suggests that Shariati made key contributions to the discourse of gender fairness. In articulating his perspective on women, Shariati invoked three central tenets, according to Alijani. The first tenet was the emphasis on consciousness, the second on liberation and the third tenant was the freedom of movement, particularly from one's home.[90]

The post-Islamist discourse on Shariati advocated by Susan Shariati, Alijani, and others including Ehsan and Sara Shariati argue that Shariati conceived a political discourse of Islam that is humanistic, spiritual and egalitarian in nature. To them, Shariati's thought supports the discourses on gender, and is in contrast to the ideology of Islamism. For Saffari, this distinction can be made by identifying the responses of Shariati and Qutb for instance towards the modern and colonial condition.[91] In another important study, Mahdavi discusses the differences between the ideas of Shariati and Khomeini by evaluating their articulation of the notions of radicalism, public religion, and state and democracy.

---

84   Susan Shariati, *Zanan ra be Naghd-e Ghodrat Fara Mikhand: Arman Emrouz*, 2021.
85   Ali Shariati, *Zanan dar projeh-e Shariati*, 2009.
86   Shariati, *Zanan dar projeh-e Shariati*; Shariati, *Zanan dar cheshm-e va del-e Shariati*.
87   Saffari, *Beyond Shariati*.
88   Ibid.
89   Ibid.
90   Ibid.
91   Ibid.

While in subsequent years, the discourses of Islamic feminism and post-Islamist Shariati thought have encountered severe challenges and limitations, they nevertheless remain fundamental and relevant discourses in many institutions and spheres. These perspectives also represent vibrant and compelling intellectual currents and movements existing in Iran. Furthermore, such discourses serve as the link, between firstly the religio-political discourse of the pre- and post-revolutionary years and periods, secondly the ideas and perspectives of Shariati on women, and thirdly the contemporary intellectual, social and political currents that continue to shape and redefine the discourse on the women question, women's rights and advancement, and gender justice, in Iran today.

4 Conclusion: Contestations and Reform in Iranian Political Discourse

Ali Shariati has always divided opinion, and will continue to do so in the years and decades to come. This is inevitable, and will persist in line with critical and experimental scholarship on Iranian political and intellectual, and Shi'i Islamic thought as it continuously develops. Such is the significance and richness, as well as the open-ended nature of Shariati's social and intellectual thought. These viewpoints and ideas also serve as the crucial link between political narratives and discourse before, and after, the 1979 Iranian revolution.

Shariati's ideas, writings and rhetoric are partly the source of the religio-political discourse, as well as partly the consequence of this discourse in Iran. In this context, his political ideas serve as both the starting point and dividing line, and additionally grey area, between competing and conflicting, discourses within the discursive field and the interaction of political Islamic thought and Shi'i Islamic theological thought in Iran. Shariati's perspective of women in Iran is one of the instances and manifestations of these contestations, and is also part of the radical and innovative space that his political ideas and expressions have contributed to forming, as this chapter has attempted to argue and demonstrate. Subsequently, such narratives have given rise to the expansion of the discourse of the women's question and feminism, and reformism.

This chapter has focused on two of the key components of this discourse, Islamic feminism and post-Islamist reformism, which in Iran emerged as a response and critique of both the religio-political discourse and Shariati's perspective on the relation between women, politics and society. Though emerging as a critique, the Iranian Islamic feminist and post-Islamist Shariati discourse has also renewed and refined Shariati's perspective on women in society, to provide a more progressive narrative and discourse that advocates gender justice, and supports and defends the dignity and welfare of women in Iran. To what extent, such developments and processes can attain meaningful change and ends, remains to be seen as Fereshteh Ahmadi had pointed out and posed then fourteen years ago, and even today. However, as Ahmadi had additionally noted, it undoubtedly has served as a "path for rethinking gendered Islam in Iran."[92]

At the theoretical level, this chapter has also attempted to argue that the political ideas and rhetoric of Ali Shariati, and the religio-political discourse more generally, had opened up and constructed a radical space that had not existed in Iranian society earlier. It demonstrates the relation and interaction between political ideas, discourse and space. In examining the political history, traditions and landscape of society, the identification and knowledge of space is pertinent. It is in these spaces that political narratives and discourses are found, and where the ideal and material and social converge. It is through and because of space that social change and revolution take place. To articulate and espouse political ideas and values, is to make and construct space. Political ideas are the basis of space, and conversely, space is the basis and site for political ideas.

Finally, the study of intellectual history and political history enables us to understand these linkages between ideas, discourse and space. It affirms the intellectual project of Foucault who "was carrying out a historical analysis in such a manner that people could criticize the present." And in line with the need for and significance of post-Shariati political, and feminist as well as Islamic feminist discourse in Iran, such a project and discourses are a form of historical analysis and enquiry and critique that "protects us from historicism—from a historicism that calls on the past to resolve the questions of the present."[93]

Bibliography

Afary, J. (1989). On the Origins of Feminism in Early 20th-Century Iran. *Journal of Women's History*, *1*(2), 65–87. doi: https://doi.org/10.1353/JOWH.2010.0007.

Afary, J. (2001). Portraits of Two Islamist Women: Escape from Freedom or from Tradition? *Critique: Critical Middle Eastern Studies*, *10*(19), 47–77. doi:10.1080/10669920108720186.

Afary, J. (2009). *Sexual Politics in Modern Iran*: Cambridge University Press.

92   Ahmadi, "Islamic Feminism."
93   Paul Rabinow & Michel Foucault, *The Foucault Reader.* New York: Pantheon Books, 1984.

Afary, J. A., & Kevin B. (2005). *Foucault and the Iranian Revolution: Gender and the Seductions of Islamism.* University of Chicago Press.

Ahmadi, F. (2006). Islamic Feminism in Iran: Feminism in a New Islamic Context. *Journal of Feminist Studies in Religion, 22*(2), 33–53.

Dabashi, H. (2017). *Theology of Discontent: Ideological Foundations of the Islamic Revolution in Iran.* New York: Routledge.

Elden, S. (2007). There is a Politics of Space because Space is Political: Henri Lefebvre and the Production of Space. *Radical Philosophy Review, 10,* 101–116. doi:10.5840/radphilrev20071022.

Farhi, F. (2001). Religious Intellectuals, the 'Woman Question', and the Struggle for the Creation of a Democratic Public Sphere in Iran. *International Journal of Politics, Culture, and Society, 15*(2), 315–339.

Fazaeli, R. (2007). Contemporary Iranian Feminism: Identity, Rights and Interpretations. *Muslim World Journal of Human Rights, 4*(1). doi:10.2202/1554-4419.1118.

Gashtili, P. (2013). Is an 'Islamic Feminism' Possible? Gender Politics in the Contemporary Islamic Republic of Iran. *Philosophical Topics, 41*(2), 121–140.

Groot, J. d. (2007). *Religion, Culture and Politics in Iran: From the Qajars to Khomeini.* London; New York: I. B. Taurus.

J., B.DM.S. (2017). *Ali Shariati and the Future of Social Theory: Religion, Revolution and the Role of the Intellectual.* Leiden: Brill.

Jahanbakhsh, F. (2004). The Emergence and Development of Religious Intellectualism in Iran. *Historical Reflections-reflexions Historiques, 30,* 469–489. doi:10.2307/41299319.

Karimi, P., & Madani, S. (2020). Monument to an Alternate Islamist Movement: Hosseiniyeh Ershad and its Legacy. *In Cities and Islamisms: On the Politics and Production of the Build Environment, edited by* E. B. B. Batuman. Abingdon, Oxon: Routledge.

Kashani-Sabet, F. (2005). Who Is Fatima? Gender, Culture, and Representation in Islam. *Journal of Middle East Women's Studies, 1*(2), 1–24.

Khanlarzadeh, M. (2020). Theology of Revolution: In Ali Shari'ati and Walter Benjamin's Political Thought. *Religions, 11*(10), 504.

Lee, R. D. (1997). *Overcoming Tradition and Modernity: The Search for Islamic Authenticity. Boulder*: Co: Westview Press.

Lefebvre, H. (1991). *The Production of Space,* (*D. Nicholson-Smith, Trans.*). Oxford; Cambridge: Blackwell.

Lefebvre, H. (2009). *Dialectical Materialism*: University of Minnesota Press.

Lefort, C., & Macey, D. (1988). *Democracy and Political Theory,* (*David Macey, Trans.*). Cambridge, UK: Polity Press.

Mahdavi, M. (2013). One Bed and Two Dreams? Contentious Public Religion in the Discourses of Ayatollah Khomeini and Ali Shariati. *Studies in Religion/Sciences Religieuses, 43*(1), 25–52. doi:10.1177/0008429813496102.

Mirsepassi, A. (2000). *Intellectual Discourse and the Politics of Modernization: Negotiating Modernity in Iran.* Cambridge: Cambridge University Press.

Moghadam, V. M. (1993). *Modernizing Women: Gender and Social Change in the Middle East.* Lynne Rienner Publishers.

Moghadam, V. M. (2002a). Islamic Feminism and Its Discontents: Toward a Resolution of the Debate. *Signs: Journal of Women in Culture and Society, 27,* 1135–1171.

Muhammad Amin, & Bano, N. (2015). Implications of Ali Sharīatī's Political Thought for Iranian Revolution. *Journal of Islamic Thought and Civilization, 5* (2), 56–67. doi: https://journals.umt.edu.pk/index.php/JITC/article/view/299.

Najmabadi, A. (1997). *Feminism in an Islamic Republic: Years of Hardship, Years of Growth.* Oxford University Press.

Osanloo, A. (2014). Khomeini's Legacy on Women's Rights and Roles in the Islamic Republic of Iran. In *A Critical Introduction to Khomeini,* edited by Arshin Adib-Moghaddam. Cambridge University Press, 2014.

Povey, T. (2015). *Social Movements in Egypt and Iran. Basingstoke*: Palgrave Macmillan.

Rabinow, P., & Foucault, M. (1984). *The Foucault Reader.* New York: Pantheon Books.

Rāhnamā, A. (1994). *Pioneers of Islamic Revival.* Zed Books.

Rajaee, F. (2007). *Islamism and Modernism: The Changing Discourse in Iran.* Austin: University of Texas Press.

Razavi, S. (2006). Islamic Politics, Human Rights and Women's Claims for Equality in Iran. *Third World Quarterly, 27*(7), 1223–1237.

Rosanvallon, P., Castiglione, D., & Hampsher-Monk, I. (2001). *Towards a Philosophical History of the Political.* Cambridge University Press.

Saffari, S. (2017). *Beyond Shariati: Modernity, Cosmopolitanism, and Islam in Iranian Political Thought.* Cambridge: Cambridge University Press.

Shariati, A. (1977). *Hajj.* (T.B.A.B.N. Denny, Trans.). Evecina Cultural and Education Foundation.

Shariati, A. (1981). *Fatima is Fatima.* Tehran: Shariati Foundation.

Shariati, A. (1996). *Shariati on Shariati and the Muslim Woman* (T. b. L. Bakhtiar., Trans.): ABC International Group.

Shariati, A. (2009). Zanan dar projeh-e Shariati.

Shariati, A. (2018). Zanan dar cheshm-e va del-e Shariati.

Shariati, S. (2021). *Zanan ra be Naghd-e Ghodrat Fara Mikhand*: Arman Emrouz.

Tohidi, N. (2003). *Islamic Feminism: Perils And Promises.* Middle Eastern Women On The Move.

Tohidi, N. (2006). "Islamic Feminism:" Negotiating Patriarchy and Modernity in Iran. In *The Blackwell Companion to Contemporary Islamic Thought,* edited by In Ibrahim M. AbuRabiÊ. (Malden, MA: Blackwell Pub., 2006): 624–44.

Tohidi, N. (2016). Women's Rights and Feminist Movements in Iran. *Sur International Journal on Human Rights, 13*(24), 75–89. doi: https://ssrn.com/abstract=3028205.

CHAPTER 7

Redefining "Qawamoon" through Feminine Approaches toward Quranic Verses

Marzieh Mohases

1   Introduction

The discussions, viewpoints, and attitudes around women's concerns have helped shape both the historical and contemporary realities of women in Iran, along with Iranian society's customs. Anchored within such discourse, the identity construction of women shaped by Islamic teachings is one of the fundamental elements of Iranian culture and it increasingly affects the attitudes and behaviors of society in general. Islamic scholars are currently preoccupied with significant cultural changes that have interacted with the Quran's doctrines and served as the foundation for a number of theories. These theories incorporate both novel perspectives and the underlying causes of each of these events, as well as a rereading and revision of the conventional frameworks and procedures. This prompts a study to better understand how Iranian women intellectuals deal with various controversial ideologies. The topic of men's authority has been brought up frequently throughout the history of Islamic thinking, and it calls for the development of current viewpoints and perspectives. Undoubtedly, developing an effective policy to strike a balance and take advantage of modern capabilities will ease the way for theorizing and, to a certain degree, fill the gap left by earlier research.

Although many theories regarding gender differences are not exclusively derived from the Qur'an, the interpretation of Quran's verses serves to support them. The development of the understanding of verse 34 of Surah *Nisa'* demonstrates the impact of gender disparities in interpretation. This verse has attracted the attention of commentators and analysts for various reasons, especially in recent times. Contemporary scholars, unlike their predecessors, are confronted with important questions about the status of women in the family and society. To analyze these differences, they place emphasis on the system of developmental differences, which naturally results in different roles being assigned to men and women. A review of the interpretations of the verse of *"Qawamiat"* from the pre-modern era until now shows the fundamental changes that have occurred in the process of understanding and interpreting this particular verse. These developments have been the result of changes in the cultural context of Muslim societies and especially the position of women in various scientific, economic and managerial fields.

2 *Qawamiat* Verse

الرِّجَالُ قَوَّامُونَ عَلَى النِّسَاءِ بِمَا فَضَّلَ اللَّهُ بَعْضَهُمْ عَلَى بَعْضٍ وَبِمَا أَنْفَقُوا مِنْ أَمْوَالِهِمْ فَالصَّالِحَاتُ قَانِتَاتٌ حَافِظَاتٌ لِلْغَيْبِ بِمَا حَفِظَ اللَّهُ وَاللَّاتِي تَخَافُونَ نُشُوزَهُنَّ فَعِظُوهُنَّ وَاهْجُرُوهُنَّ فِي الْمَضَاجِعِ وَاضْرِبُوهُنَّ فَإِنْ أَطَعْنَكُمْ فَلَا تَبْغُوا عَلَيْهِنَّ سَبِيلاً إِنَّ اللَّهَ كَانَ عَلِيًّا كَبِيرًا

> Men are the guardians of women, because Allah has made one of them excel the other, and since they support women from their own means. Therefore, the righteous women are obedient and guard in the husband's absence what Allah orders them to guard. As to those women on whose part you see ill conduct, admonish them, and abandon them in their beds, and beat them, but if they return to obedience, do not seek a means against them. Surely, Allah is Ever Most High, Most Great.

In this verse, first of all, men's guardianship over women is confirmed. The reason for this *qawamiat* (authority) is also stated in the verse: one is the superiority of some (i.e. men) over others (women) and the other is men giving maintenance to women. This issue is also addressed in previous verses, "And do not crave what Allah has given some of you over others. Men will be rewarded according to their deeds and women ⌜equally⌝ according to theirs. Rather, ask Allah for His bounties. Surely Allah has ⌜perfect⌝ knowledge of all things."[1] After explaining the characteristics of righteous women in family life, this verse points to wife's disobedience and ways to overcome them. This verse does not elaborate on the meaning of disobedience, obedience and protection, but it has been one of the documents being used by scholars and jurists to establish the laws related to alimony and obedience, sexual disobedience and other family rights. In other words, Muslim scholars have never questioned the implication of this verse on the man's authority over the woman's body. However, the commentators, especially in the modern era, have had to explain

---

1 Surah *Nisa'*, verse 32.

the alimony system against sexual submission that they extracted from this verse using beliefs about the biological, psychological and social nature of men and women.

3 General Approaches to the Concept of *Qawamiat*

In general, the concept of male authority has been interpreted through the following approaches.

Qawamiat as guardianship in the family: a group of commentators of the Qur'an have considered the dignity of a man as the dignity of a manager and supervisor, and have used different interpretations to express their meaning. Some have interpreted it under the title of protection and guardianship,[2] others have considered this as man's guardianship over a woman.[3] Some have taken this as the domination of men over women; others went further and have even added the term "as a governor (ruler) over the subjects."[4] This approach to *Qawamiat* has drawn criticism from a legal point of view, because guardianship is the authority that a person has over another's property and life, and it includes the governorship of the father and paternal ancestor, prophet and ruler, while this is not true about the *Qawamiat* of the man in the family as his *Qawamiat* is in line with the interests and survival of the family and he does not have control over the property of the woman. What one should bear in mind is that today, the leadership of a man is more similar to performing a social duty than the exercise of a personal right. Therefore, the legislator's objective is not to grant the man superiority over the woman and to gratify his desires; rather, this leadership is entrusted to the man so that he can exercise his authority in order to preserve the interests of the family. This viewpoint that assumes men's position, as opposed to women's, is like the position of a ruler over his subject. The assumption that men are dominant over women represents pre-Islamic attitudes toward women's roles and the unquestioning dominance of men rather than reflecting Islam's perspective.

---

2 See Madrasi, S.M.T. *Man Hoda al-Qur'an*. 1st edition. Tehran: Dar Mohibi Al-Hussein, 1998; Sayyid 'Ali Akbar Qarashi, *Ahsan Hadith*. 3rd edition, Tehran: Baath Foundation, 1998; Najafi, M.J., *Simple Interpretation*, 1st edition, Tehran: Islamic, 2020.

3 Miqdad, F., *Gratitude Treasure in the Jurisprudence of the Quran*. 1st edition. Qom: World Assembly of Islamic Religions, 1988.

4 See Baha' al-din Muhammad b. 'Ali al-Sharif al-Lahiji, *Tafsir Sharif Lahiji*, 1st edition, Tehran: Nashar Dad, 2000; Shirazi, H., & Mohammad, S., *Al-Qur'an to the Mind*. 1st edition. Beirut: Dar al-Uloom, 2003.

Qawamiat as working in the family: according to a group of commentators, a man's *ghawamiat* entails standing up to the command, maintaining and caring, protecting and observing, standing up and endurance, taking care of women's affairs and being an agent, etc.[5] This approach is also very evident among the translators of the Qur'an.[6] According to this interpretation, the verse of *Qawamiat* merely alludes to resistance and not to domination. It is also emphasized that the obligation of *Jihad* for a man and the obligation to pay alimony confirm the fact that he is obliged to support and protect his wife.[7] Jurists believe that the scope of *Qawamiat* depends on custom, because in the eyes of the legislator, custom holds a special place in determining the scope of *Qawamiat*, and the heading of men over his family is different according to the customs and traditions of each community.[8] Therefore, they consider the meaning of heading as having a final say in family affairs and to upholding the interests of the family, some of which, like a woman's right to choose her place of residence and her line of work, are stipulated in the law and fall under the husband's prerogatives, and other cases are specified and implemented according to customs and habit, and the rational procedure.

Qawamiat in the sense of assigning major social positions to men: there are different views on the scope of men's *qawamiat*. Some interpret "men" and "women" to mean the superiority of all men over all women; others have also considered the *imamate* and governorship to be reserved for men by resorting to this prophetic verse.[9] This interpretation takes the scope of *Qawamiat* in the community and a wider environment than the family. This group contend that the generality of the verse shows that the ruling that is based on it (guardianship) is not exclusive to the husband towards his wife, but it is rather to the

5 Khosravani, M. & Reza, A., *Khosravi Interpretation*. 1st edition. Tehran: Islamic, 2012.

6 See Arfa, S.K. *Translation of the Quran (Arfa)*. Ch One, Tehran: Faiz Kashani Research and Publishing Institute, 2003; M. Ashrafi Tabrizi, *Translation of the Qur'an (Ashrafi)*. 14th edition. Tehran: Javidan, 2002; Esfahani, R., & Ali, M., *Quran translation (Reza'i)*. 1st edition, Qom: Dar al-Zhaker Cultural Research Institute, 2005; Ibrahim, A., *Tafsir Aamili*. Tehran: Sadouq, 1982; Farsi, J., *Translation of the Quran (Persian)*. Tehran: Domar Kitab, 1991; and Mesbah Zadeh, *Quran Translation (Mesbahzadeh)*. 1st edition, Tehran: Badragh Javidan, 2002.

7 Hijazi, M.M., *Al-Tafsir al-Shazrah*. 10th edition. Beirut: Dar Jail Al-Jadid, 1992.

8 Qomi, Y. & Ali Muhammad, S., *Family Rights*. In the Civil Code of the Islamic Republic of Iran. 1st edition, Tehran: SAMT, 2009.

9 See Tabatabaei, M.H., *Al-Mizan fi Tafsir al-Qur'an*. Qom: Al-Nashar al-Islami Foundation of Jama'ah al-Madrasin, 1982; Gholpayegani, M., & Rida, S.M. *Book of Judiciary*. Qom: Khayyam Press, 2022; Mazandarani, I.S.A., & Bin Ali, M. *Motashabih al Quran va Mokhtalifih*. 1st edition, Qom: Bidar, 1989; and Al-Sa'di, A.R., *Taysir al-Kareem al-Rahman, a tafsir of the entire Qur'an*. 2nd edition. Beirut: Al-Nahda Al-Arabiya Library, 1987.

type of women and men in general aspects that are related to the life of two tribes, such as governance and justice.

4 Innovation in Explaining *Qawamiat* Verse

At the end of the 19th century and the beginning of the 20th century, a number of different events such as the constitutional movement in Iran, the fall of the Ottoman Empire, the emergence of modern state countries, colonial rule and wider relationships between the residents of Islamic states and Westerners led to the development of new look to the relationship between religion and society. On the other hand, the religious reform movement in the Indian sub-continent, Asia Minor, the Middle East, and North Africa gave believers a fresh perspective on religion that made it easy to reconcile religiosity and moder-nity. This new attitude towards religious and modern values had a tremendous impact on interpretations. In this historical course, we will see that the inter-pretations were in line with the new gender constructions and new percep-tions of the abilities of men and women not seen in the earlier interpretations.

The evolution of the interpretation of this verse has been studied by certain Iranian women. In examining the development of interpretations of verses pertaining to women in the modern era, Forough Parsa demonstrates how the justifications connected to verse *Nisa'* 34 have found different explanations in the modern era despite not separating themselves from the prior rulings.[10] In other words, we are witnessing how the concept of gender differences, which has been the foundation of many views about the superiority of men over women and the system of alimony and subservience, has evolved in the eyes of commentators in the contemporary era. Iranian female Quran scholars have tried to show with "scientific" justifications that men and women should accept different roles in society and that this difference in roles is more "devel-opmental" and "natural" than legislative.

Some Quranic scholars have acknowledged the existence of women with intellectual, social and managerial abilities. However, they did not find a place for them in their divisions based on gender differences, and as a result, they were considered exceptions that do not disturb the general rule. For example, Banoo Amin says:

---

10   Forough Parsa, "A Feminist Reading of the Quran." *Women's Journal*, 6(4) (2014a): 51–71; and Forough Parsa, Meeting on the Fundamental Differences of Interpretation and Translation of Women and Men. Iran Book Agency (IBNA), 2014b.

God the Almighty has given men superiority over women in these aspects, and it should be known that this superiority and superiority of men over women in terms of mental strength and physical strength is generally on the whole, not inclusively on all people, because as it is known there have been and there are many women who are superior to some men in wisdom and intellect, but also in physical strength.[11]

Let me cite two examples here that provide different gender divisions by considering women who are not included in the conventional rules. These commentators have somewhat innovative views on gender differences, despite sticking mostly to what other commentators have said in their ultimate judgment of women and men. For example, Balaghi (2008) presents this division in his commentary. He states:

Men are all men (in appearance) and women are all women (in appearance), but in truth, each of them is of some categories: 1- A complete man: his sign is masculinity, courage, prejudice, and preserving the honor of himself and his wife. He is a sodomite, he does not expose his female member of the family to the auditory, visual and physical pleasure of others (and he likes polygamy). 2- A complete woman: her sign is to marry and win her husband's friendship and to obey him, protect his honor, and perform her duties as a mother (and she hates a co-wife). 3- A complete woman-like man: his sign is a woman's song and a desire to dance and obey men, and a desire to wear women's makeup and women's clothes, takes alimony and objects to co-wife. 4- A complete man-like woman: her sign is not marrying a husband and being arbitrary with men, and not obeying them, and when forced to marry, they usually end in divorce, and she will also fulfill her lust by wearing a leather penis and engaging in sex with other women. 5- A man who has some woman's features, but his man's feature is dominant, and his sign is that he has a woman and is not sexually assaulted except by chance, and most of the time he dominates the woman in maintaining his honor and in his opinions and beliefs, and sometimes he is defeated and this is when he suffers and does not turn away from dancing and wearing gold rings and wearing silk clothes and women's luxuries (and he does not like polygamy, but he agrees with debauchery). 6- A woman who has some man's features, but her woman's side is dominant, and her sign is marrying and obeying her husband

11   Banoo Amin, *Interpretation of Makhzan al-Irfan in Quranic Sciences*. Isfahan: Golbahar Publications, 2011.

incompletely and fighting with her husband and leading to multiple divorces (and she hates co-wife). 7- A man whose feminine side is dominant, and his sign is that he is more sexually assaulted and has a great desire for dancing and music, and his singing is more similar to women than to men and when married, he does not adhere to honor and hates wearing men's clothes, and he always wants to be alone with women. 8- A woman whose male aspect is dominant, and whose symptoms are similar to the symptoms of a woman whose male features are complete, but in a more relaxed manner.[12]

The Holy Qur'an only speaks about the first group, i.e. "complete men" and the second group, i.e. "complete women", but "the rest should be forced by these two groups to accept this natural, creative and psychological truth that comes from the mentioned verse."[13] Balaghi is also one of the few who specifically noted that according to the verse, God has made "some men" superior to "some women", not all men over all women.[14] The importance of rhetorical explanation is that it places gender differences in a "spectrum" and imagines eight genders (instead of two genders). Even though he only places two groups of men and women in ideal gender roles, he brilliantly manipulates the current stereotyped categories to provide each group an opportunity to demonstrate different tendencies.

Another example is Seyyed Mohammad Hossein Fazlullah. While rejecting the intellectual superiority of men over women, he argues that the attribution of *ghawamiat* (and differences in martyrdom) are due to both the predominance of affection in women and the educational circumstances of women. He argues that "as evidenced by the current examples, many women who experience personal and social situations that are comparable to those experienced by men have demonstrated their aptitude for comprehending both intellectual and practical issues."[15] Fazlullah's words are significant because he takes empowered women seriously and does not view them as exceptions to the general rules of gender differences. Instead, he sees progress for men and women as being a result of educational circumstances, with the result that some gender characteristics will change if the educational circumstances change. From

---

12   A.H. Balaghi, *Hojjat al-Tafaseer and Balagh al-Aksir*. Tehran: Hekmat Publications, 2008.

13   Ibid.

14   Ibid.

15   S.M.H. Fazlullah, *Tafsir Man Wahi Al-Qur'an*. (2nd ed.). (Beirut: Dar al-Mala, 1998), 235–236.

his perspective, the variations between the sexes are not just developmental but also to some part educational making them flexible and non-universal.

As the paradigm for protecting women's rights began to take shape in the 14th century, Muslim women in all parts of the Muslim world as well as in Western nations "had a different approach from men in these verses."[16] This view has it that "part of the Qur'anic verses which is related to women are thought-provoking to women themselves, while a male commentator may easily ignore them."[17] Women claim that the Qur'an is a reformist scripture with reforms throughout. The entire Qur'an exhibits both these structural and content improvements, as does the spirit that directs the text. The Qur'an has summoned all believers to these reforms, regardless of gender, and has made righteous deeds the standard of faith for both men and women. Belief, intellectual, moral, social, and devotional reforms are the essence of the verses. One of the fundamental and unbreakable tenets of the Holy Quran is the equality of faith between men and women, notwithstanding the functional and experiential distinctions between the sexes.

It should be noted that philosophers associate this stream of patriarchal interpretations of verses related to women with methodological shortcomings in such interpretations. In fact, women themselves believe that the commentators of the Qur'an have so far interpreted these verses with the method of sequential interpretation without paying attention to the verses that appear before and after them. As a result, they have not been able to maintain the structural and thematic coherence of the Qur'an. Such a sequential interpretation of the verses fails to accurately depict the status of women in the age of descent and is unable to predict the rulings necessary for Muslim women today. A person's comprehension of the Qur'an is directly influenced by their mental presumptions, inclinations, interests, context, and living environment.[18] The term "women's reading," a modern account of the interpretation of female commentators, does not imply abandoning accepted criteria of comprehension; rather, it is based on the same epistemological principles as men's interpretation.

Therefore, women commentators in their interpretation equally emphasize the revelation of the words and meanings of the Qur'an, the immunity of the Qur'an from verbal distortion, the immortality and universality of the call of

16   Parsa, "A Feminist Reading of the Quran," and Parsa, Meeting on the Fundamental Differences of Interpretation.

17   Akhwan Moghadam, *The Fundamental Differences of Interpretation and Translation of Women and Men*. Iran Book Agency, 2004.

18   Parsa, "A Feminist Reading of the Quran," and Parsa, Meeting on the Fundamental Differences of Interpretation.

the Qur'an, the comprehensiveness of the Qur'an, the possibility and permissibility of understanding and interpreting the Qur'an, the authenticity of the Qur'an's appearances, the permissibility of *ijtihad* in the interpretation, Qur'an possession of multi-levels meaning, the validity and reliability of different readings of the Qur'an, the interpretability of similar verses, the obsoleteness of the rulings of some verses, the lack of internal and external contradictions and contradictions of the Qur'an, and the strictness of the order and proportion between the verses and chapters of the Qur'an, like the male exegetes had emphasized. They pay the same amount of attention as men to the validity and accuracy of understanding present in their exegesis and others'. It goes without saying that some theological presuppositions, the use of hermeneutics in the interpretation of the Qur'an and attention to the gender nature of the language of the Qur'an have more nuances in the thought of women commentators.

5 Munirah Gorji Fard[19]

Despite being a traditional Quran scholar, Munirah Gorji is a proponent of women's rights in the Holy Quran. Her modern approach to the Qur'an, particularly regarding women's issues, and her use of the Qur'an-to-Qur'an method to comprehend the verses as well as her genuine avoidance of using hadiths in the

---

[19] Munirah Ali, known as Gurji Fard, was born in 1933 in Tehran. With seminary education as well as self-proclaimed traditional studies, she came forward as a *mujtahid* woman and rose to fame by participating in the Assembly of Experts in 1980; although this decision drew a lot of criticism from the traditional clerics. But her study of the Quran and exceptional command of its passages are her most notable scientific attributes. She is one of the former social activists in Iran who, since 1963, attended religious lectures in different cities of Iran, and after the revolution, gave speeches at international gatherings, set up interpretation classes and has pursued her Quranic activities with the focus on women's studies in academic centers such as Khadijah Kobri (PBUH) Seminary and Shahid Rajaee Teacher Training Center, and then in her home in recent years. Her very close acquaintance with the leaders and officials of the Islamic Republic as well as her relationship with women in high-level management in the governments has made her an effective figure in Quranic teachings to the extent that her students in the governments have key positions in women's affairs, and this spiritual attachment has caused her to maintain her resistance in the years 2015 and 2016. Also, her efforts in the strategy of defending women's rights have made her the founder of the field of women's studies in Iranian universities. Only one book has been published by her entitled "Attitude of the Qur'an towards the Presence of Women in the History of the Prophets" and the basis of the text of this book is taken from her oral interpretations and some additions have been made by the editor. This book was published for the first time in 1374 by the Institute of Women's Studies and Research, and it was reprinted many times by other publishers.

interpretation of the Qur'an have elevated her to the level of a contemporary intellectual commentator and given her a feminine reading of the Qur'an in spite of her lack of familiarity with academic sciences and the foundations of modern sciences. Several courses of oral commentary in her house, along with her spiritual and intellectual attraction and method of *ijtihadi* interpretation has given her gentle face a complete boost and has attracted many students to her thoughts. In 2007, I had a full conversation with her in two sessions of interview regarding the discussion of women in the Qur'an, from which, I have selected the discussion of *Qawamoon* and present it for the first time in this chapter. Of course, Gorji has presented some of her thoughts during several interviews. In various interviews that were held in her commemorations, she has statements that I will present in this paper and I will discuss my interview with her later in the course of this chapter.

Gorji, like most female commentators, believes that "there is no difference between men and women" in the Holy Quran.[20] She believes that the Qur'an has been interpreted in a masculine way, while even the Messenger of God, with all his greatness, introduced himself in Qur'an as not a man but a human being and said, "I am a human like you."[21] That is, he has called himself genderless. Therefore, the man (in the Qur'an) is neither ahead nor behind the woman. Gorji avoided the literal interpretation of the Qur'an with human terms, emphasizing the understanding of the Qur'an with verses and referring to the narration of the Messenger of God, who said, "Al-Qur'an explains some things" and has used the same way of interpretation to understand the vocabulary related to the discussion of women. For example, she considered the word *Rijal* in verse 108 of *Surah* Toba (referring to the Iranian constitution about the characteristics of the presidency) not in front of *Nisa'* but as a general noun and says:

> one of these men is Fatimah (AS) and one is Ali (AS). The domain of this word is not the discussion of men and women, but rather a description; just like we say "elders" or "old men" in Farsi. This term "old man" is not a male, but an experienced person ... Here, too, it is a common man, that is, anyone who has acquired intellectual and experimental power.[22]

It is surprising for Gorji to give in to this interpretation or jurisprudence attitude that Islam is a religion against women and considers such an explanation

20   Monirah Gorji, "Unsaid Stories of the Only Woman in the History of Assembly of Experts," Mahtab Mohammadi interview, Vice President of Women and Family Affairs, 2016.
21   Monirah Gorji, Interview with ISNA, 2015.
22   Ibid.

of religion as an example of interpretation of opinion. This finding, that prior to the movement of the prophets mentioned in the Qur'an, there were woman or women who provided the platform for their great movements, is one of the most serious views of Gorji. She rejected this petrifying idea that in Islam women do not have a complete soul and spirit, by interpreting several verses of the Qur'an that speak of righteous women, believing women, Muslim women, etc. She believes that the Qur'an even exaggerates the high status of women and deliberately hides it under various topics. From her point of view, the commentators' emphasis and insistence on the lack of equal efficiency of women and men is a sign of their fear of their great power. She believes that although in the Qur'an, the institution of marriage is emphasized, despite being a wife and becoming a mother, God in no way excludes a woman from the experience of being a complete human being and does not deprive her of the presence in social and political, economic, cultural, judicial, leadership and sovereignty arena, or eliminates her from the experience of spiritual and mystical unity. Gorji believes that the Quran should be freed from the heavy burden of the past, and the progress of the contemporary world should also become the source of another explanation of the divine verses.

Gorji's approach to the interpretation of women in the Qur'an is related to the existence of great women who were on the educational path of the prophets and always accompanied the great missions of the prophets. She maintains, "The woman of the same house that gave birth to Moses, the same woman sat waiting for the mission of Moses (pbuh), the same woman who is Pharaoh's wife in Pharaoh's house, the same woman moves side by side with Moses."[23] The role of women in the great mission of Moses, i.e. the mother and sister of Moses, the wife of Pharaoh and the daughters of Shoaib, cannot be removed in the upbringing of Moses and cannot be ignored. In criticizing the incorrect translation of Quranic words about women, especially about the word *Qawamoon* in verse 34 of *Nisa'*, she first refers to this word in verse 8 of *Maeda* and raises the question, does the concept of *Qawamoon* in the verse

كُونُوا قَوَّامِونَ لِلَّهِ [24] mean guardian? The word *Qawam* in the Qur'an has its own meaning, and *Qayyim* has its own meaning. For what reason have we taken

---

23   Ibid.

24   The full verse is:

يَـٰٓأَيُّهَا ٱلَّذِينَ ءَامَنُوا۟ كُونُوا۟ قَوَّٰمِينَ لِلَّهِ شُهَدَآءَ بِٱلْقِسْطِ ۖ وَلَا يَجْرِمَنَّكُمْ شَنَـَٔانُ قَوْمٍ عَلَىٰٓ أَلَّا تَعْدِلُوا۟ ۚ ٱعْدِلُوا۟

هُوَ أَقْرَبُ لِلتَّقْوَىٰ ۖ وَٱتَّقُوا۟ ٱللَّهَ ۚ إِنَّ ٱللَّهَ خَبِيرٌۢ بِمَا تَعْمَلُونَ

O believers! Stand firm for Allah and bear true testimony. Do not let the hatred of a people lead you to injustice. Be just! That is closer to righteousness. And be mindful of Allah. Surely Allah is All-Aware of what you do.

the word *Qawamoon* for guardianship? Couldn't God himself have used the word "guardian"? She believes that paying attention to the words of the Qur'an along with the context of the words and the interpretation of similar verses has drawn the path of their meaning.

In verse 34 of *Nisa*, Gorji interprets the word *Qawamoon* by relying on "Ali" which means transcendence and states that "Qam Ali" means "rising over ..." and not "dominion over ..." or "organizer of ..." or "director and supervisor of ...".[25] She believes that in the Holy Qur'an, all righteous or rebellious men such as Abraham, Moses, Jesus, etc. have grown and flourished alongside women, and without their presence, their uprisings would not have been realized. For example, the role of five women next to Moses, and the role of Mary next to Jesus, shows the reliance of men on women in carrying out great revolutions and movements. By emphasizing the weight of exaggeration and association with the word Ali, the verse of *Qawamoon* shows the presence of women in the growth and development of men. Therefore, the verse says that men stand on the shoulders of women and have found a place. In this verse, they need women to establish a family, not that they establish women or dominate them or manage them. According to Gorji's explanation of this word, "a man ascends from the lap of a woman" and nothing else.

6   Zilla Movahed Shariat Panahi[26]

Movahed Shariat Panahi (1951) in an article entitled "The Outline of the Character of a Muslim Woman" maintains that:

> This issue (the ideal woman) is an issue that has been remained unclear.
> Because the vast majority of Qur'an commentators have been men. Also,
> due to the lack of awareness that men have had about women through-
> out history, the plan that men have presented about women is not a

---

25   Gorji, Unsaid Stories.
26   Zhila Movahed Shariat Panahi graduated from Sharif University of Technology in 1992
      with a degree in Science Engineering, and was one of the first radioactive material experts
      to work at the Atomic Energy Organization. She is now a scholar of the Qur'an and has
      written a two-volume book entitled Discreet Justice or "A new Analysis of Women's Rights
      from the Perspective of the Qur'an", the second volume of which has not yet been pub-
      lished. She is one of the active members of the One Million Signature campaign to change
      discriminatory laws against women and teaches volunteers in some of the campaign's
      workshops. Zhila Movahed Shariat Panahi is also a member of the National Peace Council
      and a member of its inspection board, and a member of the convergence of the Iranian
      women's movement. http://bestbiography.rozblog.com.

complete plan. Therefore, in order to be able to find a correct and relatively authentic image of women, we have to go back to the verses that are in the Qur'an and also to the hadiths that are in harmony with the Qur'an or do not contradict it. Finally, we neither find any verses about a subject nor an authentic hadith, we should go back to the academic, experimental and practical science of today (these three qualities must be combined).[27]

She continues, "two verses of the Qur'an's enlightening verses have been misused throughout history, and generally, those two verses have been considered the reason for the superiority of men over women. One is verse 34 of Surah *Nisa'* and the other is verse 228 of Surah *Al-Baqarah*. In both of these verses, there are two words, grace and rank."[28] In her review of verse 34 of *Nisa'* in an independent article, by examining the views of 12 early and late commentators, she explained the vocabularies in this verse including the interpretation of the concept of "*Qawamoon*" and stated:

> Unfortunately, there is a major difference (in the interpretation of the word *Qawam*) in diverse interpretations. In this way, "they are the guardians and masters and dominate over women", "they are the supervisors in planning and life and dominate the upbringing and education of women", "they have dominance", "men are in charge of women", "do some important tasks for others" ،قيام على النساء بالحماية و الرعاية و الولاية، و الكفاية.[29] "strengthening and protecting", "guardian and servant." Despite all the differences in the interpretation of the word Qawam, after careful consideration of the above meanings, one can infer the following common meaning from each of them: Qawam = responsible for establishing the family system due to the provision of expenses, support and protection and necessary things.[30]

She then benefits from the dictionary and by digging into the dictionaries, she contends that *Al-Qawam* means handsome, tall, and the plural of which is *Qawamoon*, emanating from the root "*Qam*" which means to rise. And then,

---

27   Movahed Shariat Panahi, Zilla, A New Analysis on Women's Rights in the Quran. (Tehran, Nashr Peek, 2008), 73.

28   Ibid., 109.

29   This verse says that man is responsible for women's protection, care, guardianship, and sufficiency."

30   Zilla, Movahed Shariat Panahi, Influential Women in the First Two Centuries of Hijri. (Tehran: Samadieh Publishing, 2012), 195–196.

based on these books, she enumerates the other meanings of this word.[31] Then, by mentioning the word *Qawamoon*, which is mentioned twice in verses 135 of *Nisa'* (31) and 8 of *Maedah*, she says:

> Through consideration of the meaning of these two verses and paying attention to more than 500 other verses, in each of which there are words with the same root as "Qam," we come to the conclusion that among the mentioned meanings, the closest meanings to the word "*Qawam*" are "standing", "consistency", "supporter", "protector" and the most distant meanings to this word are the expressions "dominant", "conqueror" and "superiority."[32]

Then she stated the final result of the meaning of this word from her point of view to be equivalent to "material support and physical support."[33] While Movahed believes in the equality of men and women in purity, goodness, and the possibility of equal access to education, research, job promotion in decision-making positions, she believes that women should maintain their positive feminine traits and they should brag about it. She is of the idea that these feminine traits should not be considered as a weakness and cause women to deprive themselves of some privileges and, as a result, dislike their feminine traits.[34] In this sense, she believes that "*qawamoon*" is a male thing and argues that "according to this honorable verse, the main pillar of an ideal family is a man. He is the one who should raise his financial ability based on his physical and intellectual abilities to the extent that he will have the courage to start a family before deciding to get married. This suggests that he has sufficiently developed the two qualities of 'strong' and 'trustworthy' in himself."[35] However, Movahed believes that there are selfless women who, in addition to fulfilling their sensitive and heavy female duties, also bear the heavy burden of stability and with this sacrifice prevent the collapse of the family system.[36]

Movahed considers the role of society to be as significant as a family in raising a man to become a "*Qawam*." In addition to intellectual education, she points out that their physical education is also important. She states:

---

31   Ibid., 198–200.
32   Ibid., 201.
33   Ibid., 202.
34   Ibid., 56.
35   Movahed Shariat Panahi, *A New Analysis on Women's Rights*, 78.
36   Ibid.

In a proper educational environment, boys should be raised to be hard-working and resilient. In the family, primary school, high school and university, in addition to developing intellectual abilities, sufficient attention should be paid to developing physical strength.[37] Society, as it is obliged to, should give proper material and spiritual respect to the work of a doctor, engineer, scientist, etc. It should also give due respect to the work of a farmer, industrialist, fisherman, worker, technician, etc.[38]

According to Movahed, every man should do manual work in addition to his mental work to become stronger. Because, by cultivating this divine grace (more physical strength than a woman), he should always be able and ready to perform the worship of *"Jihad* for the sake of Allah" in an efficient manner during the attack of the enemy. He considered Ali (a.s.) to be a perfect example and a practical example of steadfastness, who dug a well for a Jew and spent money from the same wage, and was the strongest in the field of *Jihad* and the richest in the field of cultural struggle.[39]

Therefore, according to Movahed, the first step in the way of men's *Qawamiat* is to reform the family system to raise boys and transform them from pampering to being economically productive by developing their intellectual and manual abilities. This is how, she argues, the main pillar of the family will be strong and stable.[40] She believes that girls should also be raised to virtue based on kindness and mercy, by developing their intellectual and emotional abilities, in addition to teaching them science and art to enable them to secure their financial independence. This will make them temporarily the financial pillar of their family in case of unexpected events such as *jihad*, long journeys, emigration, martyrdom, divorce, illness or death of men.[41]

This practical-legal view of the duties of men and women originates from the fact that Movahed is seeking to amend family laws and pays more attention to the drafting of laws that she wants to submit to the Islamic Council as proposed bills. She seeks to point out the inadequacies and ambiguities of executive and by-laws in connection with the amendment of laws and adapt it to the social conditions and customs of Iranian society. By discovering the legal loopholes and amending the articles of Iran's civil law and its connection with the issue of *qawamoon*, Movahed pointed out the flaws in Article 1105, which

---

37   Ibid., 96.
38   Ibid., 210.
39   Ibid., 211.
40   Ibid.
41   Ibid., 213.

states that "in the relationship between spouses, being the head of the family is one of the characteristics of the husband," should be corrected based on the verses of النساء على قوّامون الرجال[42] and بينهم شورى ومرهم[43] as follows: "In family relations, the management of the family is the responsibility of the husband based on consultation with his wife, and division of work should be according to the physical, scientific, and moral qualifications."[44]

7   Conclusion

Women commentators, with the benefit of Qur'an-centered hermeneutics, seek to separate the ideals of religion from biased interpretations and official common traditions in Qur'an interpretations that have been popularized by men. They are seeking to extract an intellectual and moral system from the Qur'an, based on which they have innovated and paved the way in some historical-cognitive problems of women and explained the basic concepts of the Qur'an such as monotheism, justice and the role of man before God without the function of gender and update these concepts.

Adherence of women commentators to the foundations and rules of interpretation, while having a specific but different methodology in interpreting and analyzing the concept of "*qawamoon*" in verse 34 of Surah *Nisa'*, shows that they are anxiously seeking answers to the contemporary world and Muslim women in interpreting such gender concepts in the Qur'an.

Undoubtedly, a one-sided, incomplete and selective look at the verses of the Holy Qur'an leads to an incorrect and cruel judgment about the Qur'an's perspective. The unsystematic view of the Qur'an's rulings in the field of the family has caused some Muslims to consider the legal rulings of this field as discriminatory and influenced by the culture of ignorance. However, there are many verses and traditions in defense of the character, rights and effective position of women, and by putting them together, the spirit and depth of the meaning of the divine word is obtained. If we consider all these rulings in one set, it becomes clear that there is no discrimination in the Qur'an due to

---

42   Men are the caretakers of women.

43   This is a part of verse 38 in Surah *Shuraa* which reads:

وَٱلَّذِينَ ٱسۡتَجَابُواْ لِرَبِّهِمۡ وَأَقَامُواْ ٱلصَّلَوٰةَ وَأَمۡرُهُمۡ شُورَىٰ بَيۡنَهُمۡ وَمِمَّا رَزَقۡنَٰهُمۡ يُنفِقُونَ

And those who have responded to their lord and established prayer and whose affair is [determined by] consultation among themselves, and from what We have provided them, they spend.

44   Ibid., 273.

being a woman or a man. A one-sided and one-dimensional view of Islamic teachings also leads to misunderstandings and disrespectful interpretations of religious texts and creates grounds for many doubts that will cause serious damage to religious understanding. Instead, one should have a systemic approach to every issue to see restrictions and allocations alongside generalities and absolutes. The religion of Islam, based on the knowledge and absolute wisdom of God, has surrounded and paid full attention to all the real needs and dimensions of human existence and has included their provision in all the rules and laws. Therefore, Islam recognized the rights of each party and determined them based on real interests.

Although verse 34 of Surah *Nisa'* mostly refers to the rights of men and the need for women to submit and obey them, the general opinion of religion should not be extracted exclusively from this verse and ignore other texts. From this point of view, we explore the moral teachings of other related verses and traditions in the three categories of dignity, justice and good character in order to achieve an authentic Islamic approach. With a relatively short exploration, one can easily find a large number of verses and traditions in the field of family and marriage that emphasize the importance of observing moral principles in the interaction of spouses and actually explain the components of the Qur'an and Hadith of "*Qawamoon.*"

In the eyes of the Holy Qur'an, the truth is that men and women are the same things, and they are equal in various cases, and there is no difference between them in the principle of humanity. These similarities are as follows: being God's creation (45 and 46/Najm and 37 to 39/Qiyamat and 6/Zamr), worship and servitude (56/Dhariyat), human dignity (70/Isra), achieving perfections and authorities (97/Nahl) (7), creation, human nature and its accessories (Nisa'/1 and Shuri/11 and Hujarat/13 and Aaraf/189), closeness to God and worship and righteous deeds (Al-Imran/195 and Nisa/ 124 and Nahal/97 and Towba/72 and Ahzab/35), the possibility of choosing the side of right and wrong (Towba/67 and 68 and Noor/26 and Al-Imran/43), most tasks and responsibilities (Baqarah/183 and Noor/2) and 31 and 32 and Maedeh/38 and Ahzab/35), rewards (Nahl/97 and Nisa/32 and Al Imran/195), political, social and economic independence (Mutahnah/10 and 12 and Nisa/32 to 34) and Possession of family rights (Ankabut/8 and Israa/23 and 24 and Baqarah/83 and Maryam/14 and Anam/151 and Nisa/36 and Luqman/14 and 15 and Ahqaf/15).

From the point of view of the verses, the gender of men and women does not affect the valuing of people in the society, and the human models of men and women are presented in the path of excellence and degradation (10 to 12/Tahrim), also in valuing righteous actions, the characteristics of women and man is not considered (97/Nahl and 195/Ali Imran), but piety is introduced as the evaluation of human beings (13/Hujrat). Also, in none of the Qur'anic

addresses a difference between men and women has been established and
يا ايها الناس و يا ايها الذين آمنوا [45] gender segregation has not been done; therefore,
superiority and supremacy of one gender over the other cannot be deduced
from the verses of the Holy Qur'an.

Bibliography

Akhwan Moghadam, Z. (2004). *The Fundamental Differences of Interpretation and Translation of Women and Men.* Iran Book Agency.

Al-Sa'di, A.R. (1987). *Taysir al-Kareem al-Rahman: A Tafsir of the Entire Qur'an.* (2nd ed.). Beirut: Al-Nahda Al-Arabiya Library.

Amin, N.B. (2011). *Interpretation of Makhzan al-Irfan in Quranic Sciences.* Isfahan: Golbahar Publications.

Arfa, S.K. (2003). *Translation of the Quran* (Arfa). Ch One, Tehran: Faiz Kashani Research and Publishing Institute.

Ashrafi Tabrizi, M. (2002). *Translation of the Qur'an* (Ashrafi). (14th ed.). Tehran: Javidan.

Balaghi, A.H. (2008). *Hojjat al-Tafaseer and Balagh al-Aksir.* Tehran: Hekmat Publications.

Esfahani, R., & Ali, M. (2005). *Quran Translation* (Reza'i) (1st ed.). Qom: Dar al-Zhaker Cultural Research Institute.

Farsi, J. (1991). *Translation of the Quran* (Persian). Tehran: Domar Kitab.

Fazlullah, S.M.H. (1998). *Tafsir Man Wahi Al-Qur'an* (2nd ed.). Beirut: Dar al-Mala.

Gholpayegani, M., & Rida, S.M. (1981). *Book of Judiciary.* Qom: Khayyam Press.

Gorji, M. (2015). Interview with ISNA.

Gorji, M. (2016). Unsaid Stories of the Only Woman in the History of Assembly of Experts, Mahtab Mohammadi interview, Vice President of Women and Family Affairs.

Hijazi, M.M. (1992) *.Al-Tafsir al-Shazrah.* (10th ed.). Beirut: Dar Jail Al-Jadid.

Ibrahim, A. (1982). *Tafsir Aamili.* Tehran: Sadouq.

Khosravani, M. & Reza, A. (2012). *Khosravi Interpretation.* (1st ed.). Tehran: Islamic.

Madrasi, S.M.T. (1998). *Man Hoda al-Qur'an.* (1st ed.). Tehran: Dar Mohibi Al-Hussein.

Mazandarani, I.S.A., & Bin Ali, M. (1989). *Motashabih al Quran va Mokhtalifih.* (1st ed.). Qom: Bidar.

Mesbah Zadeh, A. (2002). *Quran Translation* (Mesbahzadeh). (1st ed.). Tehran: Badragh Javidan.

---

45   O People and O Believers.

Miqdad, F. (1988). *Gratitude Treasure in the Jurisprudence of the Quran.* (1st ed.). Qom: World Assembly of Islamic Religions.

Movahed Shariat Panahi, Z. (2014). Conference specializing in 40-year-old experiments and achievements of Sharif University Graduates.

Movahed Shariat Panahi, Z. (2012). *Influential Women in the First Two Centuries of Hijri.* Tehran: Samadieh Publishing.

Movahed Shariat Panahi, Z. (2008). The Outline of the Character of a Muslim Woman. In Zilla Movahed Shariat Panah (ed.). *A New Analysis on Women's Rights in the Quran.* Tehran, Nashr Peek.

Najafi, M. J. (2020). *Simple Interpretation* (1st ed.). Tehran: Islamic.

Parsa, F. (2014a). A Feminist Reading of the Quran. *Women's Journal*, 6(4), 51–71.

Parsa, F. (2014b). Meeting on the Fundamental Differences of Interpretation and Translation of Women and Men. Iran Book Agency (IBNA).

Qomi, Y. & Ali Muhammad, S. (2009). *Family Rights (in the Civil Code of the Islamic Republic of Iran).* (1st ed.). Tehran: SAMT.

Sharif, L., Bin Ali, M. (2000). *Tafsir Sharif Lahiji.* (1st ed.). Tehran: Nashar Dad.

Shirazi, H., & Mohammad, S. (2003). *Al-Qur'an to the Mind.* (1st ed.). Beirut: Dar al-Uloom.

Tabatabaei, M.H. (1982). *Al-Mizan fi Tafsir al-Qur'an.* Qom: Al-Nashar al-Islami Foundation of Jama'ah al-Madrasin.

CHAPTER 8

Rereading the Position of "Banoo Amin:" Religious Feminism throughout the History and Contemporary Culture of Iran

Zeinab Shariatnia

المراة ريحانة، ما اكرمهن الا الكريم، و ما اهانهن الا اللئيم؛

A woman is a fragrant flower; only noble people respect her and only ignoble people insult her (the Holy Prophet).

∵

1   Introduction

For many years, investigating the place and the determining role of "women" next to men has been an important issue in the context and core of thinkers' activities. Throughout the thousand-year history of Iran, due to issues such as the autocratic nature of governments and burdensome traditions, women have always been prevented from active social presence and subsequently acquiring knowledge and awareness. Historical evidence demonstrates that women who even slightly opposed the common thinking and rulers' ideal conditions of their era were harassed and deprived of many of their natural rights. Nevertheless, we have always witnessed the presence of women who have had their own style and principles, whose main goals were to eliminate any inequality related to physical differences and promote the social role of women. These women, indeed, carved a name for themselves and made a wide and undeniable range of achievements in different fields. One such woman is "Seyedeh Nosrat Beigam Amin", known as "Banoo Amin", a wise and courageous lady who happened to be one of the female Shiite scholars in Isfahan. Despite social restrictions and a lack of scientific opportunities for women back then, she was one of the first women who achieved the high position of *ijtihad*. She can be assumed as the initiator of a pragmatic movement in an era when the position of women was not only different from that of men but also was less valuable and unequal.

During the period that her personality was forming, which was concurrent with the end of the Qajar era and the beginning of the Pahlavi era in Iran, Banoo Amin, also known as the "Iranian lady" took the first steps to influence women in various fields. She organized her activities based on the changing of women's life relationships and the promotion of women's dignity as "human beings." The prevailing condition of society of the time and the absence of positive motives, especially for women, prompted Banoo Amin, the precious mujtahid to take an effective and enlightened step in the path of the growth, development, and enhancement of women in society. She did this with scientific and practical efforts and performing effective activities, such as training many students, writing numerous books, and establishing free schools for the education of women, and creating scientific circles. She also succeeded in abrogating the derogatory thinking about women's talents and invalidating beliefs that women are unable to follow the path of integrity unlike men.

Although she never assumed herself as a part of feminist movements, she can definitely be identified as one of the pioneers of "religious feminism" in Iran, who used religious instruction to defend women's rights. Simply put, feminism means believing and supporting political, economic, social, and theological equality of the genders, which defends the rights and benefits of women through organized actions. "Religious feminism" refers to the theology that is inspired by the feminist movement and is found in various religions, including Islam. It reviews traditions, practices, the holy book, and the principles of jurisprudence from a "feminist" point of view.

Against this backdrop, this chapter evaluates and rereads the discourse of Banoo Amin and her enlightened methods in various scientific, cultural, political, and social fields. Therefore, this chapter attempts to analyze the enlightening methods of Mujtahid Banoo Amin with the historical-analytical method. After providing a brief introduction about Banoo Amin, her methods of enlightenment will be investigated by various approaches, and her efforts and activities in this way will be expressed and explained.

2   The First Theme: a Glimpse into Banoo Amin's Life

Mrs. Seyedeh Nosrat Beigam Amin, known as "Banoo Mujtahid Isfahani" and the "Iranian Lady", the daughter of Muhammad Ali ibn Hasan ibn Muhammad ibn Masoum ibn Masoum Hosseini Isfahani, whose nickname was Amin Tojjar, is one of the few women who have reached *ijtihad* degree in a scientific position. Her mother Zahra, was Haj Mehdi's daughter, known as "Jenab." The Jenabi family was one of the scholars and artist families of the Safavid era. She was born in an ancient and religious city in Isfahan in 1895.[1] The lifetime of this honorable lady can be divided into two periods:

1.   The first forty years were the period of emergence of her talents, inner perfections, and their flourishing.
2.   From the age of 40 onwards was the period of fulfillment, releasing the external works resulted in her perfection and her appearance in society.[2]

Banoo Amin was born at the end of Nasereddin Shah Qajar's reign. Despite all the existing barriers in girls' education in that era and the prevailing condition in Iran at the time when only a few families would send their daughters to school to pursue education, her intellectual parents sent her to school at the age of four. At the age of 15, she married her cousin Haj Mirza, also known as "Moinotojjar," and began to raise her children. When she was 20, she started studying religious sciences, including jurisprudence, principles, exegesis, theosophy, and the Arabic language, and her husband supported her in this journey.[3] She studied in Isfahan with some eminent figures such as Sheikh Mohammad Reza Isfahani, Ayatollah Najafabadi, Ayatollah Sheikh Morteza Mazaheri, and Haj Agha Hossein Nezamoddin Kachoui. Some disasters such as losing her eight children to different causes could not hurt the will and determination of this mujtahid lady. Ayatollah Seyyed Mohammad Najafabadi puts:

> Once I heard that her child passed away. I thought that the lady would cancel the lesson; but on the contrary, the day after that, she sent someone to me to go to her house and teach her. I was surprised by her eagerness to study and pursue education.[4]

Her effort and diligence to acquire knowledge and awareness led to the approval of her academic rank and mastery at the age of forty by contemporary scholars and authorities. She succeeded in obtaining the degree of *ijtihad* from the great scholars of that era such as Agha Mirza Estahbanati, Ayatollah Haeri, and Ayatollah Marashi.[5] At a time when there was still a debate in many circles and meetings on whether a woman is a human being on the same level as man, and are the perfection traits only attributed to the men or can they

1   Seyed Javadi, A.S., Khorramshahi, B., & Fani, K. *Encyclopedia of Shiism* (Vol. 2). (Tehran: Shahid Saeed Mohebi Publications (n.d.), 106.
2   Mohamamd Hossein Riahi, *Famous Women of Isfahan*. (Isfahan: Publications of the Organization of Culture and Islamic Guidance, 1996), 75.
3   *Encyclopedia of Shiism*, 106.
4   Ali Mardani, *Zolal e Hekmat: The Life and Behavior of Arif Be Allah, Banoo Mujtahed Nosrat Beigam Amin*. (Tehran: Vozara Publications, 2011), 14.
5   Alawieh Homayouni, *Biography of Iranian Lady*. (Isfahan: Golbahar Publications, 2007), 272.

also be assigned to the women? her scientific status and achievements as a "woman" reached such a point that the great scientists and cultural figures and scholars of the era corresponded with her and also went to see her. One such scholar was the great philosopher Mohammad Taghi Jafari who stated that:

> To encourage and praise, she can definitely be introduced as one of the prominent scholars of the Shiite world whose scientific methods are completely comparable to other scholars. Noticing her high spiritual stature, she should be considered as an elite scientist. In addition to acquiring knowledge, she also achieved a rebirth in her life. This eminent scholar's book "Seir va Soluk" clearly shows that the knowledge and philosophies of the words did not deteriorate her soul; rather, it attracted those kinds of insights and knowledge that "knowing" them is often associated with "becoming." Banoo Amin's nobility and awareness of important facts are combined with a kind of scientific conscience that unfortunately few scientists achieve.[6]

In her profound life, Banoo Amin authored many books on various topics to show the excellence of women's thoughts. The authoring of the book "*Arbaein-e Hashemiyyeh*" was the commencement of her scientific manifestation.[7] She never wrote her name on her books; rather, she published them under the name of "Iranian Lady." Among her other works are *Jami al-Shetat, Resurrection or the Last Journey of Mankind, Makhzan al Layali, Seir va Soluk in the Way of Olia* and *Soada* each of which show her intellectual taste, power of thinking, and attitudes. In addition to authoring valuable works, Banoo Amin was able to influence many students with her teaching and guidance. Under the influence of Banoo Amin and her instructions and achievements, these students played an important role in deepening and promoting Islamic sciences and realizing their religious and intellectual goals. Zinatosadat Homayouni, Effatozaman Amin, Robabeh Elahi, and Badrosadat Modares Khatunabadi are some of her students. Banoo Amin passed away in 1983 and was buried in the family cemetery of the Amin family.

---

6   Salavati, F., *Women in the Works of Mujtahid Banoo Amin. Memoir of Banoo Mujtahid Hujjat al-Islam va-al Muslemin Seyyedah Nosrat Amin.* Center for Research and Cultural Studies. (Tehran: Publications of the Ministry of Culture and Islamic Guidance, 1995), 173.

7   *Encyclopedia of Shiism*, 106.

3   The Second Theme: the Cognitive and Intellectual System
       of Banoo Amin

To know the political, social, cultural, and behavioral positions of each philosopher, their intellectual and epistemological foundations should be identified.
Banoo Amin is a philosopher who has embedded all her thoughts, paradigms,
goals, and plans in her life in the revelations and teachings of the Quran and
the *Sunnah* and shaped her life by adhering to the theoretical and practical
aspects of this tradition. This characteristic can be presented in two aspects of
theory and practice, and can be perceived from her students' works and words.
Her intellectual and epistemological system is based on the determined and
explained epistemological foundations in Islamic philosophy, which is on the
flow of the Quran and *Sunnah*. This suggests that she is a realist regarding
the possibility of cognition and like the great Islamic philosophers including
theologians, philosophers, and mystics, she accepts the proven realization of
reality and the possibility of acquiring its knowledge for all human beings,
both men and women. In order to achieve knowledge and awareness, Banoo
Amin in her book "*Seir va Soluk*," considers human beings to be trainable and
emphasizes the role of "will" in the growth and integrity and attaining knowledge for humans.[8] She believes that life is a collection of thoughts and feelings
that lead a person to the path of happiness or misery. Human beings have two
paths ahead of them: a way to a higher level of humanity and a way to nature.
Banoo Amin believes that firstly human's will controls their actions and secondly they are attributed to good or bad deeds; and basically, if there was no
free will, the classification of human actions as good or bad would be senseless.
If a person tends towards the higher world willingly, external obstacles did not
prevent them, achieved progress, and gradually acquired sciences and knowledge, then, the desire for perfection that is inherent in human nature will lead
them to a path of attaining perfection and proximity to the inhabitants of
omniscience zone. It continues until they gradually elevate from a level to a
higher one and from a position to a better one. Then, little by little, divine light
will radiate on his heart[9], and both women and men are equal in this matter. In
Banoo Amin's opinion, the key to humans' happiness is knowing themselves:

> Knowing the self is the key to happiness, the means of acquiring good
> morals, and the source of all noble virtues and moralities. The first step
> that we should take towards happiness is to know ourselves and our

---

8   Banoo Amin, *Seir va Soluk*. (Isfahan: Golbahar Publications, 1944), 61–64.
9   Banoo Amin, *Makhzanolerfan in Exegesis of Quran*. (Isfahan: Golbahar Publications,
    2010), 14.

minds and souls, then, to study the attributes and properties of the ego. Therefore, we should examine what kind of creatures we are; are we among the scientific creatures? or from inferior organisms?[10]

She considers the Quran, *Sunnah*, and reason as effective sources and means for reaching integrity for humans, and believes that the Quran and *Sunnah* show the same way that reason achieves by attempting and organizing evidence.[11] Banoo Amin tried to adapt her ideological content to the principles of a monotheistic worldview and knowledge of Islamic culture. Therefore, her intellectual system was established based on Islamic principles and values and was centered on human integrity and improvement, which leads to personal and social development. Her efforts in learning the Quran and *Sunnah* instructions, her serious and continuous efforts in learning Islamic philosophy, and understanding great scholars and philosophers' instructions to enter the field of interpretation and exegesis of the Quran and its revelation knowledge, are some of her behaviors stemming from her beliefs. Her behaviors are not limited to these cases, because teaching Islamic sciences throughout many years, as well as providing knowledge and wisdom to the seekers of Islamic knowledge and subsequently training many students in this school, is another aspect of her cognitive and behavioral system.

4   The Third Theme: the Position of Women in Banoo Amin's Era

Any kind of sociological study about the cultural and social situation of women requires the study of the political and historical atmosphere of Iran. Banoo Amin's lifetime (1895–1983) coincided with thirty-three years of the Qajar era, fifty years of the Pahlavi dynasty, and almost five years of the Islamic Revolution. The history of Iran in these nine decades witnessed unique events that definitely influenced the life and personality of Banoo Amin. Cultural characteristics, historical contexts, and Banoo Amin's lifetime conditions did not provide an opportunity for the serious presence of women in the field of science, especially religious science. Back then, women and girls were not allowed to leave the house, and writing was considered a shame for women, and they had to stay indoors.[12]

---

10   Banoo Amin, *Ethics and the Way of Felicity*. (Isfahan: Golbahar Publications, 2016), 1 & 11.
11   Banoo Amin, *Makhzanolerfan*, 2.
12   Ali Asghar Shamim, *Iran during the Qajar Dynasty*. (Tehran: Behzad Publications, 2008), 354–356.

Generally, at the end of the Qajar dynasty, the influence of the Western world weakened the domination of religion on society more than before, and the traces of this influence could be seen even in words that carry a religious meaning. As a case in point, intellectuals and educated people of that period changed the concept of "nation" from a religious society to a non-religious concept of "nationality."[13] The intellectuals considered religious dogma as opposed to rational and scientific thinking and believed that true knowledge is not acquired through revelation and religious education. Rather, it is obtained through wisdom and modern sciences.[14]

Naser al-Din Shah also imposed more restrictions after the tobacco crisis. He ended the period of growth and expansion of Dar ul-Funun and banned the construction of new schools.[15] In such an atmosphere, education, especially religious education, was very difficult even for men. During the course of this period, women had far worse conditions and were considered second-class citizens who spent most of the day preparing food and doing other household chores.[16] The position of the Iranian women in the society of that period did not allow them to participate in different fields and most of the women knew nothing about the outside world. Women usually knew about their society's issues through their husbands or close relatives.

> If they (women) are free to exit home, it is clear where things will end. Instead, women must never leave the house, except to go to the bathroom, cemetery, mosque, and religious ceremonies. Otherwise, they should stay at home. If they are of noble families, they should take care of the household affairs, and if they are of the middle class, they should be engaged in their own business such as tailoring and taking care of the household chores. They should take care of their children.[17]

Throughout this period, it was very difficult for women to pursue education. Women were always deprived of a position commensurate with their dignity and abilities. According to the general belief, on the one hand, literate women were considered dangerous to society. On the other hand, they believed that women's brains are not capable of acquiring knowledge. This explains why the

---

13   Ervand Abrahamian, *Iran Between Two Revolutions*. Trans. A. Gol-Mohammadi & M.E. Fatahi. (Tehran: Ney Publications, 2017), 66.

14   Ibid., 80.

15   Ibid., 59.

16   John Foran, *Fragile Resistance: The History of Iran's Social Reforms*. Trans. A. Tadayyon. (Tehran: Rasa Cultural Services Institute Publications, 2015), 207.

17   M.R. Asgarani, *Culture and Cultured in Isfahan*. (Isfahan: Cheshmeh Afarinesh Publications, 2020), 201.

establishment of girls' schools was not necessary or meaningful for them. Most people also believed that women should not learn to read and write. Therefore, literacy was a disgrace and if a woman was literate, she tried to conceal it. At the end of the Qajar period, *Tamaddon* newspaper in its 12th issue wrote about the restrictions of women quoted from a woman:

> We were sent to Maktab from the age of five. Not all girls, only a few of us. When we were nine years old, we were no longer allowed to continue maktab. If we read books or write calligraphy, our dear fathers would impound our books and pens, and they would tear the books, break the pens, and throw them away because they believed that it is nonsense for a girl to write something.[18]

It goes without saying that some people agreed with the growth and education of women during this period. *Zayandeh Roud* newspaper, under the management of Mirza Abdul Hossein Khansari, wrote in an article entitled "Tarbiat-e Nesvan" (Training Women):

> The first educators of humans are mothers being the gardeners of the humanity garden. It is obvious that they are not capable of educating children who are the tots of our homeland when they themselves are unaware of science and do not receive suitable education. In England which is the most civilized country, among every one hundred women, there are not more than two illiterate and uneducated ones. If it is determined to choose between the education of men and women, the education of women is more beneficial to the country than the education of men.[19]

After the overthrowing of the Qajar government by Reza Khan, the situation of the society and women did not significantly change; however, the type of restrictions and pressures changed. Having visited Turkey, under the influence of its conditions and the actions of Mustafa Kemal Atatürk, the then President of Turkey, Reza Shah attempted to improve the position of women. His decree had it that educational institutions can allow girls to register and study, and if public places such as cinemas, cafes, and hotels discriminated between men and women, they had to face a pecuniary punishment. However, these actions were practically useless for women bound by religious rules since in 1935, Reza

---

18   Beheshti Seresht, "Reviewing Social and Cultural Studies of Women in the Press of the Qajar era (with an emphasis on women's letter journal)." *Women in Culture and Art Journal*, 7(3) (2015): 328.

19   Asgarani, *Culture and Cultured*, 205.

Shah ordered the removal of the hijab and banned wearing *chador*. Most of the people did not consider this action as "freedom" but a form of oppression. Throughout this period, due to the pressures of the Pahlavi dynasty, the number of religious students decreased from 5984 to 785.[20] The Pahlavi government used every means to secularize and Europeanize Iranian women and believed that due to the removal of the hijab and secularization, women as a part of the society are allowed to prove their talents and creativity, and present and participate in cultural and social areas. Accordingly, the conditions governing the era in which Banoo Amin grew and developed, are divided into two periods:

In the first period, which spanned about 33 years of Banoo Nosrat Amin's life and coincided with the last 40 years of the Qajar period, education was completely impossible for women except for a few ones and in a few cases. Of course, those few were allowed for a short period to only pursue reading and writing. In this case, Banoo Amin was lucky because she was born into a pious and wealthy family that enjoyed a bright vision and taught her the Quran and Islam from the age of four. Remembering those days, Banoo Amin maintains:

> When I went to school at the age of 6 or 7, my teacher would always tell my mother: A girl is like slow-cooking meat (hard to teach and change). Teaching her is useless and nothing will occur in the end. Do not send her to school futilely.

Nevertheless, Banoo Amin did not cease studying. After marriage, she was able to continue studying at home and reached the degree of *ijtihad* when she was forty.

The second period coincided with the beginning of the Pahlavi dynasty, and as it has been discussed earlier, due to the removal of the hijab and the pressures from the government, religious women could not even leave the house until they were allowed to demonstrate their scientific status. In such a difficult condition, Banoo Amin was able to achieve her religious education goals and also fought against the removal of the hijab and the European policy of subjugating Iranian women, which restricted the growth and integrity of religious women. Simultaneously, Banoo Amin was able to write and publish her works, thanks to her financial resources and her family's social status. She definitely affirmed her scientific position among other intellectuals and scholars.

Given these conditions and her serious and fruitful participation in the education and learning field which was against the common opinion of her era, and noticing her intellectual and cognitive doctrine, she can be considered one of the leaders and social-political fighters during this period playing

---

20   Abrahamian, *Iran Between Two Revolutions*, 179–180.

an important role in women's movements to achieve equal rights and make social changes. From this point of view, she can be considered a social activist and one of the prominent representatives of religious feminism in Iran. Banoo Amin's educational, social, and moral views towards different issues, in addition to making a change in the attitude of the contemporary people, led to the improvement in cultural-social attitudes towards the position of women in that era.

5   The Fourth Theme: Banoo Amin's Influence on Women's Position in Society

Nosrat Beigam Amin's thought principles are rooted in Islamic doctrines and her personal experiences. When she was younger, noticing her experiences and the position of women in society in those days, she shaped her thoughts based on progressive ideas and social justice. Emphasizing the importance of education and knowledge, gender equality, and intellectual freedom, Banoo Amin paid attention to the realization of women's rights and social changes in Iranian society. She also examined the role of women in society, paying attention to women's rights, and gender equality through the interpretation and recitation of religious concepts. She tried to make changes in society's attitude towards women through reinterpreting religious concepts and examining Islam from an analytical and fair perspective. Of the concepts and values that were prominent in Nosrat Beigam Amin's thought and practice the following cases are prominent:

1. **Gender Equality:** One of the basic principles of feminism accepted by Islam is the principle of equality between men and women as "human beings." Human is a word that receives improvisation of its meaning from the improvisation of its example. "Talking animal" is the philosopher's famous definition of human. Banoo Amin defines humans in this way: Talking animal is the answer to الانسانُ ما هو ؟ (who is human?) By using the word "animal" his common dimension with other animals is defined, and with the word "talking" which is his special characteristic and title is distinguished from other animals.[21] Therefore, both the nature of man and his level of existence are perceived. According to the following verses of the holy Quran:

---

21   Banoo Amin, *Ethics*, 13.

يا أَيُّهَا النَّاسِ إِنَّا خَلَقْنَاكُم مِن ذَكَرٍ وَ أُنْثَى وَ جَعَلْنَاكُم شُعُوبًا وَ قَبَائِلَ لِتَعَارَفُوا إِنَّ أَكْرَمَكُم عِند
اللَّه أَتْقَاكُم (حجرات / 13)[22]

أَنِّي لَا أُضِيعُ عَمَلَ عَامِلٍ مِنكُم مِن ذَكَرٍ أَوْ أُنْثَى بَعْضُكُم مِن بَعْضٍ (آل عمران/ 193)[23]

كُلُّ نَفْسٍ مَا كَسَبَت رَهِينَة (مدثر/38)[24]

she believes that men and women are both human beings and have the same substance and identity; at the same time, they are independent in will and action. Therefore, every human being, male or female, is responsible for his/her own actions.[25] She believes that men and women are not separated in the definition of human. Emphasizing the necessity of knowing one self's truth and human blessedness, Banoo Amin stated the following about the superiority of men over women:

> It cannot be said that all men are generally superior to women. There are women like Fatima (peace be upon her), Khadijah, and Saint Mary, and many other women who were better than many men. The supremacy that God has assigned to men in some issues is general, not individual. One of the imperfections mentioned in the Quran for women is stated in a verse. It is maintained that women cannot resolve disputes and if they are supposed to judge, they cannot persuade other people. Another shortcoming is that women tend to show off and flaunt and they are less concerned with sensual perfections. Of course, this is an instinct that God has placed in them, and the philosophy of hijab is certainly based on this principle. All in all, these are general issues and there are certainly some women who are exempt from these characteristics and this is not the case with all women. For example, there are some women who can eliminate hostilities or judge.[26]

---

22   "O mankind! We have created you from a male and a female, and made you into nations and tribes, that you may know one another. Verily, the most honourable of you with Allah is the most pious of you" (Surah Al-Hujurat, 13).

23   "I do not waste the work of any worker among you, whether male or female; you are all on the same footing" (*Surah* Al-Imran, verse 193).

24   "Every soul, for what it has earned, will be retained" (*Surah* Al-muddathir, verse 38).

25   Banoo Amin, *Makhzanolerfan*, 316.

26   Banoo Amin, *The Way of Fecility*. (Isfahan: Rashad Publications, 2018), 116.

Banoo Amin believes that except in natural cases that God willed, there is no difference between men and women in terms of nature and creation, and no one
is superior to the other except for their piety. In some cases, men are stronger
than women and vice versa. In the exegesis of some verses, especially verses
from Surah Nisa', she refers to the power of women and believes that (نَفَحْتُ
فِيهِ مِن رُوحِى)[27] we are all from the Spirit of God, and that (خَلَقَ مِنها زَوجَها)[28]
from everything that Adam was created, his wife is also created. She believes
that originality is in action, faith, and reasoning, and it is not in sex and gender.
She tried her best to make women aware of their true position. To achieve this
goal, she encouraged women to continue studying and promoted education
and awareness among women. Her advice to the women who were planning to
continue their education was to bear the difficulties during their studies and
continue studying because the lack of committed and knowledgeable people
is clearly felt in many societies.

   2. Education and Study: Banoo Amin gave importance to the social life of
women and considered education and knowledge as presuppositions to such
a life. She believed that women were forced to acquire knowledge to get rid of
the chaotic cultural and social conditions.[29] Therefore, one of the highlights
of Banoo Amin's life is giving importance to learning science and knowledge
and its centrality in life and special efforts towards knowledge acquiring and
promoting it by women; especially, when even men rarely cared about learning
science let alone women. Banoo Amin not only walked into this path herself
but also encouraged other women to follow suit and helped them as much
as possible. However, she believed that such education should be performed
in a sound atmosphere to lead them to the intellectual, moral, and spiritual
enhancement of women. She believes:

---

27   This is part of the verse 72 of *Surah* Sad which means "God has breathed His soul into
     every human being."

28   This is part of the first verse of Surah Nisa' which reads:

يَـٰٓأَيُّهَا ٱلنَّاسُ ٱتَّقُواْ رَبَّكُمُ ٱلَّذِى خَلَقَكُم مِّن نَّفْسٍ وَٰحِدَةٍ وَخَلَقَ مِنْهَا زَوْجَهَا وَبَثَّ مِنْهُمَا رِجَالًا
كَثِيرًا وَنِسَآءً ۚ وَٱتَّقُواْ ٱللَّهَ ٱلَّذِى تَسَآءَلُونَ بِهِۦ وَٱلْأَرْحَامَ ۚ إِنَّ ٱللَّهَ كَانَ عَلَيْكُمْ رَقِيبًا

     O humanity! Be mindful of your Lord Who created you from a single soul, and from it
     He created its mate,1 and through both He spread countless men and women. And be
     mindful of Allah—in Whose Name you appeal to one another—and ˹honour˺ family
     ties. Surely Allah is ever Watchful over you.

29   Ibid., 105.

Science is the best thing that a human may have. Since the human mind is different from other creatures, we are supposed to expand and develop our reasoning. This does not mean that when we move toward acquiring knowledge, we should not be satisfied with the little amount, or seclude ourselves; in fact, this is the beginning of our path; we should always move forward and we should also return to the people.[30]

A part of Banoo Amin's concern about women's education and influencing them was due to her effort to explain the attitude of Islam toward women. The other part was in reaction to the Western-style extremists and groups defending women's social freedom whose approach was not favored by Banoo Amin.[31] She paid attention to education and instruction as a tool to empower women and develop society. Banoo Amin advised housewives to give importance to their education and try to reach higher positions and opportunities in society so that their own and their families rights are not disregarded due to their ignorance.[32]

In addition to her efforts in learning science and raising awareness noticing the value of science in the social position, especially in the women's class, Banoo Amin realized the limitations of education for girls, in spite of the unfavorable social situation at that time. She suffered from witnessing the condition of women, especially the limited area for Muslim women. She contended that if women knew their own value, were aware of their role and position in the system of creation, and understood God's endowment to them, they never stand these humiliations.[33] Therefore, as a committed teacher, she felt responsible for their rights demands, and while suffering from the plights of women, she established a religious school in 1965 called "Fatemeh (peace be upon her) Maktab" known as "Banoo Amin's Maktab" in which 600 to 1000 students registered. In that school, in addition to Islamic sciences, other fields such as jurisprudence, principles, wisdom, theosophy, and philosophy were taught, and gradually a scientific-cultural movement emerged and continued among women. When women became motivated to study religious sciences, and scholars realized the importance of women's education, other scholars tried to establish a religious education center for women. In this way, Fatemeh (peace be upon her) Maktab, which was known as the Maktab of Banoo Amin, became a center of nurturing and growth of religious schools in other cities.[34]

---

30   Salavati, *Women in the Works of Banoo Mujtahid Amin*, 177.
31   Homayouni, *Biography of Iranian Lady*, 130–134.
32   Banoo Amin, *The Way of Felicity*, 105.
33   Ibid., 104.
34   Homayouni, *Biography of Iranian Lady*, 134.

This Maktab did not charge any tuition fee and all their expenses were paid by Banoo Amin. Furthermore, since religious families prevent girls from continuing their education in other schools, she began to establish high schools for girls. The establishment of these two scientific centers and Banoo Amin's lectures served as a permission for the active and not passive presence of women in the scientific and social fields. Moreover, these activities increased the self-esteem and enthusiasm of women in entering the scientific areas. It encouraged some of the women of that era to avoid apathy toward the occurrences around them and perhaps saved them from drowning in ignorance. Consequently, with the hard work and perseverance of this noble lady, the path of education was paved for many girls.

3. **Freedom of Thought and Expression:** according to feminist views, one should pay attention to the difference between "Sex" and "Gender." "Sex" is related to the biological difference between men and women, but "gender" shows the social difference between them. Therefore, what has been problematic for humans is their gender, not their sex. Nosrat Beigam Amin believed that gender cannot be an obstacle to the thought, moral, and spiritual growth and development of women. Freedom of thought and expression should be guaranteed for all members of society. She believed that without the freedom of thought and expression of opinion, social change and justice cannot be achieved.

With the establishment of Reza Shah's modernist government, the project of modernizing Iranian society began, and subsequently, the challenge between modernism and the religious values of the society also commenced. Immanuel Kant's definition of enlightenment in his article titled "What is Enlightenment" in a way forms the main context of modernity: "Enlightenment is that man has come out of everything that is not the guardianship of reason."[35] That is, humans can reach enlightenment when the originality of reason plays a role in their decision-making. After the construction and reconstruction of the elements and components of the Enlightenment in Iran, Pahlavi (1) defined his policies based on modernity but denied the fundamental principle of modernity, which is "autonomy" and "subjectivity" which means independence and individual authority. This caused the deterioration of Pahlavi policies in a long-term period and instead of modern developments, Iranian society entered the "semi-modern" era. This issue not only did not lead to national unity but also brought about the collapse of the system.

Reza Shah, who founded his new ideals on modernism and extreme nationalism on the two principles of denigrating the culture and works of Islamic civilization as well as returning to Iran before Islam, passed the "Unveiling Act."

---

35   Immanuel Kant, "What is Enlightenment?" *Berlin Monthly*, (1784).

According to this law, Iranian women and girls were prohibited from using chador, scarves, and veils in schools, universities, and governmental and official centers. In fact, macro politics in this era was controlled by the concept of authoritarian modernity, and Pahlavi's policymakers completely neglected two of the most important and fundamental components of modernity, which were "subjectivity" and "autonomy." This caused women who were bound to Islam and gained self-awareness in the atmosphere of modernity, to be deprived of the right to selection and autonomy, and this "deprivation" was placed under the title of modernity and enlightenment. In order to oppose this Unveiling Act which sought to question the personality and identity of Iranian Muslim women, Banoo Amin chose the title of "Iranian Lady" to emphasize her Iranian identity while adhering to the principles of Islam.[36] This action showed both the character and nature of the cultured and noble Iranian Muslim woman and represented the thinking style of an oppressed class of the society who before and more than other groups, was exposed to the adversities of the times and the wrong policies between the traditional and modern view towards women. By taking this action, Banoo Amin began to defend Iranian Muslim women in one of the most critical periods of Iran's contemporary social history. In defense of women's rights, specifically religious women, Banoo Amin opposed Reza Khan's Unveiling Act in two ways: a) through public opposition and protest against government decrees: the Pahlavi (1) government invited the nobles and famous businessmen of the city with their unveiled wives. Moinotojjar, Banoo Amin's husband was one of these invitees but Banoo Amin did not attend this party to declare her protest against the Unveiling Act. It was this issue that prompted her to immediately migrate to Qom; b) through the culture and raising the level of awareness: at this stage, she eliminated all the doubts about the destruction of the hijab written by the press at the time, by explaining the issue, broadening the level of women's knowledge, holding ethics and exegesis meetings, and writing the book "*Ethics: The Way of Felicity*" in simple and understandable language for all classes of the society.

In her writings, the Iranian mujtahid lady both eliminated the doubts that existed in her time and were raised by the intellectuals to promote removing hijab in society, and to enlighten and inform the women's society about the rational reasons for wearing the hijab with a simple, sincere, and imperative expression. For example, the proponents of the hijab removal claimed that the hijab hinders women's progress, deprives them of every virtue, and prevents them from acquiring sciences, industry skills, and commercial activities. She responded:

---

36   Mousavi Khalkhali, *Nosrat Beigam Amin. Dictionary of Women of Iran and the World* (Vol. 1). (Tehran: Ertebatat Novin Publications, 2015), 195.

Every knowledgeable person knows that teaching, learning, and acquiring knowledge are not inconsistent with hijab at all, and hijab is not related to the intellectual and scientific development of women. Girls and boys study in separate schools and women can learn science and crafts at home with regarding their modesty and decency.[37]

She also believed that:

Civilization and objective progress are not inconsistent with religion; in addition, acquiring welfare is the prelude to human happiness. Moreover, for the independence of the country, the preservation of Islamic civilization, and to meet the needs of society, by studying new sciences progress should be made. However, we should always be careful that these progress and welfare affairs are not harmful and do not destroy the original values. The problem is that in Iranians' opinion civilization, objective progress, and new instructions are against religion; while an important part of Islamic teachings is about pedagogy, organizing social affairs, and learning sciences.[38]

Mujtahid Banoo Amin created a relationship between religion and science and broke the misconception that the hijab is an obstacle to progress. Despite many difficulties, she alone and without any encouragement sincerely stood for a holy and sublime goal, founded this movement, and opposed those who thought that hijab was an obstacle to progress and development, or those who claimed that women cannot reach high positions in spiritual and scientific affairs and contrary to the logic of Islam, considered women deprived of human value and reaching the position of caliph. This arduous standing paved this troublesome path for others. In fact, the modernist government's understanding of the new civilization was the modern-like behaviors and manners and change in appearances, not the flourishing of thought and culture. As an Iranian female subject and based on her view, Banoo Amin concluded that the modern politicians of the Pahlavi era not only do not lead to the freedom and autonomy of the Iranians but also violated the purpose.

4. **Social justice:** Justice is one of the most comprehensive and general laws of human society, which is the foundation and governing of society. The people's social order and unity depend on it. For Banoo Amin, achieving social justice in

---

37   Alimardani, *Zolal e Hekmat*, 132–134.
38   Farzin, *Unique in the Era: A Review of the Scientific and Practical Life of Arif Banoo Mujtahid Amin.* (Tehran: Hasti Nama Publications, 2010), 45.

society was important. She believes that based on هنّ لباس لكم و انتم لباس لهنّ[39] and لهنّ مثل الذى عليهنّ بالمعروف[40] the following verses of the Quran, men and women are equal in all social affairs such as business, inheritance, trading, agriculture, teaching, learning, and laws except for what is assigned to one of them.[41]

Banoo Nosrat Beigam Amin believed that men and women should be equal in society and should be given equal opportunities and access to equal legal rights. If a woman does not participate in some activities, it is not due to weakness or deficiency; her specified duties such as raising children have prevented her from doing so, and God has established equality between men and women regarding their rights in all aspects. Therefore, it cannot be said that men are more important than women in society since everyone is responsible for a part of human social affairs and they are specified for a particular activity. In Surah *Baqareh*, verse 238 God stated:

وَ لَهُنَّ مِثْلُ الَّذَى عَلَيِهِنَّ بِالمَعْرُوف "Women have rights towards men, just like men who have rights towards women." According to Islam, society is built by the family, and each family consists of two parts, female and

---

39   This is part of verse 187 of *Surah* Baqareh which reads:

أُحِلَّ لَكُمْ لَيْلَةَ ٱلصِّيَامِ ٱلرَّفَثُ إِلَىٰ نِسَآئِكُمْ ۚ هُنَّ لِبَاسٌ لَّكُمْ وَأَنتُمْ لِبَاسٌ لَّهُنَّ ۗ عَلِمَ ٱللَّهُ أَنَّكُمْ كُنتُمْ تَخْتَانُونَ أَنفُسَكُمْ فَتَابَ عَلَيْكُمْ وَعَفَا عَنكُمْ ۖ فَٱلْـَٰٔنَ بَٰشِرُوهُنَّ وَٱبْتَغُوا۟ مَا كَتَبَ ٱللَّهُ لَكُمْ ۚ وَكُلُوا۟ وَٱشْرَبُوا۟ حَتَّىٰ يَتَبَيَّنَ لَكُمُ ٱلْخَيْطُ ٱلْأَبْيَضُ مِنَ ٱلْخَيْطِ ٱلْأَسْوَدِ مِنَ ٱلْفَجْرِ ۖ ثُمَّ أَتِمُّوا۟ ٱلصِّيَامَ إِلَى ٱلَّيْلِ ۚ وَلَا تُبَٰشِرُوهُنَّ وَأَنتُمْ عَٰكِفُونَ فِى ٱلْمَسَٰجِدِ ۗ تِلْكَ حُدُودُ ٱللَّهِ فَلَا تَقْرَبُوهَا ۗ كَذَٰلِكَ يُبَيِّنُ ٱللَّهُ ءَايَٰتِهِۦ لِلنَّاسِ لَعَلَّهُمْ يَتَّقُونَ

It has been made permissible for you to be intimate with your wives during the nights preceding the fast. Your spouses are a garment 1 for you as you are for them. Allah knows that you were deceiving yourselves. 2 So He has accepted your repentance and pardoned you. So now you may be intimate with them and seek what Allah has prescribed for you. 3 ⌈You may⌉ eat and drink until you see the light of dawn breaking the darkness of night, then complete the fast until nightfall. Do not be intimate with your spouses while you are meditating in the mosques. These are the limits set by Allah, so do not exceed them. This is how Allah makes His revelations clear to people, so they may become mindful ⌈of Him.⌉

40   This is part of verse 228 of *Surah* Baqareh which means that women have rights similar to those of men equitably.

41   Banoo Amin, *Makhzanolerfan*, 311.

male. If everyone fulfills their duties properly, human social affairs will be well-organized. Banoo Amin stated that:

> Men should not reckon that God created women only to satisfy them. If an important part of life which is to meet living needs is on the man's shoulder, the more important part, which is raising children and managing the home, is the exclusive duty of the woman.[42]

She made a lot of efforts to eliminate social discrimination and inequalities, especially between men and women, and promoted equal rights and opportunities. It is obvious that these "practical" efforts were based on her "theoretical framework" that we call the concept of "religious feminism." According to this framework, religion is not the basis of gender discrimination; rather, based on the critical reading of Banoo Amin, "equality" is the principle of interaction between men and women in the context of society, and anything other than this interpretation is considered a kind of suppression of the principle of equality between men and women, which is the underpinning of true religion from her point of view.

6   Conclusion

Examining the role of women directly or indirectly in long eras can provide proper examples of women's talents and capabilities and their influence in various fields. Reviewing the history of women's presence in various social, cultural, scientific, and political fields, one can undoubtedly argue that Banoo Amin is one of the prominent figures and female fighters in the contemporary history of Iran. Given the social-cultural conditions of the Qajar and Pahlavi eras, the effectiveness of her activities and her continuous endeavors deserve attention. Banoo Amin had a rationalist personality which was obvious in all of her affairs. In fact, reason and thought dominated her feelings. This characteristic resulted from her religious studies along with rational sciences and philosophy. As can be perceived from her writings, she was very far away from dogmatism and petrification, and emphasized the advantage of reasoning and matching actions with logic and reason. She paid equal attention to *Sharia* and schools, and therefore, she aimed at moderation in religion and dealt with it far from any extremes. As a forerunner of "religious feminism" in Iran, she is a figure who had organized her intellectual and behavioral system (i.e. education, teaching, research, and student training) with the aid of the

---

42   Banoo Amin, *The Way of Felicity*, 100.

revelation teachings of the Quran and *Sunnah*. She considered fighting for religion to improve women's conditions as her religious responsibility in society. Banoo Amin emphasized that there is no contradiction between the religious duties of women in wearing hijab and their scientific advancement. Rather, a woman's scientific and moral ability and potential are at a level that she can acquire knowledge and awareness in any situation, and staying at home is not an obstacle to acquiring knowledge and awareness. Banoo Amin believed that women should be present in society and serve it, and be aware of what occurs in society in such a way that their primary duty of being a mother and a wife will not fade away.

In her opinion, looking down at women in traditional society, and looking at them as commodities in the modern world were inconsistent with Islamic teachings and Islam's view about women. Therefore, Banoo Amin established a direct relationship between these two types of views: "traditional" and "modern." In this relationship on one side, there are socially inhibiting thoughts that exploit every means and tool to prevent women from acquiring science and technology. On the other side, there is a period in which learning and acquiring knowledge were considered free, obligatory, and compulsory for everyone either women or girls. However, the field for the growth of religious women was still restricted. By defending women's rights and providing education opportunities for religious women, Banoo Amin's arguments provided enough reasons for men to reconsider their attitude toward the abilities of the other half of society. She proved that women can study science in a social environment with an Islamic hijab and enjoy social rights.

Bibliography

Abrahamian, E. (2017). *Iran Between Two Revolutions* (A. Gol-Mohammadi & M.E. Fatahi, Trans.). Tehran: Ney Publications.

Ali Mardani, N. (2011). *Zolal e Hekmat. The Life and Behavior of Arif Be Allah, Banoo Mujtahed Nosrat Beigam Amin*. Tehran: Vozara Publications.

Amin, N.B. (1944). *Seir va Seluk*. Isfahan: Golbahar Publications.

Amin, N.B. (2010). *Makhzanolerfan in exegesis of Quran*. Isfahan: Golbahar Publications.

Amin, N.B. (2016). *Ethics and the Way of Felicity*. Isfahan: Golbahar Publications.

Amin, N.B. (2018). *The Way of Felicity*. Isfahan: Rashad Publications.

Asgarani, M.R. (2020). *Culture and Cultured in Isfahan*. Isfahan: Cheshmeh Afarinesh Publications.

Beheshti Seresht, P. M. (2015). Reviewing Social and Cultural Studies of Women in the Press of the Qajar era (with an emphasis on women's letter journal), *Women in Culture and Art Journal*, 7(3).

Farzin, M. (2010). *Unique in the Era: A Review of the Scientific and Practical Life of Arif Banoo Mujtahid Amin*. Tehran: Hasti Nama Publications.

Foran, J. (2015) *Fragile Resistance: The History of Iran's Social Reforms*. (A. Tadayyon, Trans.). Tehran: Rasa Cultural Services Institute Publications.

Homayouni, A. (2007). *Biography of Iranian Lady*. Isfahan: Golbahar Publications.

Kant, Immanuel. (1784). What is Enlightenment? *Berline Monthly*.

Mousavi Khalkhali, E. (2015). *Nosrat Beigam Amin. Dictionary of Women of Iran and the World* (Vol. 1). Tehran: Ertebatat Novin Publications.

Riahi, M.H. (1996). *Famous Women of Isfahan*. Isfahan: Publications Organization of Culture and Islamic Guidance.

Salavati, F. (1995). Women in the Works of Mujtahid Banoo Amin, Memoir of Banoo Mujtahid Hujjat al-Islam va-al Muslemin Seyyedah Nosrat Amin. Center for Research and Cultural Studies. Tehran: Publications of the Ministry of Culture and Islamic Guidance.

Seyed Javadi, A.S., Khorramshahi, B., & Fani, K. (n.d.). *Encyclopedia of Shiism* (Vol. 2). Tehran: Shahid Saeed Mohebi Publications.

Shamim, A.A. (2008). *Iran during the Qajar Dynasty*. Tehran: Behzad Publications.

CHAPTER 9

The Tudeh Party and the Social and Political Revival of the Iranian Women's Movement in the 1940s

Saeideh Torab

1 Introduction

The secular policies of Reza Shah and his grip on the clergy community in Iran prompted Iranian women to make a significant change in their political and social life. Concurrent with this change, the government made efforts to play a key role in the development of women's affairs. Equal opportunity for education and amendment of family law were two such cases. However, in Mohammad Reza Shah's reign, amid the occupation of Iran by the Allies, and the concomitant democratized political space as well as the rise of new groups and parties' activities, conservatives and religious people attacked women's rights issues. Tudeh Party was formed in these circumstances and later played a key role as the most important and effective political force in Iran in the 1940s–1950s. Tudeh party attempted to encompass all social classes of Iranians as a party. Apparently, the left-wing considered women as an important and influential force. Hence, in addition to including women's political and social rights among the general goals of the party and establishing special organizations for women, the party sought to pay more attention to the unity and solidarity of Iranian women's activities against regression. The women's organization directed by Maryam Firouz was among those institutions that were formed to organize and direct women's activism. This organization, somehow, represented the women's wing of the party. This chapter examines the manner and the extent of women's activity and influence in different ranks of the Tudeh party. It will address the following questions: considering the progressive approvals of the Tudeh party's central committee regarding women's rights, to what extent was the party successful in implementing and advancing these enactments? To what extent did the Tudeh Party affect the Iranian women's movements improvement to achieve equal rights? What was the women's wing of the Tudeh party and their organization's role in the revival and promotion of the other women's movements in Iran?

2   Women's Participation in Historical Arenas

The historical trend has always been based on the seclusion and withdrawal of women from the political arena. Despite the fact that women have been present in various social spheres throughout different historical periods, and have always played a significant role either overtly or covertly, their presence has generally been ignored or underestimated for a clear reason of the masculinity of historiography. Similar to other human sciences, History has not paid enough attention to women. It was male prejudices that determined what should be studied and how it should be interpreted. Throughout history, women have not been considered an independent entity of men or they have completely been marginalized. In social history studies, what pertains to the public (male) sphere has always been considered significant and noteworthy, while the private (female) sphere has been marginalized. Therefore, the analysis and explanation of women's role throughout these periods require further and more careful examination; similarly, the basic criteria in recording history need to be reevaluated since only through this approach different conceptualizations of history can be achieved. On the other hand, women are somehow ignored in political and social theory, and their actions are only described in direct comparison with men so much so that they do not appear as actors in the realm of political and social thought. Sociology does not deal with the nature, structure, and functions of the world in which women's dignity is formed. In fact, it pays attention to this world only when this is placed at the center of the intersection with the workplace or masculine world. Even psychology, by presenting gender behavioral stereotypes and analysis methods that justify these stereotypes, somehow tries to reproduce the patriarchal order. Therefore, it can be claimed that human and social sciences are not basically impartial despite their claims of objectivity and avoidance of bringing values into scientific research. Social sciences are strongly influenced by thinkers' personalities and life experiences.[1]

Every society must recognize the equal rights of women and men in all aspects of participation, especially political participation to achieve real development. Women's presence in political parties is considered one of the most important underpinnings of democracy. Women's political participation results in the liberation of half of the potential of society. Obviously, with the participation and utilization of these abilities and forces, the ground is prepared for

---

1   Homeira Mashirzadeh, *From Movement to Social Theory: Two Centuries of Feminism*. (Tehran: Shiraze Research and Publishing, 2002), 303–309.

growth, development, stability, and even justice in a society. In fact, one of the most important indicators of development is women's presence and their influence on decision-making. Capitalism in its advanced stages needed to strengthen the service sector, and with the growth of this sector, the number of related jobs increased. As a result, along with the technological advances that led to the simplification of some jobs in the service sector, the way was also paved for the presence of women in this sector of the economy.[2] On the other hand, the complexities of urban life, the increasing need for a skilled and specified workforce, and the need for these qualified people to manage the new economic and social order caused revision and reform in issues such as the right to education and the development of education, making it one of the greatest social ideals of the 19th century. As a result, increasing such efforts gradually led women to gain access to higher education levels making it possible for women to study in fields such as philosophy, theology, and sociology. It is interesting to note that these educated women later became the leaders of the women's movement. Accordingly, the level of women's activities in such parties is also important as it is one way of women's presence in reforming structures and managing affairs. Without having the right to political participation, women will not be able to play a crucial role in power distribution and participation in the power system.

3   Iranian Women's Movement: Structure and Identity

The most serious movements and practical efforts for women's political and social participation took place during the Constitutional Revolution. Despite their influence and importance, these activities did not turn into a continuous and serious flow at that time. Evidence shows that women were actively present in Iran's Constitutional Revolution and the clergy encouraged them to fight against foreign forces. Specifically, after 1864 they formed their own organizations and acted even more independently. However, they were still a part of a larger national movement that was active at the country level. In fact, the Iranian women's movement was a micro-movement that collaborated with the general movements and aimed for Iran's independence and the implementation of the constitution. Therefore, the goals that women pursued did not contradict the customs and routines of that period. In fact, during that period, the proposal of any rights for women was not welcomed and did not attract much

---

2   Ibid., 34–36.

attention.[3] Mangol Bayat Philip[4] presented a detailed description of women's role in the constitutional conflicts in Iran. She puts:

> It seems that the women's participation in the political events of 1864–1870 was spontaneous and lacked any organized movement by themselves since their organizations and political activities did not have a historical, traditional, and social background that could inspire and guide those women. Given such context, women's role in that period clearly not only expresses a new nationalism that suddenly overwhelmed them and set them in motion, but also simultaneously reflects a new and powerful tendency to be recognized.[5]

In fact, only a few constitutionalist women advocated women's rights. Through nationalist activities and efforts, they became aware of their inferior position, and these same individuals later became the main supporters of the Iranian women's rights movement which was in the early stages of its formation. It is worth mentioning that those who were present in the early stages of the formation of this movement mainly came from nationalist intellectuals' families. They were educated, informed, and open-minded women who later became an inspiration to others. However, while this movement was considered a minority and its founders belonged to the prosperous and distinguished classes of society, the ideals that they simultaneously sought and the rights that they attempted to gain were not only related to the middle and prosperous class but also included the lower ones. However, the 95% illiteracy rate of Iranian women was a major obstacle in the way of this fledgling movement. Therefore, promoting women's literacy and developing their education was considered one of their primary and very important goals. It is obvious that promoting equal rights and establishing justice among such a population was a very difficult task. Likewise, the influence of the clergy and the religious class and how they blocked the egalitarian and progressive activities of women in different fields should also be taken into account. The lack of political and economic stability should be added to these two factors. Therefore, from the beginning of its entry into the political and social fields, the women's movement in Iran encountered the restrictions imposed by this particular system; additionally, sometimes this movement had to accept these restrictions. Another important point to bear in mind is that this movement in Iran lacked public support due

---

3   Eiz Sanasarian, *Women's Rights Movement in Iran, Rebellion, Decline and Suppression from 1900 to the 1979 Revolution.* Trans. N. Ahmadikhahrasani. (Tehran: Akhtaran, 2004), 41–42.

4   An American researcher of Iranian history.

5   Sanasarian, *Women's Rights Movement*, 43.

to the support and presence of educated and upper-class women. Therefore, this movement did not have enough facilities and opportunities to continue its activity. Thus, at least in theoretical terms, the Iranian women's movement did not seem to grow and improve much like some other similar movements. However, what is truly admirable is the women's extraordinary courage, boldness, willpower, and ability to realize their great ideals. As it has been pointed out earlier, a serious obstacle in the path of this movement was religion and religious people but they were less directly criticized by women. One reason stems from the fact that by focusing on the criticism of Islam, the main axis of social oppression of women which was supported by the society and some open-minded men would remain hidden. It is even imaginable that Islam could possibly be used as a supportive means for their activities. Therefore, although hijab and the right to vote were two main demands of the women's movement for a long time, it was preferred to propose and approach them indirectly as this would expose them to less harassment and pressure. This issue even somehow shows why women, despite their awareness of political issues, did not prioritize politics and preferred to focus on other issues such as education and literacy. It is safe to conclude that the women's movement in Iran like the women's movements in other countries devoted and adhered to a set of ideals, goals, and requirements related to their society, culture, and country.

Throughout the first years of accession to power, Reza Shah did not pose any obstacles to women's organizations and activities. During this period of his sovereignty, he was more tolerant of the diversity of political and social opinions. This was probably due to the support of women's organizations and groups in the 1900s that he considered for his reformist plans about women. Plans such as women's education, the Unveiling Act, and changes in the legal system related to women are some prominent examples. I believe that the description, definition, and interpretation of the formation of the women's movement can be traced back to this important historical moment. Eliz Sanasarian, the author of "Women's Rights Movement in Iran" believes that:

> religious customs and rituals, families' traditional and strict disciplines about girls, low levels of education among women and their stable social, political, and legal inferiority in Islamic countries have led researchers to the presupposition that the women's rights movement has never happened in these countries. However, this hypothesis fails to explain the simple fact that not all social movements are visible. Some movements fail and some others change due to social and political conditions.[6]

---

6   Ibid., 14.

Therefore, she names a set of significant characteristics to identify and intro-duce the women's movement in Iran since every movement needs some mechanisms and variables to grow and pass through the initial stages. The six characteristics she takes into account are an emerging group who are frustrated with the existing social order, the intention to change the social order, regular and continuous activities to achieve these changes, the existence of opposition and obstacles against these activities, the existence of at least a quasi-structure in the social activities of that group, and finally, the common understanding and commitment to the activities.[7] However, as far as the women's movement in Iran is concerned, the external and internal conditions did not seem very suitable for its development and growth. The lack of development, the exist-ence of the gap in the political system and the power, and the influence of reli-gion were the determining factors. Moreover, organizers are very important in social movements, specifically in the emerging phase of the movement. Even leaders are not as important as they are. On the contrary, a large number of leaders can be problematic and detrimental to this movement. This is what happened to many associations, institutions, and women's organizations in Iran. When leaders were absent or they resigned, the organizations would be disintegrated and dissolved.

4   Women's Movement and Tudeh Party

One of the most important characteristics of Iran in the 1900s was political multiplicity and factionalism which provided enough flexibility and freedom in Iran's political environment to promote different groups associated with women. This relative freedom of expression gave women the opportunity to express their desires and try to make change and be publicly active like other social groups. On the other hand, it is necessary to have a glance at the role of international development. The immediate years after World War II witnessed the victory of suffrage advocates particularly in the United States and England. It is interesting to point out that the presence and dominance of the allied forces in Iran established an extensive and powerful communication network with the outside world, which provided them with vast and accessible infor-mation about the social and economic developments and changes of other countries to the Iranian society. Therefore, it can be claimed that the women's movement in other nations had a significant impact on women's movement visibility in Iran. Even the feminist press in Iran translated and published arti-cles on the topic of women's conditions in other countries and praised those

---

7   Ibid., 17.

women's legal status.[8] Following September 1940, as much as the conditions prepared the ground for a revival of political groups, parties, and publications, the reactionary groups and religious extremists grabbed the opportunity to express their dissatisfaction against those limited rights that were granted to women during the reforms of the previous era.

Since the beginning of Reza Shah's era, Iranian women's conditions improved due to the implementation of modernization plans for Iranian society in various contexts and fields such as education, promotion of activities, and social presence. The process of modernization of Iran, along with the establishment of a new official system, development, and educational reforms, gave rise to a new middle class of which women supporters of the Tudeh Party were among the most distinct groups. One can even argue that as time passed, the audience of the Tudeh party became more limited and the majority of the supporters of the Tudeh party belonged to this new middle class. However, this very important point should also be borne in mind that a little later, Reza Shah's implementation of assimilation policies which prevented the independent opinions and actions of various groups including women, seriously restricted its dynamicity and progress. When Reza Shah was abdicated from his throne, women like many other social classes and groups tried to enter this new room (intermission formed from the beginning of the 1960s to 1970s), and by taking some actions such as coming closer to political parties, paved their path to the entrance of the political and social arena. During this period, women tried to present their demands and ideals through publications and put them into practice if possible.

Mehrangiz Dolatshahi, in an interview and conversation with Shahrokh Maskoub in the form of an oral history project on Iran, mentions that in the early days of establishing the Democratic Party of Iran which was also interested in setting up some kind of women's organization, by the aid of Mrs. Dolatshahi, a meeting with some active women was held in which Mozaffar Firouz was also present.[9] This meeting was not successful as the party wanted a complete presence and activity of the organization within the party but the women wanted to maintain their independence and only be with the Democratic Party as a political organization. What women demanded from the party to maintain their independence is very noteworthy because the investigation of women's political and social activities during the movement's lifetime demonstrates that they were not very successful in realizing this demand.

---

8   Ibid., 67.
9   Mehrangiz Dolatshahi, *Memoirs, Interview with Shahrokh Maskou, Oral History Project of Iran*. Middle East Studies Center, Tehran: Safheh Sefid. 2010.

In other words, the women present in various organizations and parties were finally placed in the path of greater policies approved by the leaders of these parties; somehow, women's demands became overshadowed by those policies and sometimes even gradually it completely continued its way in the direction of their party goals.

Tudeh was the largest and most effective political force in Iran, which achieved significant success in organizing its members and supporters and it also absorbed supporters among different social classes. Establishing the Tudeh party is a product of certain social conditions in Iran. The relative growth of industries in Iran, the expansion of capitalist relations in the cities and the countryside, the quantitative and qualitative growth of the industrial proletariat, the contradiction between national and patriotic forces, and colonial policies, the urgent need to implement a series of changes and reforms in all the affairs of the country, formed the reason for the existence of Tudeh Party as the continuation of the Communist Party of Iran.[10] It should be pointed out that Soleiman Mirza, the first Head of the Tudeh party who believed in religious rituals, opposed the membership of women, although the party had promised women that if they write a membership application, they will be considered members of the party exactly from the date of application. However, when the first congress of the party was formed, some people opposed it and subsequently the history of women's membership is estimated after the date of Soleiman Mirza's death.

The first institution that emerged to organize the affairs of women applying for membership was called the Women's Democratic Organization. Zahra Eskandari, Badri Alavi, Mehrangiz Alavi, Maryam Firouz, Alieh Sharmini, Homa Houshmand Rad, Azam Soroush, and Jamileh Sedighi were among the activists of this organization. After a while, this organization became a member of the International Federation of Democratic Women. The main figures of the women's organization at the beginning of its establishment were next of kin and in-law relatives of the party members. This does not mean that the previous achievements of these women and their backgrounds in their fights should be ignored. There were some precedents for these women's political and social interests and ambitions (e.g., the women of the Eskandari family, Zahra and Taj Eskandari). Other members include Maryam Firouz, who also became a member of the party's central committee, Khadijeh Keshavarz who was a lawyer, Akhtar Kambakhsh (a doctor), Badr al-Moluk Alavi, Alieh Sharmini, Loretta (the famous actress), Sedigheh Amirkhizi, Homa Houshman Rad, and Najmi

---

10   Tudeh Party of Iran. Documents and Views of the Tudeh Party of Iran, from its Inception to the February Revolution of 1979. (Tehran: Binna, 1981), 44.

Alavi. All these women, despite their family affiliation and association with the Tudeh party, had a background of activity in various political and social fields, although they did not belong to a particular organization or did not follow specific principles and frameworks.

Although the Tudeh Party considered equality in its party plans at the beginning of its establishment, it also acknowledged that it is very difficult to eradicate the inequality issues. The party claimed that it is trying to grow a new generation of men who believe in the equality of men and women and fight for this slogan to make it real.[11] Therefore, the Tudeh party paid particular attention to women's issues in their first conference. For instance, it called for the unity and mobilization of women against the reactionary force. This attention and emphasis seem to originate from the fact that the left-wing basically considered women an important and influential force. Therefore, in their plans, they wanted to establish political rights for women and welfare assistance for impoverished mothers, and even equal rights regarding their jobs. Trying to develop social rights, the party announced establishing their rights in the legislative assembly (the right to be elected and participate in election), improving the economic situation, and ensuring the financial independence of women as their own plans. Additionally, they demanded equal rights for couples and revisions to the laws related to marriage and divorce. The constitution of the party stipulated that the members pay particular attention to Tudeh's organizations, including women, in their area.[12] The Tudeh party discussed some issues in the field of women, which were exactly the demands of progressive women of the time.

The Women's Democratic Organization was declared illegal after the Shah's assassination in February 1948. However, after a while, it continued its activities under the title of Iranian Women's Organization. What draws particular attention in the Tudeh party's development process is that apparently in attracting the mass of people including women, strata from the middle class of the society including intellectuals and low-grade employees were also taken into account. The influence of Tudeh among the middle-class salary earners was also very noticeable.[13] The party's focus was also set on educated women. It is essential to note that at the beginning of the founding of the party, Soleiman Mirza Eskandari, one of the founding members, refused to officially accept women into the party; so, women worked unofficially and on the sidelines of

11   Ibid., 13.
12   Ibid., 164.
13   Homa Katouzian, "The Campaign against the Anglo-Iranian Agreement of 1919." *British Journal of Middle Eastern Studies*, 25(1) (1998): 5–46.

the party until his death. In her memoirs, Najmi Alavi states that at the same time that Soleiman Mirza declared his opposition, some leaders believed that women should be allowed to enter party activities in order to confront and encounter the religious extremism trends and fight for their rights. Ultimately, those informal initial meetings led to the establishment of the Tudeh Women's Organization.[14] Specifically, the women's organization of the party, whether in the form of the Women's Democratic Organization or the Iranian Women's Organization, raised the same issues in drawing their policy.

These positions were: stopping violence against women in all its forms, liberating women from patriarchal and class constraints, ending religious and cultural compulsions against women (e.g., compulsory hijab), women's obedience to men, and forced marriage. Also, the freedom of women in choosing their clothing, job, and spouse; freedom to study and unconditional participation in political and social activities were among the other progressive ideals of the party's women warriors.[15] However, the important fact of this historical period was that at the same time as conditions were facilitated for political groups, parties, and various publications, regressive and extremist groups exploited the same ground to oppose those limited rights that were granted to women during the previous reforms. Since progress has been made specifically in women's education, the issue of removing the hijab, and opening the gates of universities and offices to women has turned into reality. In the political conquests of the 1960s and under the conditions of the Allies' presence in Iran, the regressive also exploited the provided atmosphere to confront these changes. It was under these specific conditions and an important turning point in Iran's history that a resolution was issued in a conference that the Tudeh party held in Tehran in October 1942, adding new articles to the party's plan in addition to the party's tactical policy, financial reports, and statutes. For instance, one such article was granting political rights to Iranian women through which the necessity of amending the election law and granting political rights to women was emphasized. At this conference, they also decided to form special organizations for women and youth.[16] Attempts to develop social rights, the establishment of women's rights, the right to be elected in the legislative assemblies and state and municipal associations, improving the financial conditions, ensuring women's financial independence, establishing and increasing

14   Najmi Alavi, *We Have Rights in this House: The Memoirs of Najmi Alavi*. (Tehran: Akhtaran, 2004), 60–61.

15   Documents and Views of the Tudeh Party, 68.

16   B. Tirani, *Political Parties in Iran*, Tudeh Party. (Tehran: National Library and Archives of Iran, 2005), 41.

institutions to support mothers and underprivileged children, equality in couples' rights, and revising the marriage laws to eliminate the current injustices,
were among the other resolutions of this congress.[17]

In 1944, only a few months after the establishment of the women's organization of the Tudeh Party, some former members of the Women's Party[18] created
a new organization called the Women's Party which had similar goals to the
goals of the women's wing of the Tudeh Party, however, it was not as radical.
Apparently, even the Women's Party and the Tudeh Party women's organization signed an agreement and emphasized their mutual struggle against the
disordered conditions of oppressed women. They even agreed that they would
confront the opponents of women's education and conduct programs and
speeches to raise awareness in different classes of women. They also planned
for women's financial independence and their participation in social affairs.
From then onward, women and political activities and movements can frequently be traced in the reports and correspondence between government
and security institutions; particularly, among the members affiliated with
Tudeh women's organizations who were actively promoting and enhancing
the party's goals. The range of their activities had expanded even to some of
the farthest parts of Iran such as Kermanshah. For example, on 2nd July of
1943, some women gathered at the Tudeh party in Rasht and raised demands
regarding food, health, and jobs. In a speech, the lack of attention to the rights
and demands of women was criticized. On the sidelines of this event, the present women were invited to register at the party.[19]

In another report that was sent by the Central Police Office to the Ministry
of Interior, the traveling of one of the women affiliated with the Tudeh party
named Banoo Ebrahimi was discussed. She arrived in Qaemshahr (formerly
known as Bandar Shahi) from Tehran in May 1945 to organize and lead the
Women's Party and gave a speech at the Workers' Union Club about women
uniting and taking action to achieve real freedom. The report further stated
that she ended her speech with the slogan "Long live the Red Army." In addition, on the same day, she gave a speech about women's freedom in front of
some women affiliated with the Tudeh party and announced that she planned

---

17   Documents and Views of the Tudeh Party, 145.
18   The Woman's Party was the first women's organization that was formed by Reza Shah's
      decree, and its goals were changing the moral system of women, teaching modern meth-
      ods of housekeeping and raising children, creating charity centers and encouraging
      women to consume domestic products. This organization was thoroughly supported by
      the government.
19   National Library and Archives of Iran. National Archive of Iran. (n.d.).

to travel to Sari and Behshahr to preach.[20] In June of 1945, in a report from the Ministry of Interior to the General State Railway Company of Iran, it was stated that Mrs. Rousta, who is associated with the (former) Soviets and is a member of the Tudeh party, influenced in the Jariyah section, which is one of the most sensitive sections of the railway. She has employed some employees of the Tudeh party and brought them there, paid them high salaries, and when she is present there, the workers do not respect their bosses. In addition, as soon as they realized that someone was not a member of the mentioned party, they would be accused and fired. Moreover, it is mentioned in the report that she spent an hour of her time promoting the Soviet Union and the Tudeh party every day.[21]

In June 1946, the women's organization held a meeting in Arak and through giving some speeches, they requested to raise awareness amongst women about their duties and conditions; furthermore, women were simultaneously invited to register.[22] In the fall of the same year, some reports from police headquarters indicate that the Tudeh party conducted a large-scale registration among women in Kermanshah, specifically female students. Women with diploma degrees and some teachers were in charge of leading them and managing the community.[23] Female students welcomed this enrollment very remarkably and they even chose leaders from some educated women for themselves; while some of their teachers were also engaged in promoting leadership positions. In November 1945, the Central Committee of the Organization wrote a letter to the Cabinet of Ministers and asked for a commitment to issuing passports for three women of the Organization's participation in the International Women's Congress that was held in November 1945 in Paris; the candidates were Maryam Firouz, Shah Zanan Waziri, and Zahra Eskandari.[24] In February 1945, through a confidential report sent by the 12th police station of Tehran to the Ministry of Interior and the General Police headquarter, the speech of some forerunners and members of the Tudeh party, including Zahra Eskandari who spoke at Dr. Erani's grave was recorded.[25] In another report on June 29th 1946, it is mentioned that the party women's organization opened an office in Arak, and through the speeches made at the opening ceremony, the present women demanded similar activities and jobs to the men.[26]

---

20   Tirani, *Political Parties in Iran*, 1185.
21   Ibid., 10.
22   National Library and Archives of Iran.
23   Ibid.
24   Ibid.
25   Ibid.
26   Tirani, *Political Parties in Iran*, 1268.

It is noteworthy that according to the specified documents and remaining reports, the activity of women affiliated with the party was not limited to promotion or recruitment. When Mohammad Ali Sharmini[27] was arrested in June 1946, the women's organizations strongly protested against the central governor and the judiciary of Gilan. They explicitly demanded the investigation of the central government and even the summoning and accountability of the governor and the judiciary officials of Rasht.[28] However, throughout the years 1941 to 1948, many members of the party considered the quantitative expansion of the party to be slow. They believed that people associated with the party joined it for reasons such as family ties, friendly relationships, or even affiliation with members who were present in the Tudeh party. For some others, it was the tendency towards the Soviet Union and Marxism.[29]

5   Tudeh Women's Organizations

Although the establishment and expansion of new branches and party-affiliated organizations, including youth and women's organizations, can be considered as an attempt to strengthen the party foundations during its early life, the establishment of trade, cultural, and social institutions was done exactly with this purpose. In fact, the intense organizational and promotion activities among different strata of women, including workers and intellectuals, were a continuation of the traditions of the Communist Party of Iran. Tudeh considered the Communist Party as one of the founders of the women's freedom movement. The party claimed that it was successful in bringing Iranian women to the path of awareness, awakening, and striving, and played a crucial role in presenting the correct policy of trade union struggle to Iranian women.[30] Anyway, in 1948, after the Shah was assassinated, the Tudeh Party and the Women's Democratic Organization were declared illegal; then, the Iranian Women's Organization was formed as its successor. Of course, this newly established institution was able to obtain a license and legally continue its activities throughout the era of Dr. Mossadegh. Its Secretary General was Homa Houshmand Rad and during the clandestine activity of the party, women's organization members were active in organizing protests, sit-ins, and even communicating with the

---

27   One of the high-ranking members of the Tudeh party.
28   Tirani, *Political Parties in Iran*, 940.
29   B. Tirani, *Political Parties and Organizations, Eight Articles on Political Parties, Organizations, and Groups in Iran*. (Tehran: Publishing Company, 2017), 442.
30   Documents and Views of the Tudeh Party, 11.

families of prisoners. In the period of public activity, they were very active, specifically, in girls' high schools.[31]

The party became a major political force, especially during 1951 to 1953. Maryam Firouz, one of the most prominent women in the party, who was by default sentenced to prison, secretly published *Jahan-e Taban* newspaper during this phase of her life and continued to raise women's demands in the field of women's rights. Firouz and a group of other women activists initiated this activity in a secret publishing press. With an announcement that was published by the women of the party, the members were still invited to continue the activities until the achievement of the basic goals of the party, and dealing with women's condition was definitely declared as one of these goals. It should be noted that in the second congress of the party that was held in May of the same year, in addition to the central committee, an advisory committee was also appointed for the party and Maryam Firouz was one of this committee members. Maryam Firouz, a former aristocrat and current warrior, was one of the most well-known and simultaneously most controversial women of the Tudeh party. Investigating the viewpoints and opinions of Maryam Firouz, who went on to become a member of the party's central committee and inevitably influenced women's organizations, can reveal some less-discussed aspects and angles of these organizations.

Before joining the party, Maryam Firouz used to hold numerous gatherings and meetings in her ancestral home with intellectuals such as Bozorg Alavi, Abdol Hossein Noushin, and Sadeq Hedayat. Reports suggest that not only Maryam Firouz but also other female members of the party and founders of women's organizations had political interests and ambitions before joining the party. Although part of these circumstances was still related to their family ties to high-ranking men of the party, their entry into the party was rooted in their previous experiences of struggle. Surprisingly, Maryam Firouz had a thoughtful opinion about these women. She considered them as inexperienced and novice women lacking a clear understanding of the goals; those whose kinship merely had attracted them to the organization. In her memoirs, she states that the first time Bozorg Alavi introduced her to a group of women close to the Tudeh party, they themselves formed their own gatherings since the party did not accept her as a member. During the second meeting, she met the Eskandari family and proposed to establish an organization.[32] The spark for the establishment of a magazine was created in these gatherings. Since

31   Tirani, *Political Parties and Organizations*, 466–7.
32   Maryan Firouz, (1994). *Didegah (Perspective)*. (Research and Publishing Institute, Tehran: Information, 1994), 40.

only Zahra Eskandari met the requirements for obtaining the license, she went to the Ministry of Culture that was under the supervision of Dr. Ghani, and obtained permission to publish the magazine entitled "Bidari ye Zanan" (The Awakening of Women). It was published in June 1944 with the slogan "We also have a right in this house."

As it has been mentioned earlier, at a time when regressive and radical religious groups also dared to express themselves, forming any organizations or institutions under the titles related to women was only considered a preliminary step, and a significant portion of women's ability and effort had to be focused on removing these obstacles. The content of organization meetings, activities, and publications including "Bidari ye ma" (Our Wakening) magazine, are good indicators of these efforts. In the editorial that was published in the first issue of the magazine, four main goals for women's organizations were listed: first, women's awareness by publishing books, and articles, and illustrating their social rights; second, organizing Iranian women to demand their rights with unity, sympathy, and organizational solidarity; third, fighting against the decayed thoughts that wish to keep women in slavery; and fourth, requesting for laws that guarantee women's rights and make them free.[33] A very emphatic subject of this magazine was women's education and reforming the curriculum of girls' schools to prevent the spreading and promoting of superstitions and to reopen schools that were closed in different areas under the pressure of religious forces. However, the magazine finally fully followed the organization's goals and reflected the ideas of the Tudeh Party. It should be noted that this magazine was no longer published independently from January 1944.

6   Maryam Firouz: An Aristocratic Warrior

In her memoirs, Maryam Firouz considered joining the Tudeh party as the only way forward for her as a female political activist. While admitting that she did not have a specific theoretical study, she considered observing the campaign plans of the party as an effective factor in attracting her to the party. She even confessed that she never took the courses of the party school and thus did not know about Marxism and its theory.[34] In other words, she did not have the theoretical mastery over the philosophy that she invited other people to

---

33   Sedighe Babran, *Special Women's Publications, A Historical Overview of Women's Publications in Contemporary Iran.* (Tehran: Roshangaran and Women's Studies, 2002), 101.

34   Firouz, *Didegah*, 103.

follow. She believed that in this party, women possessed the same rights as men and thus, the Tudeh party was the only platform that could realize its efforts and dedication to the restoration of women's rights.[35] She even refers to the responses and opinions of her spouse Nuroddin Kianouri about many political and theoretical issues. As one of the most prominent women of the party, Maryam Firouz admitted that she knew nothing about many political and party relationships, even related to the Tudeh party. Using sentences such as "I was unaware, I was not at that level, or I had no knowledge whatsoever" from a female political activist and a prominent party member is very surprising. However, she insists on introducing herself and the women's organization party as a completely independent organization from the main party, focused on fulfilling the demands and ideals of the women's movement. For example, she considered her travel to the Soviet Union in 1946 which was also attended by Kianouri and Ehsan Tabari, as a completely independent business trip that was done due to the invitation of the Iran-Soviet Cultural Association. Firouz wrote about how she communicated with the International Women's Organization. She states that:

> In the first years of our activity, the International Women's Organization was formed in Europe. I was informed about such an organization and met one of the representatives of France named Marie Gedvayan Couturier during my trip to Paris and asked her about the possibility of our organization's membership. Of course, after returning to Iran, I consulted with others.[36]

At the same time, she admits that during the second trip to the Soviet Union which took place during her and her spouse, Nuroddin Kianouri's self-imposed exile, she was engaged in the management of home affairs and housekeeping, while Kianouri became a member of the Moscow Academy. On the other hand, through within-party relationships, despite the progressive demands raised by the party regarding women's rights, the recognition of Maryam Firouz as a high-ranking member encountered many ups and downs. Her aristocratic descent as the daughter of Abdul Hossein Mirza Farman Farma and her marriage to Kianouri exposed her to numerous attacks from her fellow party members. It continued until she was even accused of treason and having a relationship with Britain. Even her membership which was proposed and approved by the advisory board of the second congress had many

---

35   Ibid., 32.
36   Ibid., 72.

opponents. They used her insufficient experience in the party as an excuse and threatened her with expulsion. Apparently, they not only ignored this choice but also appointed Homa Houshmand Rad as the secretary of the women's organization. In her memoirs, she referred to this issue and stated that she decided to apply for membership in order to end these oppositions and grudges, and restart her activity in the education field.[37] Later, during the 4th plenum in 1957, when Kianouri himself became a member of the executive board, Maryam Firouz's right as a consultant was recognized. Throughout the next years when the party was still alive, she achieved high levels of promotion and became a member of the party's central committee. It was said that she was promoted with the support of her spouse. The interesting point is that even when she stayed in Iran in the years after banning the Tudeh party and secretly continued her activities, she was still suspected by her opponents, and her honesty, commitment, and loyalty to the party were still considered with suspicion.

7 Tudeh Party and Women's Movement Revival

The main purpose of mentioning these events is to point out the obvious and serious inconsistency between the progressive constitution of the Tudeh Party and the ongoing events within it, especially regarding women and their participation in the party. Regarding what the Tudeh party specifically did to revive the women's movement, it is necessary to mention again that women were present in organizations that emphasized manifesting their activities independent of the party. Najmi Alavi clearly stated that the women who initially joined the party, entered this arena according to their own experiences and backgrounds, including a motivation to prosecute Reza Shah's actions or oppose the patriarchal nature of their families. She differentiates the initial movement of these women from what later officially took place in the women's organizations of the Tudeh party.[38] She introduced "Bidari ye ma" magazine as the witness of her claim because all of the women who work in the magazine were not the members of the party. She admits that the policy of the party was interesting for these women and their demands did not show any consistency with what the party proposed in the women's area; nevertheless, they were completely independent. These women were only interested in pursuing their enlightened and progressive demands in women's area through the magazine, and only a

---

37   Ibid., 52.
38   Alavi, *We Have Rights in this House*, 62.

few of them participated in party activities. Except for these women, most of them in the magazine were not interested in participating in political organizations. The interesting point about "Bidari ye Ma" magazine was the precise investigation of deficiencies and gaps existing in the constitution that were considered as a violation of the equal rights of men and women in the opinion of the women's movement.

These women believed that these wrong laws make us "appear to the world as lacking a correct and realizable logic of the new principles, and thus we must break these incorrect laws at any cost and establish the principles consistent to the new world in their place."[39] According to the principles of the constitution, it is impossible to consider the country's powers to be derived from the nation and also deprive women, as this nation's members, of their social, political, and natural rights.[40] In these remarks, the women specifically addressed the members of the National Assembly. Another significant problem and posed a question about pursuing women's issues is the party's own actions in this regard. After including progressive materials and resolutions in its constitution, what practical steps did the Tudeh party take on this path? Maryam Firouz believed that the party could not take any action, enact, or implement an effective law. The party only called for fighting but could not take action to achieve its goal. Since the party is a small unit in a big community and women are members of that great community, they must fight against the wrong laws.[41]

This is inconsistent with the fact that in the manifesto, some goals were clearly defined for realizing women's rights. The available reports from the second congress of the party which was held in May 1948 show the extent of the party's progress and success in achieving goals defined to realize the ideals of the women's movement. These reports are noteworthy because they accurately reflect the viewpoints and opinions of the party and the central committee. During this Congress, the party fraction in the women's organization asked to expand the women's movement seriously and turn it into a passionate and broad movement. Moreover, the party fraction was obliged to adhere to the perfect goals of the party at the same time, fight against any hypocrisy, schism, and divisions within the women's organizations, strengthen the sense of social and organizational collaboration among women, and create a friendly work environment within the women's democratic organizations as priorities of their actions. In addition, the central committee was advised to provide any

---

39   Ibid., 66–67.
40   Ibid., 69.
41   Ibid.

assistance to the women's democratic organization unconditionally, since it is considered the only democratic and progressive women's organization in Iran and it is even a member of the International Women's Democratic Federation. After that, the party congress ordered the comrades to lead their female relatives to these organizations unconditionally to develop the women's movement and consider it as one of their party duties. At the same time, the women members of the party were obliged to join the women's organizations to fight for their union. Finally, it was emphasized that the second congress did not recognize any organization or population related to women, except for the women's democratic organization.[42]

Two important points can be concluded from this resolution. First, according to the statement of the party itself, when several years passed since its establishment, this political organization had defined some of the most advanced goals and demands of women among its fundamental objectives in its constitution and was not successful in realizing these demands. Even the women's organization itself encountered internal disputes and troubles. Second, it seems that until then, membership in the party did not necessarily mean membership in the women's organization. Similarly, there was no need to be a member of the party to participate in women's organizations. This fact can justify some weaknesses and internal disputes of the women's organizations, as well as the presence of some politically active women who had no relationship with the Tudeh Party but interacted with its organizations. The resolution also stated that the women's movement has developed less than expected. The leaders of the party were accused of not paying enough attention to the progress of the women's movement. If a little change has been made in it, it would only take place in the central organization, not in the small towns. According to the content of this report, despite passing 5 years of its establishment, the women's organization did not have a stable organizational foundation. Moreover, internal disputes made organizational cooperation difficult.

An important part of these problems was related to the central committee of the party. As mentioned in the resolution, the leaders did not sufficiently cooperate with the organization and assist it, and this relative stagnation could only be resolved with their collaboration.[43] These hints are enough to prove the lack of independence in women's organizations. In fact, one of the reasons for the organization to encounter these problems and issues can be attributed to this dependency on the party. It means the female activists who were present in the party had to sacrifice their demands and ideals for the macro-demands

42   Documents and Views of the Tudeh Party, 141.
43   Documents and Views of the Tudeh Party, 284.

and policies of the Tudeh Party. The focus of the Tudeh party was on educated women; therefore, it was naturally expected that firstly, Tudeh's goals and ideals would be implemented in the field of progressive and pioneer women; secondly, since these women were educated, advanced, and responsible for the party's membership and support, they would react more persistently, seriously, and differently regarding pursuing and implementing women's goals. However, in the end, what happened is usually limited to their silence and relative passivity. In other words, there is not much balance and harmony between party women's demands and their practical activities to achieve their goals; as the demands of the women of the party and the macro-politics followed by Tudeh, sometimes did not have any harmony.

As much as the Tudeh party appeared diligent with the women's suffrage proposal in the 14th parliament, we observed their relative silence regarding important issues such as marriage and divorce laws or polygamy. This silence may be considered purposeful for various reasons. Despite the insistence of Maryam Firouz, Najmi Alavi, and others, the women's organization was not independent of the party. Had that been the case, steps would have been taken to align with the progressive ideals mentioned in the manifesto; however, with the change in the policies of the party, the women's organization also moved in the same direction. At the preliminary stages of establishment, the Tudeh party attempted to move towards equality in its party plans, however, eradicating inequality was a very laborious task since the approach of the women of the party can be considered a political approach not a gender-oriented one. That is, gender demands and requirements were not the priority of the women's organization and the women's organization moved exactly in line with other parts of the party and even changed its direction with any change of priorities posed by its leadership and the entire party.

Studying women's organization approach cannot demonstrate its selection and action independence. These women's activity was a function of the Tudeh Party and its policies in such a way that if party activities needed it, these women's demands would be completely marginalized and their movement's ideals would be sacrificed for party demands. Perhaps, this is the reason why women's issues have not been discussed much in the historiography of the party. Additionally, in the party's performance, activities, memoirs, notes, and documents narrative, women are not considered important. Abrahamian attributes women's organizations' silence about women-specific issues (e.g., marriage and divorce laws) to male leaders' control over the organization.[44] As elaborately

---

44   Ervand Abrahamian, *Iran Between Two Revolutions*. Trans. A. Gol-Mohamadi& M.E. Fatahi. (Tehran: Nashr-e Ney, 1998), 276.

mentioned earlier, the most famous woman present in the top cadre of the party was Maryam Firouz, whose name was called only with criticisms and attacks to herself and her husband, Nuroddin Kianouri, and Firouz's family lineage. On the other hand, from the beginning stages of the party formation, its leaders behaved conservatively regarding the clergy class; that means they tried to keep themselves away from non-religious programs as much as possible to prevent any incitement and displeasure to religious people.[45]

An important point that should be borne in mind is that there was a kind of pessimism and even hatred among the public towards the Soviet Union, the left wing, and communism. Perhaps, inaction and passivity towards some of the most important rights and demands of women and enacting laws against women can be justified by noticing this fact. In addition, there was a popular belief among the party that it is not possible to deal with the inequality of women's rights until class inequality is resolved. If equality and social justice are achieved, many other inequalities including women's issues, will automatically be resolved. It should still be emphasized that addressing this issue should not allow one to ignore the achievements and efforts of the women's organization. As far as activities within the party are concerned, Tudeh party women were very advanced. For the first time, the Tudeh party maintained women's organizations in its organized and systematic form, even during the banning period of the party's activity, and then throughout its exile period. Women were given the chance to partake in the high ranks of the party despite the abovementioned obstacles. Moreover, the manifesto of the party and the proposed organizations are considered progressive for the political and social presence of women as well as realizing their goals. The party women were completely informed, advanced, and demanding in the true sense of their era; however, their demands were not the priority of the party. Therefore, if we put aside some exceptions such as the women's right to vote in the 14th parliament, the Tudeh party was somehow conservative regarding women's issues for the reasons mentioned earlier. While the party was fully aware of the existing flaws and contradictions, even in the constitution regarding women's civil rights, it avoided involvement in particular issues that might irritate religious people. For example, the laws related to marriage and divorce were completely mixed with jurisprudential laws; therefore, any request for modifying or reforming them could lead to a real religious controversy.

Not only the Tudeh party but also other parties and groups that raised issues and goals in women's area did not go far regarding taking action to promote the women's movement and demands; however, they also intended to change

---

45   Ibid., 279.

women's life conditions. Despite this fact and noticing all the defects and problems in all activities and efforts regarding the women's movement that was performed by the women in Tudeh party organizations, the years between the 1960s
and 1970s is the decade of renewal and vitality of the women's movement. The
Tudeh party, at least in the form of manifestos and resolutions, made efforts to
pay particular attention to women's issues and demands; however, this revival
and activities were brought under control and became limited. Some of these
restrictions were imposed by the party itself since party activities have their
own conditions and requirements in any case. The other part of the troubles
was imposed by the environmental conditions and the specific cultural context of the society in which the members lived. These restrictions should not
be considered specific to women and the women's movement because in an
environment where all political and social parties and groups were gradually
under pressure, censorship, and monitoring, women and their demands were
pushed back more than others and encountered serious obstacles.

Another important point is that, although women's movements and organizations in Iran, regardless of their party and political tendencies, had all the
characteristics of a movement to start their motion, they had particular characteristics that were a serious obstacle on its path. Tudeh women's organization was not an exception to this rule and had similar characteristics. For
instance, it consisted of educated, middle-class, and upper-middle-class
women. In addition, it mainly concentrated on its central unit, (i.e. Tehran).
As mentioned earlier, this organization was formed in a specific cultural environment. In this atmosphere, the women's movements did not receive much
public support because these were not all Iranians' demands, and these goals
were limited to the intellectual groups. In fact, the social and cultural environment of this period was considered an obstacle for Tudeh and the women's
party, which decreased the effectiveness of activities and efforts. The Tudeh
Party consciously sought to use the political and social power of women as
half of the country's population. Therefore, from the very beginning, they put
men's and women's social, political, legal, and economic equality at the top of
their plans and policies.

Women who supported the party and were members of it also had a correct
understanding of many deficiencies and defects in women's issues. Therefore,
it can be claimed that women played a crucial role in raising gender awareness
in society. Holding adult education (*Akaber*) and literacy classes proves their
awareness of the different stages and the journey that they should step into and
meet the demands and ideals of other women. They knew that this difficult
path should be paved through women's awareness and increasing their education. In 1944, for the first time, "Bidari ye Ma" Magazine received permission

from the Ministry of Culture to hold the *Akaber* classes. The women of the movement believed that literacy and thus increasing the level of knowledge and awareness of women can prepare them for a serious fight to get rid of superstitions, ignorance, and injustice. Furthermore, it could help them to restore equal rights compared to men. In other words, literacy can pave the way for freedom and fast progress for Iranian women.[46] The party and the women members truly prioritized increasing their education level and promoting literacy because they correctly realized that there is a close relationship between meeting their demands and increasing women's awareness level about their society. In 1951, when it was announced that Tudeh party prisoners had been transferred from Qasr prison to Yazd to be exiled, the women of the party held a protest demonstration as a solution; however, since the Tudeh Party was outlawed, no protest demonstration had been organized or held. Therefore, a small number of prisoners' families as well as members of women's organizations came together in front of the parliament and even some of them entered the parliament as representatives of the protesters and staged sits-in there.[47] Somehow, it can be concluded that restarting the party's protests and activities after banning it in 1948 was realized by women.

Throughout this year, actions were taken to revise the constitution. The women's organization of the Tudeh party made an extensive effort to restore women's right to vote. For instance, through *Jahan* newspaper, women tried to receive attention to their demands by collecting signatures, holding meetings and protesting demonstrations. Even the Iranian Women's Organization (former Democratic Women's Organization) sent a letter to other women's groups and they requested taking some kind of common and united action to achieve the right to vote. The next step was to write a letter to Iranian famous people to receive their support and cooperation. For example, Ali Akbar Dehkhoda responded positively to their letter. Finally, these efforts failed to bear fruit in the short term and women's right to vote was still ignored in the new election law. After these events, the women telegraphed the United Nations and stated their protest and demanded and asked for obliging the Iranian government to respect the United Nations Charter and the Universal Declaration of Human Rights by international institutions. Later, when the right to vote was granted to women in the 1960s and during the White Revolution, the Tudeh Party considered this achievement not to belong to the monarchy and the government, but to the decades of efforts and struggles of women's movements such as the

---

46   Alavi, *We Have Rights in this House*, 72–73.
47   Firouz, *Didegah*, 76.

women of the Tudeh Party.[48] It seems that not only the Tudeh party but also other parties and groups that were active in the field of women's issues, finally intended to change the conditions and status of women; however, they were not interested in taking any practical action to expand the women's activities and their independence.

Women, in fact, were never given priority in party activities. The women's movement in Iran met all the requirements and characteristics of a social movement at the beginning. Women's presence as a dissatisfied group, the purpose of these women in challenging social order, their continuous activity to make needed changes, public opposition against their activities, existence of a quasi-structure, commitment to the main goals, and a common understanding of these goals, are the necessary features for creating a movement all of which were discernable in women's movement in Iran. However, the women's movement in Iran also possessed two special features that led to its failure: first, it consisted of upper-middle-class women in Tehran and several other big cities and these intellectual women and men were its leaders too; second, it was a movement without any public support. In fact, what was proposed and followed in the Iranian women's movement were the wishes and hopes of the intellectual society, not the common people of Iran. Although the 1960s is considered a prosperous time in the history of the women's movement, the political ups and downs, turmoil, and instability that the Tudeh party itself encountered were considered serious obstacles in the way of the women's movement. In fact, due to expediency and caution, political ups and downs, and disturbances and instability in the party, the women members were deprived of the necessary solidarity, integrity, and unity to continuously pursue their demands.

The women's organization of the Tudeh party was inspired by the experience of women's groups and organizations in other parts of the world. The global women's movement continued with unity and sympathy and tried to achieve women's rights, including the right to vote and equal rights between men and women and to some extent, it succeeded in these areas; however, the women's organization of the party apparently was not willing to follow these movements. The reason can be attributed to the fact that the belief was not yet formed among these organizations that they would advance their opposition independently from the party's activities and in a similar way to other women's groups. It was mentioned that the dominant approach of the women's organization of the Tudeh Party was corporatist and political and not gender-oriented. In other words, it followed the macro policies of the

---

48   *Documents and Views of the Tudeh Party*, 246.

party; however, the interests of the party were preferred to the wishes and ideals of women. In other words, women were working in line with the party's official policy, and the gender demands of the women's organization were marginalized due to changes in the party's plans and goals. There is no doubt that women such as Maryam Firouz, Homa Houshmand Rad, and Khadijeh Keshavarz were fully aware of their violated rights but they followed the policies announced by Tudeh during their official activities in the party. If we trace the policies followed by the women's organization during this period, we see contradictions and ups and downs in its plans in such a way that if the party targeted tradition, women would have followed the same procedure; and if the party fought against imperialism in a period, the same policy would be followed in women's organizations.

Apparently, the women of the party, regardless of their knowledge, abilities, talents, and advanced ideals, were only in the vanguard of the party's official and macro policy and prioritized the interests of the party. This may explain why in the documents published by the party itself, which try to examine its performance through published works, there is nothing about analysis of the results of women's presence and activity in the party. Similarly, there is no information about the results of the investigation or mentioning the possible achievements regarding women's issues. Of course, the party itself admits that imitating the political approach of the party and practicing leftism in the activities of women's organizations is considered one of their major deficiencies.[49]

However, despite the fact that the party did not achieve many demands and ideals regarding equality for women and did not even approach this objective, there are some important advantages embedded within women's activities in the party. First, for the first time in the political culture of Iran, women's participation in political parties was officially accepted and women's political and social activity found its place in a framework called "party." Another important advantage is that women's discourse and right to political participation reached some degree of maturity and growth that became a law in the form of granting the right to vote to women throughout the next decade. Therefore, it is impossible to name some specific achievements regarding the identified goals for the Iranian women's movement during this critical decade in the contemporary history of Iran. What was achieved during the 1960s was the result and outcome of women's cumulative efforts and approaches in the 1940s of which the Tudeh party's women were also a part.

---

49   *Documents and Views of the Tudeh Party,* 279.

Bibliography

Abrahamian, E. (1998). *Iran Between Two Revolutions* (A. Gol-Mohamadi & M.E. Fatahi Trans.). Tehran: Ney Publications.

Alavi, N. (2004). *We Have Rights in this House: The Memoirs of Najmi Alavi*. Tehran: Akhtaran.

Babran, S. (2002). *Special Women's Publications, A Historical Overview of Women's Publications in Contemporary Iran*. Tehran: Roshangaran and Women's Studies.

Dolatshahi, M. (2010). *Memoirs, Interview with Shahrokh Maskou, Oral History Project of Iran*. Middle East Studies Center, Tehran: Safheh Sefid.

Firouz, M. (1994). *Didegah*. Research and Publishing Institute, Tehran: Information.

Katouzian, H. (1998). The Campaign Against the Anglo-Iranian Agreement of 1919. *British Journal of Middle Eastern Studies*, 25(1), 5–46.

Mashirzadeh, H. (2002). *From Movement to Social Theory: Two Centuries of Feminism*. Tehran: Shiraze Research and Publishing.

National Library and Archives of Iran (n.d.). National Archive of Iran.

Sanasarian, E. (2004). *Women's Rights Movement in Iran, Rebellion, Decline and Suppression from 1900 to the 1979 Revolution*. (N. Ahmadikhahrasani, Trans.). Tehran: Akhtaran.

Tirani, B. (2005). *Political Parties in Iran, Tudeh Party*. Tehran: National Library and Archives of Iran.

Tirani, B. (2017). *Political Parties and Organizations, Eight Articles on Political Parties, Organizations, and Groups in Iran*. Tehran: Publishing Company.

Tudeh Party of Iran. (1981). *Documents and Views of the Tudeh Party of Iran, from its inception to the February Revolution of 1979*. Tehran: Binna.

CHAPTER 10

Women's Subjectivity and the "Woman, Life, Freedom" Movement

Seyed Javad Miri

1 Introduction

Upon the death of Mahsa (Jina) Amini in September 2022, a "movement" was formed in Iran. "Woman, life, freedom" has become the most important slogan of this movement in which women played a significant role in its leadership. Besides the national dimensions, this movement has rapidly gained regional and international dimensions and was discussed in various circles from various points of view. A number of politicians and thinkers referred to this movement as a "revolution" and others simply called it a "riot." Adopting each of these positions needed particular requirements and led to many consequences.

Before delving into the main issue, it is important to address these questions: Was this movement a "revolution" or a "riot?" How do these movements occur? Throughout the last century in Iran, in the Qajar and Pahlavi eras, or the Islamic Republic, the first reaction after each event would be to call it a conspiracy orchestrated by Iran's foreign enemies. For example, during the Constitutional Revolution, some elites also considered the Constitution a conspiracy of foreign enemies. What is inevitable after the movements is the exploitation of the status quo by the various national, regional, or international activists in the field to reach their goals. Taking this approach toward movements will lead to a negligence of their real contexts. It goes without saying that other parties also participate in the formation or expansion of a movement and try to exploit it to gain their own benefit. The main question that behoves one to pause and consider is why movements occur in societies. This question has been neglected and not much reflected upon. Are the movements a negative sign or a sign of social trouble? Is movement a sinister phenomenon? Or is the emergence of a movement a sign of activity, vitality, and dynamicity of a society? An alive society moves forward, and has a kind of vitality and a common voice to bring a collective identity message. Can such an issue per se be classified as a bad or good thing? Why did women basically play an important role in the "Women, Life, Freedom" movement? What caused this female agency? Was this movement formed in opposition to the "1978 Revolution" in Iran? What religious understanding and approaches have become the basis for the formation of the women's movement in Iran?

This chapter attempts to respond to such questions from a conceptual and theoretical point of view. Considering the importance of "subject and subjectivity" in the concept of "revolution," the actualization of the subjectivity of Iranian women is emphasized. Then the ratio of this concept to the "Woman, Life, Freedom" movement is examined, and some social and religious contexts of this movement are also investigated.

2   The 1979 Revolution and Subjectivity

"Revolution" might be defined as toppling a regime by a number of people and their movements, and then creating a new regime. Such a definition cannot be correct and does not hold any value. In the field of critical philosophy and social science literature, the concept of revolution is tied to the emergence of the "subject." The subject means "a person who is aware of the self, history, society, and is powerful or willing enough to transform the current status." From a sociological point of view, one of the modern societies' characteristics is activity and dynamicity. In other words, the occurrence of rapid changes and transformations in a society is one of the modern societies' characteristics. In traditional societies, people would also "rebel" but their rebellion was not taken as a "revolution" and subsequently quick changes would not happen. Iran of a few centuries ago, certainly, witnessed rebellions by various peasants and farmers in different parts and civilizations; however, these rebellions were not meant to impose the people's will on the society. For example, the goal of the rebellion was not to abolish the monarchy and replace it with a republican system. If they deposed a king due to his tyranny, then, his son, uncle, brother, or one of the relatives of the same king was placed on the throne. No one thought in their wildest imagination that it is possible to remove the "Monarchy." Removing the monarchy was not possible since the monarchy was an endowment that God naturally bestowed upon some particular people. In other words, the king had a divine Farrah; or put it differently, the king was supported by the Holy Spirit. As a result, in traditional societies, peasants never "revolt" but they only "rebel." It is the "subject" that can revolt; therefore, the revolution is a contemporary phenomenon. In other words, "revolution" is a phenomenon that has happened throughout the last two centuries of human history as in the contemporary era, a kind of human understanding is formed which is called "subjectivity."

Revolution means the emergence of a "subject" and the subject itself is a person who is aware of his society, self, and history and is willing to make transformation and change. The subject is determined to change the foundations of society and to alter what he finds inappropriate in it, and what he considers to be against his own self, social, and historical awareness. For example, when a verse such as إن لله لايغيرُ ما بقومٍ حتى يغيروا ما بأنفسهم ("Allah does not change people's lot unless they change it themselves")[1] was recited in Muslim societies, but why did it not prompt people to change their destiny at the time? This verse was undoubtedly recited in previous centuries in Muslim societies but why did it not lead to revolution and social transformation at the time? When the Muslims overthrew the Umayyad government, they established the Abbasid government instead of imposing their own will on the society. This stems from their peasantry attitudes lacking an awareness of the "self" and "society;" and they did not have the self-centered will to transform society and continue this transformation.

Between 1961 and 1979, Iranians achieved this self-awareness and historical knowledge to form a system in which the will to change and transform was manifested. Following such an idea, the republican system was formed; in other words, a contemporary Iranian subject was created. In the initial stages of the revolution era when the Iranian subject was formed, there was no difference between men and women in terms of subjectivity. It was not the case that only men came to the fore as Iranian subjects and women were marginalized. Considering the literature and various denominations amid the revolution such as Islamists, leftists, communists, nationalists, etc., one can fully realize that the male gender was not the addressee of the subjectivity discussion. In other words, there has not been such an opinion that only men can be aware of history, themselves, and society, and be willing to make a change and social transformation. However, after the formation of the Islamic Republic, the system of alternative discourses gradually overcame the discourse—the subjectivity of all the Iranians—that emerged from the revolution. Consequently, this issue engendered many restrictions and limitations for half of the Iranian society. These restrictions gradually became "structural" and gained sanctity; therefore, it impedes changes and transformations resulting in the society's difficulties and complications for every change and social transformation.

To examine Iranian society, specifically in relation to the "Women, Life, Freedom" movement, the questions that come to mind are "Was this movement formed to be against the 1978 revolution? Or did this movement itself

---

1   The Holy Quran, *Surah Rad*, verse 11.

originate from the same revolutionary subject of the 1979 revolution?" Many of those who were incensed and concerned about this movement in Iran considered it a counter-revolutionary movement. However, if we reconstruct the movement conceptually and from a theoretical point of view, we may reach different results. Most of the arguments and interpretations that have been raised since the formation of this movement almost lacked any theoretical and conceptual dimensions. Analysts and Iranian national media considered this movement as counter-revolutionary, anti-regime, and a negative factor, and referred to it as a "riot." On the other hand, in the international atmosphere, this was taken as a movement and revolution. As a result, two theories were proposed that were completely against each other.

This movement was, apparently, neither a riot nor a revolution. Rather, it happened to be a movement along the revolutionary subject. In other words, the will of that layer of the Iranian society—which should have structurally been manifested in these four decades but its will and subjectivity had somehow been ignored—has now evolved and emerged. For instance, the term "political man" in Iranian society was a common term to refer to a politician irrespective of sexuality. However, the term gradually became a reference only to males, hence, a woman could not become a political man. During the formation of the 1979 Revolution, the male and female sexuality issue was not raised at all; rather, the discussion was about how the revolutionary subject can have maximum participation in social changes and transformations. In the wake of the revolution, some religious scholars and authorities asked Ayatollah Khomeini whether women could participate in protests and demonstrations without their parents' approval. Ayatollah Khomeini emphasized the presence of women in demonstrations because he believed that women have become subjects like men. Women are not objects or subjects under someone else's control anymore. Women were also equal to men in constructing the society. However, after the revolution, the political readings linked to political men led to a negligence of women's subjectivity. As a result, instead of enhancing all the revolution's ideal situations and capacities, they were degraded due to personal desires and tastes. Simply put, the revolution was based on subjectivity but after the revolution, the level of its ideal targets was lowered to the level of some people's realization instead of achieving the intended ideas and ideal situations of the revolution.

What has still been neglected and unknown is that the "Women, Life, Freedom" movement was neither a revolution nor a riot. Rather, this movement was a kind of "social transformation." Looking at all the differences and confrontations between the proponents in Iran and the opposition parties outside of Iran, one commonality sticks out: neither of them discerned the social transformation. This movement shows that society and social affairs do not proceed according to the will of a particular person; rather, social movements are formed according to a set of components. One of these components is "globalization of the new world" which is also referred to as "modernity," "new world," and "postmodern world." This new world is a place where "servant" and "peasant" are not formed in it; instead, the "subject" as a person who is aware of the self and history, and is willing to change is formed in it. If governments and political systems are flexible and can adapt accordingly, they can remain stable and achieve unity and integrity.

The nature of this movement shows that the Iranian society which was a society composed of various subjects has been voiceless for a long time. Instead of consulting this community, the community has been asked to oblige. It is now time to raise this society's voice. A society that has not been allowed to raise its voice for years and has been stuttering, is now speaking loudly through this movement. This may now sound strident but one can argue that society is gradually returning to the same idea of the revolution. This return is not a regression, rather, the society is returning to those political ideals and is researching them.

3   The System of the Islamic Republic of Iran and Women's Subjectivity

To realize social developments, we need to understand the context in which the events take place. For instance, why were women in the "Women, Life, Freedom" movement prominent? and what is its relationship with the structure and context of Iranian society? What happened in Iranian society? There seems to be a difference between "system" and "revolution." Concepts such as "revolutionary government" and "revolutionary system" are concepts that cannot be woven together. Revolution means the emergence of a subject while "system" refers to the formation of a government a narrative of which has highlighted that revolution. In 1979, Iranians tried to manifest their desires and thoughts in the public sphere through their own awareness of the society, self, and history. Iranian society and the system that was formed in 1979 maintained a part of that philosophy but made an effort to restrict Iranians' goals and hopes. One of these restrictions is related to women. Before or during the revolution, women were free and had subjectivity as Ayatollah Khomeini emphasized the participation and presence of women in the revolution. Therefore, a part of the revolutionary forces entered the revolutionary movement with the "dynamic jurisprudence" motto. However, when the Islamic Republic system was formed, some tried to guide and manage the Republic system and the dynamic society of Iran with "traditional jurisprudence." This explains why "revolution'" and "system" are now two different concepts. Now this begs the question: what is the relationship between the Iranian women subject who has been manifested in the "Woman, Life, Freedom" slogan and the Islamic Republic system?

As noted earlier, the emergence of women's subject in Iranian society is a result of the "revolutionary discourse" that inspired a kind of subjectivity in Iranian society in 1979. The patriarchal dimension of that subjectivity established the "system." The dominance of the patriarchal discourse led the system to interpret the female element or components in a traditional *Sharia* manner, suppress and oppress them, and put them under the men's wardenship. On the other hand, due to gender segregation, the Islamic Republic's policies required women to manage those "women-specified places." Therefore, the Republic brought women into places such as exclusive women's parks, women's clubs, women's schools, women's universities, and women's environments where women were appointed to manage the places. This led women to practice subjectivity in a laboratory manner where they mostly got rid of that traditional patriarchal control which was decorated and glossed by a layer of *Sharia* and religion. Consequently, Iranian society was provided with an opportunity for matriarchal revival or the women's subjectivity revival against suppressive patriarchal subjectivity. These two types of subjectivity are still in conflict. As a result, Iranian society will not move towards absolute feminization, nor will it walk in the direction of continuing patriarchy. Rather, in the future, Iranian society and even the Muslim world will witness the integration of feminine and masculine affairs to balance the social ground and society structure.

Therefore, the Islamic Republic has somehow contributed to the generation, growth, and emergence of the Iranian women's subject and has accelerated its development process. After the establishment of the Islamic Republic of Iran, some people with pre-revolutionary and traditional jurisprudential interpretations tried to bring women back to the pre-revolution conditions. However, gender segregation in different social fields such as sports, clubs, schools, universities, and hospitals, practically caused Iranian women subject to reenter the public stages differently. This Iranian woman's return was in a new form in which the Islamic Republic system had intensified its subjectivity strength. Therefore, the activity and agency of Iranian women were promoted and strengthened. On the other hand, families in Iranian society would like the girls to enjoy equal opportunities as boys and want them to pursue higher education. Pursuing higher education has postponed marriage and thus the age of marriage has gradually increased. As a result, in Iranian society, about ten to twelve million girls and women are either single or on the threshold of lifelong singleness. This had a dramatic impact on their subjectivity and agency issues so much so that many of them would not stay under their male relative wardenship such as a father, husband, or brother anymore. They have taken control of their own destiny, and the Islamic Republic of Iran has accelerated this process. Therefore, the recent movement and social developments of Iranian society show that the Islamic Republic, either intentionally or unintentionally, has contributed to this modernization.

The "Woman, Life, Freedom" slogan accentuates the femininity of this movement more than previous movements. This movement does not seem to be simply about "erotic" discussions, although there may be slight traces of that aspect because there are different social strata in every movement. In fact, this feminine movement has somehow challenged the patriarchal structures and necessarily wants to portray the female agency or women's subjectivity in the future of Iran. In other words, two women are no longer considered equal to one man or they are not the second-class gender in the present, here, and in the future of Iran. Women, in the future of Iran, are considered equal to men, not only in political activities but also in the whole society.

The political field is also rooted in both the cultural foundations of Iranian society and the patriarchal system. Thus, it is no wonder that it can engender political discrimination without disrupting the "society" field seriously. Since fathers usually take a patriarchal approach, the patriarchal view is dominant between husband and wife, brother and sister, father and wife, and father and daughter. The recent movement targets a "female" agency and tries to represent it. It emphasizes that we need the equal presence of both men and women in the community to establish democracy in the future. The "Women, Life, Freedom" movement does not seem to be an "anti-revolutionary" standpoint; rather, it is consistent with the slogan of the 1979 Revolution of Iran which follows some other slogans such as "transcendence," "monotheism," "unity of mankind," and "justice;" not only justice in the economic policies, but also in the issues related to gender differences, education, and politics. Those who chant this slogan are looking for the revival of forgotten slogans and forgotten hopes that were formed in the field of social affairs in Iranian society in the 1979 Revolution. These slogans and hopes have gradually faded after the establishment of the "system." Throughout the second, third, and fourth decades of the Islamic Republic, the pre-revolutionary jurisprudential interpretations prevailed and tried to decorate and glitter this discriminatory policy with a layer of sanctity stating that this issue is basically rooted in Islam and religious orders. However, this was not sought by the religion, and the revolution basically had no intention of such a discriminatory structure.

The main reason for the prominence of women in this movement can be probably traced to the fact that the Iranian revolution was not merely limited to Iranian borders. The three great revolutions in the world include the French Revolution, the Russian Revolution, and the 1979 Iranian Revolution. Each of these three revolutions has global dimensions and is not merely related to their own countries. In the French Revolution, when the subject emerged and the system was formed, the system concluded that it cannot always be in an ideal or agitated state. Therefore, one should choose among "liberty," "equality," and "fraternity" systems to construct an ideal society. They concluded that there should be freedom at first, then, equality and fraternity will come along naturally. However, this did not happen practically, and "colonization" was born in France, Europe, and outside the European civilization's borders. In Russia, the post-revolution system also concluded that freedom as a central idea cannot lead the society to its target. However, if there is equality and justice in society, fraternity, and freedom will be created consequently. This idea did not work in Russia as well.

Upon a profound reflection, one can argue that the emergence of the revolution in Iran meant that freedom and justice criteria would not lead to an ideal society. Rather, books which have been published between the 1970s and the middle of the 1980s, revolved around "monotheistic classless society," "monotheistic economy," and "monotheistic politics." "Monotheistic" here means "unity of mankind" that is the lack of discrimination in society. Equality and no discrimination in society always lead to freedom, independence, justice, and synthesis. This goal was not practically achieved in Iranian society too, where discriminatory policies were used to treat men and women from different social classes. However, the highest and most systematic discrimination was imposed on women. At least, men's subjectivity is theoretically accepted in Iranian society, but women are not still considered as subjects. A woman should still obey her husband, father, or other male relatives. Due to this discrimination, the role of women became more prominent in the recent movement.

4   Jurisprudential Dimensions of Religion and Iranian Women's Subjectivity

In common law, femininity has internalized subjectivity, but does government jurisprudence recognize female agency as well? We know that the "Hijab" is one of the issues raised in the "Woman, Life, Freedom" movement. Shariati in his book "*Ensan-e- Bikhod*," talks about "Islam in culture" against "Islam in

Maktab."[2] He believes that to achieve social mutation, we need to shift from cultural Islam to *maktab*'s Islam.[3] One of the symbols of Islam as an "ideology", was the *maktab*'s hijab of women, which created a third model between Muslim women's traditional clothing and Western women's clothing. However, what distinguished Shariati's book *"Fatimah Is Fatimah"* from the other two models was "women's self-awareness" in which she chose hijab based on ideological awareness.,[4] However, the discourse with which the state uses to force women to have hijab has no trace of ideological self-awareness. This discourse has it that hijab is a religious obligation which government has turned into a law, and those who deny its obligation, will face legal punishment. It can easily be perceived that the sign of the *maktab*, which was subjectivity, awareness, self-awareness, and choice, has been sacrificed to *Sharia*-jurisprudential commitment; this is, in fact, the core of tension. This point was related to the distinction of hijab in Shariati's discourse, which formed the framework of turning hijab from a traditional covering to a revolutionary symbol and at the same time drew a line between the covering of capitalist and consumer societies. Hijab in the second, third, and fourth decades of Iran's contemporary history, which has been deeply consumerist and capitalist, has nothing in common with the hijab as a revolutionary symbol. That is the reason why the official authorities pose *Sharia* obligation, call it even a social issue, and assume that its opponents are opposed to the law.

There seems to be five trends of Islamism after the Iranian revolution in Iran:

1. Islamism with jurisprudence reading
2. Islamism with a liberal reading
3. Islamism with a socialist reading
4. Islamism with a democratic reading
5. Islamism with a fundamentalist or Salafi reading

Among the above-mentioned trends, the only movement that was able to establish a system and build its own institutions was "Islamism with jurisprudence reading." One cannot deny that Iranian women have a thousand-year history, identity, and culture, and how the 1979 Iranian revolution paved the way and prepared public areas for meeting the demands of women and men. It also actualized the agency, and the actuality of the Iranians and the Iranian woman was turned into a subject. Nowadays, an Iranian woman does not define herself under male constraints, however, the legal and jurisprudential

---

2   Ali Shariati Mazinani, *Ensan-e-Bikhod*, (*Alienated Man*). Tehran: Qalam Publications, 2013.
3   Ibid.
4   Ali Shariati, *Fatima is Fatima*. Tehran: Qalam Publications. 2016.

structures by the means of Islam and *Sharia* try to return the Iranian woman to her previous position.

Islamic jurisprudence has different readings and interpretations. Figures such as Ayatollah Khomeini, Taleghani, Motahari, Beheshti, and Bahoner believed in "dynamic jurisprudence" wherein the time and place requirements were considered. However, others committed themselves to "traditional jurisprudence." Fifty years ago when religious thinkers and intellectuals talked about the time and place requirements under the title of "dynamic jurisprudence," they took a big step forward compared to "traditional jurisprudential" approaches. However, after fifty years, the status quo is suggestive of the fact that dynamic jurisprudence has not been very successful in taking the time and place requirements into account. The jurists in time and place requirements discussions seem to have only considered two concepts and components of "time" and "place" under the title of "metaphysical time and place." Their justification is since one direction of jurisprudence is defined in relation to religious laws, the time and place should be fixed and cannot be changed. However, many did not perceive "social time and space" as a new phenomenon has happened in the world. That is, the social affair is generally a new phenomenon that the jurists have not thought about before. One of the dimensions of this matter is nation-state discourse. The nation-state will be stable when the national will and sovereignty are consistent.

The barrier seems to be a gap between social time and calendar time in terms of the jurisprudential framework that dominates the discourse. This means that the jurisprudence that has formulated the political philosophy of sovereignty encounters a gap and rupture. We should consider the fact that it is the 21st century and the conceptual tool that we are currently talking about is not a peasant; rather, it is a self-aware and socially-aware subject. The jurisprudential structure considers the Muslim believer and all believers a community. This structure also defines the law according to *Sharia*'s definitions for the believers' community. However, Iranian society is not indeed a believers' society; it is not even a Muslim and believers' society. This statement does not mean that Iranians are irreligious and unfaithful. This dominant discourse justifies social riots and revolts out of which colonialism might appear and exploit. Therefore, the formation of Iranian society is an Achilles' heel itself. It seems that what needs to be reconsidered is the question of whether only relying on the time and place requirements in the jurisprudence field can formulate social affairs, have an understanding and interpretation in accordance with social transformations, and then spread among political and governmental organizations and institutions. Apparently, the jurisprudence field cannot do such a thing. Rethinking can be fulfilled when policy a) takes a sociological view and b) has a philosophical imagination. In other words, the social time and place that forms the common law and also the human normal realization enter the political mechanism. As long as the government resists this process, such riots will be increasingly intensified. Social events should be interpreted socially. We may refuse to listen to the logic of "reason" for many reasons, but our renouncement will not resolve the problem at all. Social events cannot be interpreted with jurisprudential interpretations because jurisprudence is responsible for believers' rights; however, social logic deals with a more general phenomenon called society.

If we look at Iranian society, we will realize that what was intended by chastity and hijab law is not approved by society and does not exist anymore. The current demands of society, specifically women's needs, are not "hijab," and women are seeking to achieve all their disregarded rights. However, when the system of the Islamic Republic was formed and established its systems and institutions by reading Islamic jurisprudence, it ignored women's subjectivity, and gradually "traditional jurisprudence" was replaced by "dynamic jurisprudence." This is suggestive of its return to the same jurisprudence that conflicted with women's subjectivity or to the same jurisprudence formulation that basically was not related to revolution and the system that emerged from it. At this point, the system of the Islamic Republic is gradually formed in the stature of a patriarchal system. This mental and intellectual structure does not accept women and their subjectivity, self-awareness, social awareness, history awareness, and finally their willingness to change and transform. Since women encounter many discriminations in such a structure, they played a more prominent role in the formation of the "Women, Life, Freedom" movement.

The important questions to address are "What approach can the government adopt to deal with this transformation and movement? Should this movement be suppressed?" Regarding the effects of repression, Freud maintains that when you suppress an instinct, it may be repressed at that moment temporarily, but it will certainly return with more intensity (in his interpretation: The Return of the Repressed). That repressed instinct will return much more violently and when it returns, it will have a higher destructive power.[5] The question that arises is "Is it possible to treat women like servants and confine their movement in a certain framework in such a way that these frameworks are also completely derived from jurisprudence and have no relationship with the changes that have occurred in today's world?"

---

5   Sigmund Freud, "The Unconscious Mind." Trans. Shahriar Vaghefipour. *Organon journal*, (21) (2017).

Benefiting from the term "cultural engineering," some people try to engineer the cultural and social conditions that have emerged during this movement. This indicates that "cultural engineering" is one of the keywords with which a part of the field, engineers, or those who had engineering thought and were able to dominate the country's culture think that they can engineer the culture. However, what we need is "cultural management." One of the fundamental differences between these two approaches is that "cultural engineering" first considers a template as an ideal standard and then requires all society to fit in this "template." For instance, women are asked to act according to this standard, men should behave in this way, acting in the office should follow such standards, people should act like this in society, and so on. Now, the relationship between this format and the history, culture, background, and Iran's ecosystem and territory is placed at a secondary level. However, the society in "cultural policy" and "cultural management" is considered as pluralistic and diverse. Consequently, in the management of a pluralistic society, all the people are not supposed to be similar.

Throughout the past fifty years in Iran, there was a class called the "Clergy class." This clergy class had a "clergy lifestyle" which means that they had a particular way of life in different fields. For example, they should bear suffering and hardship in life, be virtuous and righteous, do the recommended religious acts, avoid abominable acts, hold the discernment celebration, teach how to benefit the Quran in raising children, have a particular model of haircut, respect specific dress code and so on. Now, when this clergy class moved from the cultural area into the political area, it gradually set this "clergy lifestyle" as a general criterion. In other words, the lifestyle of the clergy class became a general standard and directed society to its own path. However, in the process of social changes and transformations, the clergy class itself gradually forgot about their own lifestyle. The clergy class expects the whole society to adhere to the "clergy lifestyle" while this lifestyle is a special living manner resulting from historical changes that the *Shiite* clergy (similar to many clergy classes in other religions) respect. This lifestyle cannot be generalized to the whole society because if you generalize it to the various institutions and social sections, a conflict will arise and this conflict is the result of "cultural engineering." I think in order to escape and find a way out of this impasse on the path ahead of Iran's society, it is necessary to move past the field of cultural engineering and step towards "pluralist management." The clergy lifestyle is specified and tailored for the clergy class while the society, especially Iranian society, is basically pluralistic. Iranians have lived with different religions, Islam, Shiism, etc. for centuries and they have had different lifestyles. Throughout these centuries, the clergy had never tried to impose the "clergy lifestyle" on society, and that is the reason for its success. Imposing clergy lifestyle is caused by "Islamism with jurisprudence reading." Is jurisprudence reading higher and more practical than other readings and approaches? One of the philosophers and thinkers who classified sciences in Islamic civilization was Farabi. In Farabi's "classification of sciences," does jurisprudence possess the highest ranking or philosophy? According to Farabi, philosophy occupies a higher position compared to jurisprudence because the method of philosophy is to use evidence and reasoning; however, jurisprudence is in line with prophecy. Since the prophet addresses all the people, he uses the method and language of metaphor, but the philosopher addresses some particular people, therefore, he uses the language of proof and reasoning. Farabi states that the highest level of cognition is a philosophical one.[6] However, some people in "The Age of Reason" consider jurisprudence the highest form of cognition. Although jurisprudence is partial and individualistic in nature, it is not an "individualistic philosophy." This means that jurisprudence is not based on philosophy; rather, it is based on jurisprudence.

The understanding of the jurisprudential epistemological system of mankind, time, and requirements is not realistic. As mentioned earlier, one of the advantages and priorities of "dynamic jurisprudence" over "traditional jurisprudence" was that in dynamic jurisprudence requirements of time and place are taken into account. Although in relation to traditional jurisprudence, this was a step forward and a necessary and important move, it was not enough. Sociology teaches us that when the two components of time and place are considered timeless and placeless (i.e., metaphysical), it does not pay attention to the fundamental principle of social affairs. It means that to pay attention to social issues, only the calendar or calendared time and place is not enough. "Dynamic jurisprudence" does not pay attention to the requirements of "social time and place" (let alone "traditional jurisprudence"), and this is one of the weak points and problems that can be found in all fabrics and layers of the system.

5   Conclusion

Like Iranian men, Iranian women, became subjects since the 1979 Iranian Revolution because revolution basically means the emergence of the subjects. In the initial stages of the 1979 Iranian Revolution, the Iranians' subjectivity

---

6 Mohammad bin Mohammad Al-Farabi, *Ihsâ al-'Ulum*. Trans. Hossein Khadiv-jam. Tehran: Scientific and Cultural Publishing House, 2002.

was not assigned to a specific gender. After the 1979 Revolution, jurisprudential Islamism reading of religion established the system. This approach separated itself from the main ideas of the revolution by ignoring pluralities and diversity, and imposing restrictions and discrimination. Meanwhile, on the one hand, the patriarchal system that was created by traditional jurisprudence imposed more restrictions on women, and even ignored the subjectivity of women as important members of society. On the other hand, policies such as gender segregation and policies that postponed marriage strengthened the subjectivity of Iranian women in women-specified environments and other places. It continued to the point that women were forced to restore their own disregarded rights, be recognized as agents, recover their subjectivity, and launch the "Woman, Life, Freedom" movement. Therefore, this movement was neither a revolution nor a riot, but a social transformation that shows the dynamics of society and willingness to return to the original idea of revolution. Hence, instead of suppressing this movement, the policies that ignore women's subjectivity should be reevaluated. These policies firstly often arise from the predominance of jurisprudential reading of religion over society; and secondly, they stem from the predominance of traditional jurisprudence over dynamic jurisprudence, attempting to engineer culture, and imposing clergy lifestyle on the pluralistic and diverse society of Iran.

Bibliography

Farabi, M. (2002). *Ihsâ al-'Ulum*. (Hossein Khadiv-jam, Trans.). Tehran: Scientific and Cultural Publishing House.

Shariati, A. (2013). *Ensan-e-Bikhod*. (*Alienated Man*). Tehran: Qalam Publication.

Shariati, A. (2016). *Fatima is Fatima*. Tehran: Qalam Publications.

Freud, S. (2017). *The Unconscious Mind. Organon journal*, (21).

The Holy Quran.

CHAPTER 11

Women and War: A Narrative of Women's Presence in the Iran-Iraq War

Zahra Mirhosseini and Samaa Naissi

1   Introduction

Throughout history, war has been considered a masculine activity in which women have not had much engagement, have not participated as commanders and warriors, and their names have not been recorded as a warrior in history. Some people attribute this non-participation and women's prohibition of the battlefield as an impact of biological reasons and physiological differences between men and women as well as the delicate nature of women. However, Giddens believes that this sentiment is not true and that war like many other institutions has been masculinized.[1] Despite the inevitable violence in wars, battles have always started for reasons other than violence and killing such as expansionism or economic, political, and cultural domination. War and its surrounding issues also comprise cultural and ritual aspects. Uniforms, flags, and commemoration of the deceased are the cultural bases of military forces and wars. Anchored within such discourse, De Pauw (2014) believes that war is a cultural construct and one of the most important human cultural inventions, in which women like men have always played a key role, both individually and as a group, and shared its achievements and consequences.[2] However, one can witness from the comparison between experiences of male and female that women suffered from war much more than men as they had to tolerate poverty, rape, living in camps, and displacement.[3]

From a patriarchal narrative's point of view, war is the monopoly of men. Wars are generated by men and against men and belong to their territory.[4]

---

1 Anthony Giddens, *Sociology*. Trans. M. Sabouri. Tehran: Ney Publication, 2007.

2 Linda Grant De Pauw, *Battle Cries and Lullabies: Women in War from Prehistory to the Present*. University of Oklahoma Press, 2014.

3 Sosan Bastani, Farkhoneh Ilkhan, & Ali Asghar Saedi, "Women's Oral History." *Biannual Journal of Oral History*, 2(1) (2015): 24–47; Marlène Tuiningua, *Femmes contre les guerres: carnets d'une correspondante de paix*. Desclée de Brouwer, 2003.

4 Frigga Haug, "The Entry of Women into War." *Continental Thought & Theory*, 4(1) (2023): 10–24.

Women have been significantly excluded from war throughout history. Despite the changes and transformations that have occurred in the militarization and structure of the world's armies and women's presence in it, the media continues to present a masculine image of war and its manliness as an effective role. Meanwhile, feminists also believe that war is a masculine issue; one can argue that the feminist viewpoints on the relationship between masculinity and militarism are inaccurate both in the present era and in the past. Although the purpose of feminist analysis is not to trivialize the role of women during the war, the sentiments that wars are inherently masculine and women have no role in starting wars, excluded women from being part and parcel of war, and marginalized them.[5]

Nowadays the position of women in facing the field of war and militarism has changed in many countries of the world. Women, in the 20th century, were placed in the "frontline of geopolitical thinking," have written solid and thorough analyses about war and the confrontation of forces, and the consequences of war.[6] In some armies in the world, there are regiments of women who have different responsibilities. In the present era, women occupy a higher percentage of the military force compared to the past, especially in Western countries. For example, about ten percent of the United States military is made up of women.[7] However, in some countries, women employed in the army may not be employed in war campaigns and may not receive military training. Nonetheless, a large number of women who are present in the armies of the world have received military training and make up a higher percentage of the military forces compared to the past years. Women often participate in war in two groups: combatant and non-combatant. Some of them actively and directly participated in the war. Although the number of this group may be less than men, they are very effective in motivating the soldiers and improving their morale. In addition to participating in the battlefield, they mostly take responsibilities such as taking care of the wounded and supporting them, providing relief services, preparing food, and maintaining supplies and provisions on the battlefield. In the meantime, non-combatant women also help the military forces by providing support services such as preparing food, clothes, and other necessary equipment for soldiers and sending them to the battlefields. Encouraging men to actively participate in the battlefield, looking after

---

5   Ibid.
6   Patricia Owens, Katharina Rietzler, Kimberly Hutchings, & Sarah C. Dunstan, *Women's International Thought: Towards A New Canon.* Cambridge University Press, 2022; Glenda Sluga, "What Do We Learn about War and Peace from Women International Thinkers?" *Global Studies Quarterly*, 3(1) (2023).
7   Giddens, *Sociology.*

children and adopting them, encouraging the survivors, and similar cases are considered women's activities in supporting the war. These facts are often placed under the shadow of men's interpretation of war and reciting men's bravery. This is how they are marginalized and faded. Sometimes, "heroism and bravery" may also be considered a male concept like the warrior concept, intertwined with masculinity and are only attributed to men. However, during the war, there were brave and warrior women, who acted valorously beyond gender and its stereotypes. There may be many war-female heroes who are never commemorated. There are women who have made extensive efforts to establish peace and end the war. They have established peace-loving associations all over the world, have made a major contribution in providing support and humanitarian aid services to the groups involved in the war, and attempted to end the war and kill people.

De Pauw (2014) reviewed the history of women's participation in various wars and divided women's activities in wars into four general categories: the first category is women who are victims of war. The second category is supporting women who help in war preparations in popular groups. The third group is women who enter the battlefield as men and accept responsibilities regardless of gender. Women who protect their homes and children are also classified in this category. The fourth category is female warriors who enter the frontline of the battlefield.[8]

2   The Role of Iranian Women in Wars

The historical study of the role of Iranian women in the war demonstrates that Iranian women have played a crucial role in the wars, military, and defense of the country, and they have occupied a special position in epic literature, defense fields, and combat. For instance, "Ferdowsi," the epic poet of Iran, in "Shahnameh" refers to a courageous woman named "GordAfarid" fighting against Sohrab at the border of Iran to prevent him from invading; or in "Darabnameh" of Tarsusi, "Poorandokht" is the name of a warrior woman who attempted to fight against the enemy. In addition, the history of Iran has witnessed brave women who broke the male monopoly and were active on the battlefield, and even managed to be placed at the top of the pyramid of power as commanders and leaders. In ancient history and the war between Iran and Greece, the Iranian navy was commanded by a brave woman named Artemis. In the history of Iran's constitutionalism during the Qajar period, a

---

8   De Pauw, *Battle Cries and Lullabies.*

brave woman named "Zeinab Pasha," fought against the oppressive rulers with forty women in Tabriz.[9]

On the other hand, considering the importance of Islamic values in Iran, it can be pointed out that Islam also has opinions regarding the presence of women in the field of war and defense. From Islam's perspective, regarding the classification of defense into military, political, cultural, and individual, except for military defense which is reserved for men, women have the same responsibility as men in other fields of defense. In terms of military defense, some responsibilities for indirect presence and supplying frontline needs, support, and medical assistance have been assigned to women.[10] Examining the history of the early stages of Islam also shows that women would participate in wars. In a study titled "Women in the Battle: The Presence of Muslim Women in the Wars Until the End of the Umayyah Period," Azarnoush and Dehghanpour (2010) investigated the activity and direct presence of women in the frontline of war as warriors and the extent of their effectiveness in the battlefield.[11] They concluded that women at the early stages of Islam were active and effective members to assist men and were present both at the back of the battlefield and sometimes on the battlefield itself. In many instances, they even changed the course of war in favor of their army.[12]

3   Eight-Year War of Iraq against Iran

The war between Iraq and Iran, known as the "Holy Defense", "Imposed War" and "Eight Years War" in Iran, and "Saddam's Qadesiyah" and "First Persian Gulf War" in Iraq, is a war that lasted from 10th September 1980 to 29th July 1988 between the army forces of Iran and Iraq. The Iran-Iraq war started with Iraq's attack on Iran's borders twenty months after the victory of the Islamic Revolution in Iran. In fact, Iran inadvertently entered into a war that affected society, culture, and all dimensions and aspects of people's lives. Iraq's eight-year war against Iran is one of the disasters of human history in the 20th century. Vietnam War was the first and the First World War was the third

---

9   Abdul Hossein Nahidi-Azer, *Three Constitutional Fighters*, Tehran: Akhtar Publication, 2006.

10   Mohammad Ali Judaki, *The Role of Women in Holy Defense*. Tehran: The Islamic Revolution Document Center, 2016.

11   Azartash Azarnoush & Zohreh Dehghanpour, "Woman at Battles: The Participation of the Muslim Women at Wars Until the End of Umayyah Period," *Journal of Woman in Culture Arts*, 1(1) (2010).

12   Ibid.

longest war of the century. The Iran-Iraq war was the second longest war of the 20th century. This war ended with a temporary ceasefire between Iran and Iraq and the acceptance of UN Resolution No. 598. This ceasefire has not been broken by any side and is still consistent. On 9th December 1991, the Security Council declared Iraq as the aggressor of the war based on a report received from the Secretary General of the United Nations. This council also obliged Iraq to pay war reparations to Iran. The exchange of war prisoners between the two countries started on 17th August 1991. The exchange of prisoners between the two countries lasted for 12 years. The last group of Iranian and Iraqi war prisoners were exchanged simultaneously on March 17, 2003.

The imposed eight-year war between Iran and Iraq, in terms of nature and its period that took place in the early years after the Islamic Revolution of 1979 in Iran, is replete with complications that make it difficult for many contemporaries to understand its dimensions. On the one hand, this war is tied to concepts such as "holy defense," "martyrdom," "Jihad," and "patriotism," and on the other hand, it is related to the ramifications of war such as "displacement," "chemical bombings and respiratory diseases," "survivors of war," and the damage caused by its attrition. This caused many aspects of this phenomenon to remain unsaid and hidden even many years after the end of the war.

4   Iranian Women in the Iran-Iraq War

The history of women's presence as a military force in Iran dates back to the period before the revolution of 1979 through the Pahlavi dynasty when women for the first time were employed as the city police forces and participated in non-commissioned officers' courses and the first group of women was trained for officer course in 1969.[13] However, after the revolution, with the changes and transformations that occurred in society and its value system, women were exempted from being in the army as a military force. Finally, in 1987 after the approval of the army law, the employment of women in the army forces was limited to health and medicine services.[14]

The Iran-Iraq war began with Iraq's military attack on Iran's borders in less than two years after the Islamic Revolution in Iran while the society encountered disorders prompted by enormous revolutionary and structural changes.

---

13   D. Doaguyan, *Investigating the Factors Affecting the Efficiency of Graduates of Police Women's Higher Education Complex*. Tehran: Kosar University of Police Sciences Higher Education Complex, 2008.

14   A. Rawai & M. Rezaei Rad, *A Comparative Study of Policewomen in Iran, Germany, Belgium, Denmark and Malaysia*, Tehran: Amin Police University Publications, 2016.

During the initial 34 days of the war, the Iraqi army captured Khorramshahr, besieged Abadan, and occupied many parts of Iran. However, these parts were freed with the bravery and sacrifices of Iranian forces and they brought back happiness to all the people. Considering the time of the war and the lack of preparation to face the war, especially in the early days, the role of popular forces in defending the cities and country is very important but it has not been clarified. In the meantime, women fighters and those who experienced this war in different ways have faced a much more complicated situation compared to men.

Iranian women, especially those who lived in the southern part of the country where the war started, had a dramatic role in the war and also suffered additional problems and disasters. The war between Iran and Iraq started in the cities and villages of the southwest of the country very abruptly and without prior warning. Therefore, it took many women by surprise while they were preparing their children for school in those days. Some women were pregnant at the time, some had just given birth to their babies, and some others were preparing for marriage ceremonies or starting schools. It was in such circumstances that the war suddenly started in the cities and villages, and affected their lives. Gender, in the early days of the war, was not an issue and everyone did their best.

5   The Role of Women during the Imposed War

During the war between Iraq and Iran, women carried out various activities and took on many responsibilities, most of which are unknown to many people in the society and even to other women. The books and memoirs published by female writers in recent years can relatively reveal some of these activities of Iranian women during the war. In the following sections, a description of the Iranian women's contributions to the war by referring to these books is in order.

5.1   *Women in War Regions and the Early Days of War*
In the Islamic Republic of Iran, due to the lack of women's membership in the army and the lack of military training, women were not expected to participate in the war as military forces and fighters. However, due to the abruptness of the war, the people's forces including women gained extreme importance, and the people's mobilization force started providing military training for women. It goes without saying that the military training provided by the army and the government is different from the community forces. Nevertheless, the first war responsibility women took was to fight against the enemy. Preparing

and using the Molotov cocktail was the most basic women's military job. They later received military training during the war and equipped themselves with weapons.

Women warriors in Khorramshahr were also responsible for taking care of weapons, arming fighters, guarding the bodies of martyrs, and distributing weapons among soldiers. The situation was the same on other fronts. In Gilan-e Gharb, a Kurdish border town in Kermanshah province, a woman captured several Iraqi soldiers; similarly, in Shadegan, four women captured eight Iraqi soldiers. In Susangerd, a woman baked bread with poisoned flour and killed a number of Iraqis. In the same city, a woman invited eleven Iraqi soldiers to her house and fed them. When the soldiers rested and were asleep, she locked the door of their room, informed the Iranian military forces, and beat Iraqis with a stick herself.[15] Some other women did different types of intelligence and security activities. In the guise of aid workers and nurses, they would identify hypocrites and spies who visit hospitals anonymously, in order to find statistics of war martyrs and wounded soldiers and give them to Iraq. All in all, the main military work of women can be considered as guarding and protecting ammunition, and building trenches and foxholes.

5.2   Security and Protection of Ammunition

During the war, especially in its early months, sometimes women played an active role in moving, maintaining, guarding, and protecting the soldiers' ammunition. Some armed women in the mosques of Khorramshahr were in charge of guarding ammunition in the form of two-hour posts and sometimes distributing weapons among volunteer and community forces was also amongst their tasks. Cleaning the fighters' weapons, storing them, and discharging the ammunition from the trucks were among the preparatory activities of women on the frontlines. Some women moved ammunition trucks from danger to the safe zone during the dangerous situations of the enemy's air raid.

5.3   Building a Trench

One of the women's activities in the early days of the war was to build trenches and shelters. Some of the women who were present during the Khorramshahr resistance began to build a wall for the defenders of Khorramshahr Bridge. They also filled sandbags, built street trenches, and equipped them with Molotov cocktails in order to prevent the city from getting under the control of the enemy. In other war zones, women were active in filling sandbags to build trenches and preparing Molotov cocktails.

---

15   M. Shiroudi, "Participation of Women in the Holy Defense." *Hasson Magazine Summer* (8) (2006).

5.4   *Guarding the Bodies of the Martyrs*

One of the most difficult activities that women did during the war was guarding the bodies of martyrs until burial. Fariba Taeshpour writes in "Maryam's Boots":

> it was the evening of the second or third day when a brunette and tall sister, wearing a mantua and a scarf came to the mosque and started yelling. She said "Why don't you brothers visit the Janatabad cemetery? Why don't you help us? Why do you leave us alone with all those corpses? Dogs attacked us last night. If you don't support, at least give us a gun to kill the dogs." She said that last night the dogs took the body of a boy named Saeed and ate his arms and legs. The boy's mother came there and shouted. They sent some of the brothers to keep watching out there at night and kill all the dogs. I talked to that sister before she left. Her name was Zohreh Hosseini. From the very first day of the war, she helped the woman who worked in the cemetery to bury martyrs. She seemed very disheveled. She was not tidy and her clothes were not bloody, but she was stinking because she was dealing with a lot of dirt and corpses. Her stench was spread in the mosque. Her head, face, and hands were dirty. I envied her. She had indescribable courage. She had spent some days with the corpses and stayed in the cemetery.[16]

5.5   *Women in the Areas under Attack and Supporting the War in the Early Days*

One of the most important Iranian women manifestations in the war was their supporting and service-providing role and supplying necessary equipment for the soldiers on the frontlines. In the early days of the war, most of these services were presented spontaneously and less organized in social centers such as mosques, Hosseiniyeh (a particular section of a mosque), and schools with effective participation of women. Iranian women's activities on the frontlines of war-support headquarters were not limited to specific cases and they performed various activities according to their potential.

5.6   *Cooking: Preparing the Food and Baking*

In the first days of the war, the Grand Mosque of Khorramshahr was an important support center for the defenders of Khorramshahr and the imposed war. During these days, women were engaged in cooking and preparing food for the soldiers. A large number of women were also working in Isfahani's Hosseiniyeh

---

16   Fariba Taeshpour, *Maryam's Boots* (*Memoirs of Maryam Amjadi*). Soore Mehr Publications, 2012.

of Khorramshahr, cooking food and in some cases making sandwiches for the soldiers. Some of the women also baked bread in their homes and sent it to the soldiers.

5.7   *Food Distribution in War Zones*

Another supportive and logistical activity of women in the war which mostly occurred in the first days in Khorramshahr was women's presence in the front. Some of the supportive women in the Grand Mosque delivered drinking water to the soldiers using water tanks and pots with vans. The water tanker came from Abadan, would go around Khorramshahr and passed through the region under bombardment, cannons, and mortars. Then, if it reached the mosque safely, the women would distribute it and put the soldiers' share of water in pots and tanks and bring it with vans.

5.8   *Tailoring: Sewing Clothes for Soldiers*

Among other activities in which women actively participated were knitting, sewing, and tailoring clothes and other items that soldiers needed in different weather conditions. In the Red Crescent of Ahvaz, many women sewed clothes such as shirts, pants, and so on in large halls, and those who could not sew, engaged in patchwork. Women's sewing activities for soldiers were not limited to specific items and they also included items such as military uniforms, bags and backpacks, sheets and pillowcases, Kurdish pants for soldiers settled in the west of the country, windbreakers, anti-chemical clothing, etc. Sewing chemical clothes severely injured women's hands due to the special quality of these fabrics and cold weather.

5.9   *Laundry: Warrior Clothes and Hospital Sheets*

Another activity that women were engaged in supporting headquarters and hospitals was washing the clothes of soldiers and the wounded ones. Since during the war many supporting headquarters and hospitals were not equipped with washing machines, women voluntarily did the piles of laundry. At this time, some of the women who were not rescue experts attended the hospitals in the war zones and washed the clothes of the wounded people and hospital sheets. One of the military centers in Ahvaz was a laundry room for the bloody clothes of warriors and martyrs. Women washed, dried and darned them before sending them to the fronts.

5.10   *Collection of Public Donations*

One of the spontaneous activities of women during the war was collecting voluntary contributions and trying to provide consumable and necessary goods and other needed items for soldiers on the frontlines. Some women connected with Tehran's fabric market, collected and prepared cloth and spindle, cash, etc., and by working 24/7 under canvas tents in the courtyard of mosques, prepared clothes, nuts, pistachios, Lavash bread (a very thin kind of bread), chocolates, and sweets and sent them to the battlefield by truck.

6   Iranian Women and Participation in the War

This part of the chapter discusses the role of women across Iran and their participation in the imposed eight-year war. Women who may not have directly faced the war in their cities and villages, but have participated in different ways. The importance and necessity of addressing this issue in addition to introducing and understanding the role of women in the war process and appreciating their services and bravery during the war, can be used to improve the identity of Iranian women, accentuate their role in contemporary history, introduce them to others, and finally, help them to get rid of their marginalization.

6.1   *The First Group: Women Martyr, Veterans, and Released Prisoners of War (POW)*

It is difficult to categorize martyred and wounded women into two categories: "women martyrs and veterans" of urban warfare and urban bombings, and women who themselves became martyrs or disabled on the battlefield and were reformed as "warrior women". Therefore, in this group, both categories are generally discussed. According to the statistics of the Iranian Martyrs Foundation, between 1980 and 1988 and during the Iran-Iraq war, 6,428 women were martyred, of which 500 were on the front as female fighters, and the rest were killed in the bombing of cities. The same source shows that there were 2,500 women between the ages of 10 and 30. According to the statistics of Iran's Martyrs Foundation published in 2002, by gender and veteran groups, the total number of Iranian female veterans is 5,735 of which 3,075 were more than 25% injured and disabled. To this number, we should also add the number of women who are disabled and injured. No institution or organization is aware of their condition, and they have to live with their disability for the rest of their lives. On the other hand, the life of female neuropathic patients is always more complicated and challenging; especially, if another member of their family is also disabled and injured.

Unlike wars in the past, in new wars, chemical weapons and mass killings were also used. During the war between Iraq and Iran, a large number of women in the attacked cities were exposed to chemical weapons and bombs and had to live with the effects of these deadly tools of war for many years. In Sardasht (a city in Kurdistan), a large number of chemical victims of the war are still living with many difficulties and struggling with the consequences of the war after many years. In the history of the Iran-Iraq war, on 28th June 1988, one of the most terrible occurrences of the war happened with Iraq's chemical bombing of Sardasht wherein many were martyred, injured, and hurt by chemical bombs, and this city had a population of 20,000. These people are still suffering from wounds and pains as well as mental and psychological disorders caused by that attack for more than three decades after the war ended.[17]

In addition to women who were martyrs and disabled, there were women who were captured during the war and were called "*Azadeh.*"[18] According to the statistics Martyr Foundation of Iran, a total of 171 Iranian women were captured as a prisoner of war during this war. At the beginning of the war, five Iranian women were captured, and three out of these five women published their memoirs after their freedom; "*Eyes to Eyes with Them*" and "*Closed Doors Era: Prisoner No. 5533 Diary*" by Fatemeh Nahidi; "*I am alive*", "*Closed Doors Era: Prisoner's Diary No. 3358*" and "*An Aperture to the Sky*" by Masoumeh Abad; "*Until the Halfway*" and "*Closed Door Era: Prisoner No. 0339 Diary*" by Khadijeh Mirshekar. These five women who were prisoners of war in the initial days of the war spent 4 years of their lives in different prisons and detention centers in Iraq. In 1983, they were delivered to Iran with a group of 90 Iranian prisoners of war and were freed (except for Khadijeh Mirshekar, who was freed in 1982). During these years, they faced many problems; some of which were mentioned in their memories, but the part that is noteworthy is the harassment they bore during this period. Of the problems related to the place where they were kept, not having enough access to doctors and medicine, and the violence that they tolerated have been penned. Four out of these five women were together. After returning to Iran, a number of released women published their memories in books, among which we can mention the book "*Once Upon a Time (Released Women)*" including the interesting memories of four Iranian girls who humiliated the prisoner of Baghdad when they were captured. In a part of this book, it is stated that:

> When we fulfilled our prayer, we held each other's hands and recited the unity prayer out loud. Our voice echoes in the corridor. The guard opened the aperture of the cell, "Be quiet!" we didn't listen to. He yelled again: "Shut up!". If the others made noise, they would go into the cell and beat

---

17   Ahmad Ghyasvand, Mahdieh Mohammad Taghizadeh, & Monireh Salehpour, "The Female Face of War in the Chemical Bombing of Sardasht." *National Studies Journal*, 21(81) (2020): 109–136.

18   *Azadeh* refers to the released prisoners of war.

the prisoners, but they didn't know what to do with us. He failed. He said: "You are not our captives; we are your captives!"[19]

6.2   *The Second Group: Women Supporting and Countenancing the War*

During the Iran-Iraq war, a group of women acted in the role of supporters and protectors in the war; without their support, it would not have been possible to continue the war. This group of women carried out a series of supportive activities related to the war. Although they were redefined in the form of their gender roles, they were very effective, valuable, and supportive to the fighters. Among these actions, the preparation and cooking of all kinds of food for the soldiers and fighters of the frontline, sewing and knitting clothes, preparation of medicine and first aid equipment, and sending them to the frontline, and provision of necessities and requirements of soldiers can be named here. These women are called "home frontline activists." Furthermore, encouraging and boosting the morale of children and spouses, sending them to war, and accepting the responsibility of taking care of children alone in the absence of their fathers can be mentioned as well. Moreover, many women who worked in factories and agricultural fields and compensated for the absence of their men, have been ignored and nobody talks about them. One can argue that women from all walks of society participated in the war. The women living in rural areas created spontaneous organizations to support the frontlines, provided the requirements of the warriors, and supplied them with clothes. In the absence of men, women were also supposed to take the responsibility of managing the village affairs and fulfilling the tasks that were considered the men's duties before they left the village for the frontline of war.[20]

During the war between Iran and Iraq, many women donated their gold and jewelry to cover the financial costs of the war. These women also played a crucial role in supporting the war and defending their homeland by offering their wealth and jewelry. In addition, wives of veterans, prisoners, and martyrs are classified as the supporting women of the war. Women who overlooked their share of life, and supported their husbands to participate in the war and defend the homeland bore many hardships and took many responsibilities, especially in the absence of their husbands and raising their children. Bastani et al. (2015) in their research entitled "Women's Oral History (The Lived Experience of War Martyrs' Wives)," studied the narratives of the Iran and Iraq war martyrs'

---

19   Fatemeh Moslehzadeh, *Once Upon a Time (Released Women)*. Revayate Fath Publications, 2009.

20   E. Sam Aram, "Rural Women's Community-Based Organizations in Support of the Imposed-War Fronts." *Social Sciences*, 8(15–16) (2002): 45–69.

wives using a qualitative method and narrative analysis.[21] The results of this research show that despite being influenced by the social structure and value construction in the first years of the 1979 revolution in Iran, the wives played an active role in choosing their lifestyle. In total, these women can be classified into three types: "dependent," "independent," and "autonomous." In addition, the most central characteristic of these experienced women during the war years and after that is their "responsibility" which reflects their actions in facing their children's and society's issues.

During the war and even after that, many women in Iran took care of their veteran and disabled spouses. Some of them were married to their husbands before they became disabled or physically and mentally injured during the war. Now, they had to take the responsibility of looking after their spouses, too. Some other devoted women married their spouses after these injuries occurred, so to speak, during the "disabling" period. During the war, some girls and women tried to marry veterans because these men suffered injuries during the war while defending the country. It is worth mentioning that living with people who have amputations or disabilities, or who have physical and mental problems due to participating in the war is very hard and laborious, and this issue may affect the quality of their lives. Mousavi et al. (2009) with a quantitative method, examined the "life quality of the wives of veterans with amputation of both lower limbs."[22] The findings show that the life quality of the wives of veterans is significantly lower than normal women in Iranian society. Moreover, the length of hospitalization and the amount of physical damage in veterans affect the life quality of their spouses.

6.3 The Third Group: Women's Role in Rescuing, Nursing, and Emotional Support

When the war began, women did relief work such as treating wounded patients and nursing them more than men. In fact, the main part of women's activity was in the field of relief and assistance. As soon as they realized that the hospitals needed assistants, the women went to the hospitals and started working there voluntarily. If women volunteers did not participate in the war, the number of war martyrs would increase, and if the wounded were not treated on

---

21   Bastani et al., "Women's Oral History."
22   B. Mousavi, M. R. Soroush, M. Masumi, Z. Ganjparvar, & A. Montazeri, "Quality of Life of Spouses of Veterans with Amputation of Both Lower Limbs." *Daneshvar Medicine*, 2009.

time, their subsequent treatment would impose a heavy cost on the budget.[23] According to statistics, there were 22,808 women on the war fronts as aid workers, of which 2,276 were female doctors. At that time, many rescuers were young and teenagers when they suddenly found themselves in the middle of the war and decided to help the wounded. For instance, an 18-year-old girl "Afsaneh" who lived in Khorramshahr is one such young woman whose memories were compiled in a book called "My Home is Here" written by Golestan Jafarian and published by Sureh Mehr Publications.

> Afsaneh's family leaves the city with a van full of neighbors, but she refuses to leave the city and chooses the mosque for relief activities. She then goes to the city hospital to help the wounded and from there she goes to the Janatabad cemetery and bathes and shrouds the martyrs. There, she witnessed painful scenes that she had neither seen nor heard about before; so, she went to the Grand Mosque in the city and participated in providing services; She also worked in the operating room at the hospital for a while.[24]

7   Emotional and Spiritual Support

In war, one of the most important supporting roles that women can take on is the psychological and emotional support of warriors by boosting their morale so that they can end the war successfully. In the eight-year war, Iranian women spontaneously took the responsibility of providing spiritual support to the soldiers. This war has recorded countless and rare cases of Iranian women's spiritual support. Many mothers and wives sent their beloved sons and husbands to the front with emotional support and encouragement. A part of the emotional and spiritual support of women is expressed through poetry by female poets, and these poems have influenced the participation of soldiers on the front. Women poets such as Sepideh Kashani, Tahereh Safarzadeh, Simindokht Vahidi, Seddiqe Vasmaghi, and Shahla Ahanj encouraged the soldiers with their poems.

---

23   S. Miri, "Examining the Role of Women in the Holy Defense Based on 'Eternal Fragrance' Memoirs of Masoumeh Ramhormzi." *Holy Defense Studies*, 5(2) (2019): 49–68.

24   Golestan Jafarian, *My House is Here: Memoirs of Afsana Ghazizadeh*. Tehran: Soore Mehr Publications, 2007.

Sepideh Kashani

When can you steal my love for my country from my heart?!

Tahereh Safarzadeh

In the heavenly land of the front, no one thinks about himself.

Simindokht Vahidi

Let's floor the enemy, let's rush to the friend's place and succumb.

Seddiqe Vasmaqi

And Susangard was alone. On a hot evening in Sobhaniyeh, I saw that Palm Grove had a war song on his lips!

Shahla Ahanj

It calls me again to the sky, I am sitting here silent and cold.[25]

8   Women as War Reporters and Photographers

During the days of the war, many women bravely went to the front and took photos and videos of the scenes of war. Along with men, they shared the war news with all the people in the country. One of these journalists was "Maryam Kazemzadeh," whose memories were published after the war in a book entitled "War Reporter." Part of this book reads:

> When the Kurdistan sedition began, I went to Marivan as a reporter. Martyred Vesali had also come there with his forces. Martyred Chamran introduced me to him to record an interview about Paveh, but I received negative feedback from Asghar Vesali. He said that the reporter should see the real scenes with her own eyes, not just record what she hears.[26]

In addition to the roles that women played during the war, especially in the post-war period, the role of "women narrator and storyteller of war" can also

---

25   Shiroudi, "Participation of Women in the Holy Defense."
26   Maryam Kazemzadeh, *War Reporter*. Yad Banoo Publications, 2004.

be mentioned in the two categories of "women writer and memoirists of war" and "documentarist and filmmaker women." They have been effective in recognizing and introducing women active in war, and heroines, and revealed the significant roles played by women during the war.

9   Women and the Consequences of War

War, as a social phenomenon, affects individual, social, cultural, and economic aspects of people's lives, especially those who participated in war along with their family members. In addition, the physical and psychological consequences of war can also be observed in these people.[27] In many cases, family members take the responsibility of looking after the injured and disabled people of the war, which usually causes an increase in psychological disorders such as depression, stress, and anxiety, as well as physical consequences in the caregivers. Meanwhile, the contribution of women in caring for these people is more than men. Women's gender-related roles and gender stereotypes usually impose the task of caring for disabled and sick people on them. That is, the people injured in the war and the war wounded in Iran are respected by the people of the society because they have defended their country and land; therefore, women have often volunteered to take care of these people.

When we talk about the consequences of war, we often remember cases such as loss of homes and shelters, loss of family members, injuries, and disabling. However, the consequences of war are actually much wider and beyond the above-mentioned damages. Among the consequences of the Iran-Iraq war, were deprivation of many girls from receiving education, celibacy and loss of the opportunity to marry and have children for the rest of their lives, environmental pollution and its effect on the health of fetuses, observing terrible scenes of war and its psychological effects. War, especially for people who lose their homes and health and seek shelter in other cities or countries, often negatively affects the rest of their lives. In addition to a large number of families who were displaced and migrated from border areas, families as a group migrated from Khorramshahr and settled in Mashhad. These families still feel the effects of war due to the lack of combination and coexistence with other citizens and being confined in that town.

---

27   Arsia Taghva, Parviz Dabbaghi, Susan Shafighi, Seyyed Mohammad Ali Mortazaviha, & Vahid Donyavi "Mental Health in Spouses of Iraq-Iran War Veterans with PTSD." *Journal of Archives in Military Medicine*, 2(1) (2014); M. Dejkam & A. Aminoroaya, Comparing Mental Health Status Between Spouses of Veterans and Non-veterans with Psychological Disorders. First congress on veterans and their family's health 114, 2003.

Meanwhile, the challenges and problems of the wives and mothers of the martyrs are also important despite the support that they receive from the "Martyr Foundation." For instance, a mother hugged the body of her martyred child after many years and passed away immediately; or a woman named Farzaneh who passed away after seeing the picture of her martyred husband. Farzaneh, the hospital paramedic, was busy with the treatment and dressing of the war-wounded soldiers, and knew nothing about the destiny of her husband.[28]

Another consequence of war for women is the issue of taking care of the disabled survivors of war so-called "veterans" of the war. Research shows that women who are married to veterans, experience five different issues: psychological problems, physical problems, marital problems, social problems, and economic problems. These women take care of the veterans 24/7 without any expectations. The problems and challenges of veterans' families cannot be neglected, especially those whose percentage of disability is more than 70%. Among the other problems of veterans' wives are marital problems, which include sexual problems related to having children. Women who are married to veteran spouses also encounter some problems in having children and raising them; problems such as infertility, lack of desire to have children, and also in the field of raising children and parenting responsibilities.[29] All in all, veterans have particular conditions, and depending on the type and percentage of disability, they may experience various challenges and problems whose spouses may also suffer from illnesses and mental disorders owing to these problems. In addition, spouses of veterans also suffer from physical problems caused by looking after these patients or moving them. Physical illness refers to pains and illnesses that women with veteran spouses tolerate and mention as a result of supporting and taking care of their disabled husbands. These are only small parts of women's problems after more than 30 years since the end of the war.

28   M. Mousavi, *War And Love*. Noavar Publication, 2007.
29   Mohammad Mohammadi, Ali Rezaei Sharif, Ali Sheikholeslami, & Hussein Ghamari Givi, "A Qualitative Analysis of the Problems of Women with a Veteran Husband: A Phenomenological Study." *The Islamic Journal of Women and The Family*, 10(4), (2023): 31–51.

Bibliography

Azarnoush, A., & Dehghanpour, Z. (2010). Woman at Battles: The Participation of the Muslim Women at Wars Till the End of Omavis Dynasty. *Journal of Woman in Culture Arts*, 1(1).

Bastani, S., Ilkhan, F., & Saedi, A.A. (2015). Women's Oral History. *Biannual Journal of Oral History*, 2(1), 24–47.

Dejkam, M., & Aminoroaya, A. (2003). Comparing Mental Health Status Between Spouses of Veterans and Non-veterans with Psychological Disorders. First congress on veterans and their family's health 114.

De Pauw, L. G. (2014). *Battle Cries and Lullabies: Women in War from Prehistory to the Present*. University of Oklahoma Press.

Doaguyan, D. (2008). *Investigating The Factors Affecting The Efficiency Of Graduates Of Police Women's Higher Education Complex*. Tehran: Kosar University of Police Sciences Higher Education Complex.

Ghyasvand, A., Mohammad Taghizadeh, M., & Salehpour, M. (2020). The Female Face of War in the Chemical Bombing of Sardasht. *National Studies Journal*, 21(81), 109–136. doi: 10.22034/rjnsq.2020.104625.

Giddens, A. (2007). *Sociology*. (M. Sabouri, Trans.). Tehran: Ney Publication.

Haug, F. (2023). The Entry of Women into War. *Continental Thought & Theory*, 4(1), 10–24.

Jafarian, G. (2007). *My House is Here: Memoirs of Afsana Ghazizadeh*. Tehran: Soore Mehr Publications.

Judaki, M.A. (2016). *The Role of Women in Holy Defense*. Tehran: The Islamic Revolution Document Center.

Kazemzadeh, M. (2004). *War Reporter*. Yad Banoo Publications.

Miri, S. (2019). Examining the Role of Women in the Holy Defense Based on Eternal Fragrance, Memoirs of Masoumeh Ramhormzi. *Holy Defense Studies*, 5(2), 49–68.

Mohammadi, M., Rezaei Sharif, A., Sheikholeslami, A., & Ghamari Givi, H. (2023). A Qualitative Analysis of the Problems of Women with a Veteran Husband: A Phenomenological Study. *The Islamic Journal Of Women and The Family*, 10(4), 31–51. doi: 10.22034/pzk.2022.12534.1871 (In Persian).

Moslehzadeh, F. (2009). *Once Upon a Time (Released Women)*. Revayate Fath Publications.

Mousavi, B., Soroush, M.R., Masumi, M., Ganjparvar, Z., & Montazeri, A. (2009). Quality of Life of Spouses of Veterans with Amputation of Both Lower Limb., *Daneshvar Medicine*, Shahed University. (In Persian)

Mousavi, M. (2007). *War And Love*. Noavar Publication.

Nahidi-Azer, H. A. (2006). *Three Constitutional Fighters*. Tehran: Akhtar Publication.

Owens, P., Rietzler, K., Hutchings, K., & Dunstan, S.C. (Eds.). (2022). *Women's International Thought: Towards A New Canon*. Cambridge University Press.

Rawai, A., & Rezaei Rad, M. (2016). *A Comparative Study of Policewomen in Iran, Germany, Belgium, Denmark and Malaysia*. Tehran: Amin Police University Publications.

Sam Aram, E. (2002). Rural Women's Community-Based Organizations in Support of the Imposed-War Fronts. *Social Sciences*, 8(15)(16), 45–69.

Shiroudi, M. (2006). Participation of Women in the Holy Defense. *Hasson Magazine Summer* (8).

Sluga, G. (2023). What Do We Learn about War and Peace from Women International Thinkers? *Global Studies Quarterly*, 3(1).

Taeshpour, F. (2012). *Maryam's Boots (Memoirs of Maryam Amjadi)*. Soore Mehr Publications.

Taghva, A., Dabbaghi, P., Shafighi, S., Mortazaviha, S.M.A., & Donyavi, V. (2014). Mental Health in Spouses of Iraq-Iran War Veterans with PTSD. *Journal of Archives in Military Medicine*, 2(1).

Tuininga, M. (2003). *Femmes Contre les Guerres: Carnets d'une Correspondante de Paix*. Desclée de Brouwer.

CHAPTER 12

From Absence to Presence: Feminine Style, Voice and Power

Esmaeil Zeiny

1 Introduction[1]

For centuries, the tradition of veiling and public silence repressed Iranian women both physically and verbally. These conventions stipulated that women's physique should be concealed and their voice, emotion and concern remain unexpressed. Although Iranian women have always played crucial and representative roles in various political and historical eras, the tendency to trivialize and neglect their roles and movements has been rife. This affected Persian literature as well; women were either totally excluded or marginalized and mentioned very briefly in literature. The Iranian women had challenged these conventions, ventured into the public, and voiced their thoughts and concerns through literature but they were again marginalized and their literature was overlooked due to the so-called utilization of traditional masculine styles and tones. This sentiment gradually disappeared with the emergence of women authors whose literary works had a different style and tone than men's writings. These writings brought women from the periphery to the center as well. Since then, Iranian women authors have been producing literature to protest against patriarchy and traditional discriminatory policies. Iranian women writers in Iran have been creating a literature engaged with women's issues and gender relations. This literature modified the course of literature in Iran decisively. Men's poetry and prose writing, after centuries of literary dominance, yielded to women's writings. In Iran of the post-1979 Revolution, women not only established themselves as prolific writers but also dominated the best-selling fiction list. The number of women who have published novels is about equal to the number of men. Furthermore, women produced books that outsold the men's by far. Through these books, Iranian women writers

1 This research was supported by Xiamen University Malaysia Research Fund (Grant No: XMUMRF/2023-C11/IELL/0002). This chapter is a reworked, reorganized and revised version of an earlier draft entitled "Ecriture Feminine: Feminism and Nationalism in *One Woman's War: Da*" which appeared in *3L: Language, Linguistics, Literature*, 25 (3) (2019): 115–125.

are consciously challenging, transforming, reconstructing and negotiating histories demonstrating their own identities, rights, experiences and desired futures.

Iranian women authors have also produced significant literature in what is now regarded as formerly male-dominated genres that deal with nationalism such as war literature or "Sacred Defense Literature" which refers to the literature about the Iran-Iraq war. Women were not given any significant roles other than the mother, sister, and faithful housewife of a martyred in the male-produced war literature. Breaking the exclusive grips that men had in the literary production of "Sacred Defense," women are now narrating their sagas of endurance and sacrifices, and confrontations with Iraqi soldiers in the front. This literature could be read through the feminist lens of *ecriture feminine* by questioning and interpolating the master discourse of patriarchy. *One Woman's War: Da* (2014) (hereafter *Da*) is one such literary work told by Seyyedeh Zahra Hosseini about her experiences during the Iran-Iraq war as recorded by Seyyedeh Azam Hosseini.[2] This memoir contains three parts: the first part details the narrator's childhood in Iraq and her migration to Iran; the second part which is the core part of this memoir is a depiction of the seventeen-year-old Hosseini's volunteered activities such as nursing the wound, washing the corpses of the dead, and her role as a combatant in defending Khorramshahr; and the last part details the narrator's recovery from shrapnel injury she received from the battlefield and her married life. In what follows I bring to the surface Iranian women's journey from absence to presence and authorship. Drawing upon and reviving Cixous' notion of *ecriture feminine*, this chapter explores how *Da* constructs a feminine style of writing that defends women's rights and highlights women's roles in nation-building projects like the Iran-Iraq war.

2   Ecriture Feminine

Coined by Helen Cixous in her essay "The Laugh of the Medusa" (1976),[3] *ecriture feminine* refers to a uniquely feminine style of writing that emblematizes feminine difference and emerged in response to the exclusion of women in public discourses in a fundamentally phallogocentric culture; in a culture where the man (the ruling class) claimed: "I am the unified, self-controlled

---

2   Seyyedeh Zahra Hosseini, *One Woman's War: Da (Mother)*. Trans. Paul Sprachman. Costa Mesa: Mazda Publishers, 2014.
3   Hélène Cixous, "The Laugh of Medusa." *Signs*, 1 (4) (1976): 875–893.

center of the universe" and "[t]he rest of the world, which I define as the Other, has meaning only in relation to me, as man/father, possessor of the phallus."[4] Religion and philosophy supported this claim to centrality and language followed suit. Speaking and writing from this position, man appropriates the world and rules it through verbal mastery. Language in different contexts as symbolic discourse is also another venue in which man exerts his power to objectify the world, narrows it down to his own terms and conditions, speak instead of everything and everyone else including women.[5] Women had no voice or if they ever had, according to Robin Lakoff's dominance theory (1973),[6] it showed qualities of weakness and subordination in their language in a male-dominated society. Utilizing Lacan's ideas that the structure of language is centered by the phallus, Cixous traces the starting point of this masculine domination back to the time when a child encounters the first lack, i.e. the mother's penis. This lack of a penis and the fear of castration separate the child from the mother, make him/her renounce the mother, and make the mother the "Other." Here is when the father becomes an important figure and the Law that separates the child from the mother. Therefore, when the child discovers the language, s/he discovers the father and sees him as the pillar of linguistic structure.[7] Father is the center and the ruling principle of the whole language structure. This center is also called the phallus which stands "for all the differences that structure the symbolic order".[8] Thus, father and his penis occupy the center in the language system that impacts all other discourses.

In patriarchal culture, therefore, a text's "author is a father, a procreator, an aesthetic patriarch whose pen is an instrument of generative power like his penis."[9] This father and his penis construct a language that normalizes women as the "Other" who lacks and needs to be completed. This is a language that privileges masculine values: "a locus where the repression of women has been perpetuated, over and over, more or less consciously. ..."[10] While strong waves of feminism condemn gender difference and advocate gender equality in all aspects of life, the post-structuralist theoretical feminists such as Helen

4   Ann Rosalind Jones, "Writing the Body: Toward an Understanding of 'L'Ecriture Féminine.'" *Feminist Studies*, 7 (2) (1981): 248.

5   Ibid.

6   Robin Lakoff, *Language and Women's Place*. New York: Harper and Row, 1973.

7   Seda Peksen, "Feminine Writing as an Alternative to the Patriarchal Language." *An Online Feminist Journal*, 1 (2) (2005): 1–12.

8   Maud Ellmann, *Psychoanalytic Literary Criticism*. (London: Longman, 1994), 19.

9   Sandra M. Gilbert, "Dancing through the Minefield: Some Observations on the Theory, Practice, and Politics of a Feminist Literary Criticism," in *Critical Theory Since 1965*, eds, Adams, H., and Searle, L. (Tallahassee: University Presses of Florida, 1986), 488.

10   Cixous, "The Laugh of Medusa," 879.

Cixous, Luce Irigaray and Julia Kristeva are more concerned with deconstructing gender difference in language and text. Although these French women differ in strategy to resist masculine domination, they all agree that "resistance takes place in the form of *jouissance*, that is, in direct reexperience of the physical pleasures of infancy and of later sexuality, repressed but not obliterated by the Law of the Father."[11] Kristeva does not go any further but Cixous and Irigarary highlight that if women, who have been historically sexual objects for men—virgins or *fille de joie*, wives or mothers—speak about their sexuality in new languages, they will institutionalize a point of *difference* through which phallogocentric notions and controls can be dismantled. The emphasis on the new language is due to the fact that these women cannot voice their concerns, emotions and plights in a masculine language which sounds inadequate to their expressive needs and would put them again in a position of linguistically marginalized, dormant or silent in speech and in social signification. The only way to defeat this masculine suppression is to create a language not dominated by the phallus.

In the Lacanian Real, a stage before an infant enters the language, there is no trace of phallus and masculine domination. Kristeva calls this pre-oedipal stage semiotic to which women should return in order to create the feminine language. Whereas the Symbolic is dominated by the father, the phallus, and the law; the semiotic carries no sign of the father, the phallus, and the law.[12] Another place where the phallus possesses no strong control is the margin of the Symbolic order. Drawing upon Lacan's Symbolic Order that maintains that men are in the possession of the phallus and are therefore closer to the Symbolic, and women are located at the margins of the Symbolic Order because of the lack of penis, Cixous takes this marginal position of women to her advantage and argues that this marginality makes women far away from established meanings and reasons, and takes them closer to the imaginary and fantasies (1976).[13] The return to semiotic and the imaginary in the margins of the Symbolic Order help women to create a language that escapes the constraints of fixed meanings and reasons which are phallogocentric. Anchored within such discourse, Cixous (1976) introduces the concept of *ecriture feminine* as alternative writing for women that would pass through the restricting frameworks of phallogocentric discourse, and disrupt the conventional reading, writing and representational practices that are produced and supported

---

11   Jones, "Writing the Body," 248.

12   Julia Kristeva, *Revolution in Poetic Language*. Trans. M. Waller. New York: Columbia University Press, 1984.

13   Cixous, "The Laugh of Medusa."

by patriarchal values.[14] What makes *ecriture feminine* effective is the subversive and exorbitant character of female sexuality: just like feminine sexuality it is numerous instead of single, circulated instead of focused, and oriented towards process instead of goal.[15] *Ecriture feminine*, in fact, celebrates this openness and multiplicity, and challenges the hierarchal oppositions such as man/women that appear in masculine writing.

Cixous' refusal to define *ecriture feminine* and her contradictory statement that *ecriture feminine* comes from the female body but men can also write from this position render the concept impractical to many critics. This concept has received other criticisms as well; a critic such as Ann Rosalind Jones (1981), for instance, points out several objections to *ecriture feminine* including its tendency towards essentialism and its participation in the male-centered binary logic like Derrida's binary theory of "*différance*" to create a new binarism.[16] These critics failed to see that Cixous does not define the concept because she believes that definition, encoding and theorization belong to phallogocentrism. The fact that she mentions that men can also produce *ecriture feminine* is suggestive of her tendency not to exclude men from any discourses and therefore, she rejects essentialism and affirms plurality and multiplicity following a "both/and" logic of difference. Cixous' participation in the male-centered binary logic is to challenge it and create a new space in which, unlike the former male-created binarism, women do have a voice. *Ecriture feminine* has no intention of replacing masculine writing; it rather intends to give women a voice. What Cixous terms as "ecriture feminine" should be never confined to women's writing. As it has been noted earlier, men can also write from the position of ecriture feminine. She names male writers such as Laurence Sterne, Arthur Rimbaud, Franz Kafka, Heinrich von Kleist, James Joyce, Jean Genet, Ingeborg Bachman, Thomas Benrhard, and Osip Mandelstam whose writings can be prominent examples of "ecriture feminine."[17] Thus, both men and women, and those who are marginalized can use ecriture feminine as a medium.

The concept is usually characterized with illogicality and incoherency but according to Diana Holms (1996),[18] "*écriture féminine* will disrupt the order of the masculine text, but beneath its apparent incoherence may display a different type of order, based on the cycle rather than the straight line." I am very

---

14   Ibid.
15   Ibid.
16   Jones, "Writing the Body."
17   Cixous, "The Laugh of Medusa," 879–884.
18   Diana Holmes, *French Women's Writing, 1848–1994*. (London; Atlantic Highlands, 1996), 226.

much aware that all writings produced by women cannot be termed as *ecriture feminine* because *ecriture feminine* is originally meant to refer to a unique style of writing, especially poetry that displays gaps, silences, new images and puns. I would argue, however, that *ecriture feminine* is not eccentric, incomprehensible and inconsistent to evade the phallogocentric structure of logicality and order. Establishing new styles, themes, motifs and symbols in and of themselves undermines the masculine logic, destructs the structure of phallogocentric system and creates a new set of authentic feminine logicality and order. Highlighting the value of an authentic feminine utterance, Cixous argues that ecriture feminine is the medium that permits women, the marginalized Others of the society, to access their inner self and reclaim their liberty. Cixous believes, "writing is precisely the very possibility of change, the space that can serve as a springboard for subversive thought, the precursory movement of a transformation of social and cultural structures."[19] I am, therefore, extending the term *ecriture feminine* to any kind of writings, poetry and prose, produced by women that circumvent the phallogocentric structure through forming a feminine structure and eradicating the "silencing" and "marginalization" of women. My extension of the term is not an overgeneralization, rather I believe that feminine writings that are acts of liberation and are starting points for a female consciousness—as the main objectives of Cixous' *ecriture feminine*—can be termed as *ecriture feminine* as long as they avoid the phallogocentric structure.

3   From Absence to Presence and Authorship

The tradition of veiling and public silence kept women in Iran repressed for centuries. Their physique was mostly concealed and their voice, emotions, and concerns remained unexpressed. This imposed invisibility and enforced reticence in a patriarchal society turned women into social non-existent figures. However, there were always outspoken women who voiced their concerns about women's condition. Tahereh Quorratol'Ayn (1817–1852) is one such woman who unveiled herself in an assemblage of men and challenged the patriarchal system of the time. She spoke against the veil, polygamy and marital relations. Iran has also witnessed women's movements, associations and organizations in support of the nationalistic and anti-imperialist projects. One prime example dates back to the Constitutional Revolution of 1905–1911 when women took part in the battle against foreign forces, initiated street riots

---

19   Cixous, "The Laugh of Medusa," 879.

and strikes, boycotted the importation of foreign goods, and raised funds for the establishment of the National Bank. Despite all these initiations, movements and participation, Iranian women were denied the voting rights on the grounds that they lacked political and social insights. Iranian women's significant roles as nationalists—liberating the country from despotism and imperialism, and feminists—challenging patriarchy and questioning the conditions of their lives—are undeniable but the masculine inclination to trivialize and neglect their roles and movements, and the subsequent disregarding of women's rights has been prevalent. The cloak of imposed invisibility and enforced silence affected Persian literature as well. Women were either totally absent or they were marginalized and mentioned in passing in different genres of literature. For Instance, women in Roy Mottahedeh's *The Mantle of the Prophet* (1987), a fictional history of Iranian culture, are literally wiped out from the text. This veiling of women's voices was not confined to any particular genre of literature. For instance, Sufi Persian poetry has always been a male-dominated genre. When they appeared as the subject of men's books, they were oftentimes mentioned in passing, or portrayed as mothers, wives or queens who were bit players in politics and society.

During the Pahlavi era, when Iranian women were forced to unveil and then free to veil or unveil again, women poets and authors such as Parvin E'tessami (1907–1941) emerged. E'tessami kept venturing into the public through her poetry but the society seemed to find it hard to listen to her. Parvin E'tessami corroborates this sentiment through bemoaning of a hen in her poem entitled "The Reproach of Uncouth," who is "a captive in man's trap:" "Why tell our story? Nobody will listen/ Why recount our life? Nobody will read it anyhow."[20] Now that the Iranian woman had the chance to express herself through poetry, her voice was still unheard. To further exacerbate the marginalization of women and to accentuate the role of patriarchy, Parvin E'tessami has been "repeatedly stereotyped as a traditional recluse in the shadow of an overprotective, equally traditional father" who has "merely and passively reflected the ideas and ideals of her father."[21] Thus, women authors were marginalized and their literature was overlooked due to possessing traditional manly styles of writing. This position reaffirmed women's passivity and domesticity in public and perpetuated women's absence in literature. Even years later, the establishment of Commitment Literature—a "pervasive literary movement" to defend all the Iranians and their causes against any sort of unfair social and political

---

20   Parvin E'tessami, *Divan* [*Collected Poems*]. Reprint. (Tehran: Fardin, 1935), 58.
21   Farzaneh Milani, *Veils and Words: The Emerging Voices of Iranian Women Writers.* (Syracuse, New York: Syracuse University Press, 1992), 112.

issues—did not do much to help women writers. The Commitment Literature was set up by a group of writers and thinkers to address issues such as social welfare, social injustice, political confusion, and oppression under the Pahlavi. Hamid Dabashi argues that this literature was "a perceived notion of responsibility to supraliterary concerns, so that the artist enters the creative moment with the intention of conveying an idea, propagating an ideology, converting an audience, defending a cause, or mobilizing a mass."[22] While addressing social injustices, oppression, and Iranian nationalism, this literature failed in giving agency to women and women writers. Men who had access to literary circles and publications would still hold a firm grip on the styles, themes, tones and contents of Iranian literature, and define what Iranian literature should look like. Iranian women writers had no options but to follow suit in their writings.

In the late 1960s, this sentiment gradually faded away and women writers began to consider writing from a woman's perspective and moving away from patriarchal literary rules and styles for the first time. Known as the pioneer of Iranian female literature, Simin Daneshvar (1921–2012) shunned using the masculine styles, motifs, symbols, themes and tones of the Commitment literary tradition. Daneshvar moves away from the patriarchal literary styles and establishes her own style, themes, motifs and symbols by including garden allegory, animal imagery, and Persian myths and anecdotes intended for women readers. Avoiding a masculinity literary paradigm, she depicts women's experiences and social impediments to the progress of women. Daneshvar's feminist and nationalist tendencies appear regularly in her fictions, especially *Savushun* (1969).[23] As the first novel in Persian written by a female author, *Savushun* concentrates on a woman's experience and brings to the fore her perspectives of Iran's political unrest, anti-imperialism and anti-monarchy in Reza Shah's reign. Zari, the main character in the novel, is portrayed with fears initially but turns into a woman who fights against her loneliness, pains and sorrows and becomes a heroin of the novel. Zari is, indeed, depicted as a symbol of every-woman, making her life a paradigm of a middle-class woman's experience. Daneshvar is the first woman writer who demolished the then-existing traditionally oppressed viewpoint about Iranian women. This unveiling of the women's views comes at a time when Iranian women had to go through the state's discriminatory laws and gender inequality policies. She established a movement with which women's expression and style gained cultural currency. In a conversation with

---

22   Hamid Dabashi, "The Poetics of Politics: Commitment in Modern Persian Literature." *Iranian Studies*, 18 (2/4) (1985): 150.

23   Simin Daneshvar, *Savushun*. Tehran: Kharazmi Publications, 1969.

Alefba, she contends that "a woman must describe the situation of women."[24] She addresses women's issues in her writings and believes that "the conditions for women's struggle are very difficult. I recommend that women not give up hope and that they maintain their spirit. The struggle must not be forgotten. ... Openings will certainly appear and women will even get rid of the 'invisible nets.'"[25] Despite the social ills of society against women, Daneshvar's female characters never lose hope and never show signs of anxiety. Daneshvar admits that her work shows "the mentality of the Iranian woman."[26] Daneshvar brings women into the text to highlight the role of women in Iranian nationalism as well. While both men and women play a role in Iran's nation-building projects, women were often excluded or marginalized in such efforts. Daneshvar portrays different female characters and shows how they are vital in making Iranian nationalism. Daneshvar's new style, themes, and tone of writing paved the way for other women writers to express women's experiences. Thus, it is safe to argue that ecriture feminine in prose within the contemporary era in Iran appears to have started with Daneshvar's *Savushun*.

Equally well-known, Forough Farrokhzad (1935–1967) is another author of this era who writes about taboo subjects such as love, women's emotions and sexual desire, and women's oppression. Farrokhzad writes from a "female point of view,"[27] that is, she takes "the exclusive meaning of good poet out of the hands of middle-aged men", bound "the feminine language, mind, body, and soul with Persian literature, and change[d] its face forever and ever."[28] At a time when Iranian female poets wrote under pseudonyms, Farrokhzad had no reservation whatsoever to use her real name for poems that depict taboo subjects such as "Sin" confessing to an intimate relationship and waking up in the arms of a man who is not her husband. "Sin" is an explicit detail of her affair with a man whose speaker declares that she is a sinner but she has no feeling of repentance: "I have sinned a rapturous sin / in a warm enflamed embrace." The woman in the poem is not depicted as a victim of the lover but as a happy woman who is exhilarated by her power to arouse the man: "Lust enflamed his eyes, / red wine trembled in the cup, / my body, naked and drunk, / quivered

24   "Pa-ye sohbat-e Simin-e Danesvar" (A Conversation with Simin Danesvar). *Alefba* (Paris), no. 4 1983): 153.

25   Ibid., 187.

26   Ibid., 185.

27   Janet Afary, *Sexual Politics in Modern Iran.* (Cambridge: Cambridge University Press, 2009), 283.

28   Farzaneh Milani, *Furūq-i Farrukhzād: Zindigī Nāmah-yi Hunarī bā Nāmah kāy-i Muntashir Nashudah* [*Forough Farrokhzad: A Literary Biography with Unpublished Letters*]. (Toronto: Persian Circle Publications, 2016), 2.

softly on his breast." This is suggestive of Farrokhzad's deliberate effort to reverse a thousand years of Persian literature written by men about their lovers.[29] Her confessional and sensual style in revealing her female self and her reflections on her womanhood and femininity through a bold and blunt feminine language unique of her own characterize her poetry as ecriture feminine.

These women authors increased not only the importance of women's writing in the development of modern Persian literature but also the status of women in the patriarchal society. The women's status also owes its improvement to many women's organizations and associations that were formed for their political and cultural demands requesting equal rights, education, the abolition of polygamy and discriminatory policies towards veiled/unveiled women. Women's presence in society was now too bold to ignore. An instance of their heavy presence is the Revolution of 1979 in which women from all walks of life, veiled and unveiled, with different ideological inclinations participated in anti-Shah demonstrations and strikes. However, the abolition of the Family Protection Act, the implementation of *Sharia*, the decree demanding women to wear Islamic form of modest dress, and the Veiling Act of 1983 in the immediate years after the Revolution disappointed many women and men, and made them think that Iran is turning the clock back in respect of women's presence both in the public arena and literary world. Despite this circumstance and much to the chagrin of those who thought women would turn into a non-existent figure again under the Islamic Republic, writing by Iranian women inside Iran has increased rapidly and Iranian women carved a niche for themselves in the literary world a decade after the 1979 Revolution. The different genres of literature produced by Iranian women ever since commonly continue dealing with women's issues and gender relations which is indicative of their ongoing feminist concerns. Despite the heavy burden of patriarchal authority, these narratives articulate their protests against gender hierarchy, patriarchy and discriminatory policies and traditions. This succinct section forms the backdrop of Iranian women's journey in search of voice, presence and authorship.

4   *Da*: a Post-Revolutionary Example of Ecriture Feminine

Da (2014) bears a style that provides a good example of *ecriture feminine*.[30] To begin with, it is hard to overlook *Da*'s long descriptive passages throughout its 696 pages. These descriptive passages possess too much detail that only a

---

29   Joanna Scutts, "Feminize Your Canon: Forough Farrokhzad." *The Paris Review*, 2020.

30   Hosseini, *One Woman's War: Da (Mother)*.

woman would notice. For instance, paying particular attention to what people are wearing and how old they are, is typical throughout the memoir:

> The old couple's faces put them in their sixties and their eyes seemed glassy either from old age or cataracts. The man was tall and thin. He had a ragged turban on his head and was dressed in a faded grey and wrinkled dishdasha. His hands were unusually large, and I could tell from the calluses on them and his stubby fingers along with his sunburned face he had farmed the date groves all his life ... His son had inherited his regular features.

While women's writings are descriptive and replete with details, men's writings are usually to the point and exclude too much detail irrespective of the genre. The contemporary feminist and sociologist, Devault (1999) echoes this opinion and believes that women's descriptive skill and their meticulosity are two conspicuous elements in their writings.[31] Zahra's obsession with color terms is another feminine feature of the memoir. Zahra refers to color terms more than 100 times throughout the memoir so much so that some passages can be literally called colorful paragraphs. During the initial days of the invasion, Zahra goes to the local hospital to help and notices a small girl whose legs are in splints: "She was a beautiful girl with delicate features. Her hair, which lay on her shoulders, was an attractive brown ... She was in a yellow dress with a blue and green flower print that had turned purple from the blood."[32] The British-American Linguist, Robert Lawrence Trask confirms that this is a feminine feature and points out that women are more likely to use precise color terms.[33] Zahra includes precise color terms in her narrative as well: "Her face was olive bordering on yellow"[34] and "She was wearing a dark brown and crème colored corduroy pants."[35] Foregrounding emotions and feelings is also a feature in *Da* (2014) that makes it a good example of *ecriture feminine*. The narrator's emotions in times of her father's death,[36] her feelings upon seeing the wounded and the dead in hospital and in the front throughout the memoir, and her emotions on her brother's death[37] are just a few illustrations of women's feelings and emotions that are hardly present in men's writing.

---

31   Marjorie L. DeVault, *Liberating Methods: Feminism and Social Research*. Philadelphia: Temple University Press, 1999.

32   Hosseini, *One Woman's War: Da (Mother)*, 57.

33   Robert Lawrence Trask, *Language: The Basics*. (New York: Rutledge, 1995), 61.

34   Hosseini, *One Woman's War: Da (Mother)*, 62.

35   Ibid., 74.

36   Ibid., 168–222.

37   Ibid., 293–339.

Da (2014) also shows affection amongst family members which is an uncommon occurrence in men's writing. Zahra recalls that her "father was forever declaring his love for her [mom]. Even after having eight children, they doted on each other like newlyweds."[38] Zahra's way of greeting Ali, his brother in which she "would kiss and hug" him and "stroke his beard for a while"[39] also corroborates the existence of the warmth and closeness between family members. Another *ecriture feminine* characteristic of *Da* (2014) is the presence of rivers, trees, greenery and animals that are included to describe beauty: "Shakha was a very pretty spot watered by a branch of Tigris, which explained its lush palm groves,"[40] "Both sides of Shatt were lined with trees so lush and leafy that walking under them was like entering a tunnel sheathed in green."[41] The inclusion of these images, which are emblematic of birth and growth, in a war memoir is reflective of Zahra's willingness to refrain from following the phallogocentric structure of war memoirs mostly fraught with destruction, blood, killing and martyrdom beside sacrifice. Moreover, metaphorization of events is another vehicle that Zahra uses to establish a different writing structure than that of men: "With windows on either side of or room, we saw nothing but sky. This gave me the feeling we were living on a ship in the middle of an ocean, a ship that never reached land."[42] As an indispensable component of women's writing, nostalgia is another trait that helps *Da* construct *ecriture feminine*. Zahra's narrative enjoys the all-present flashbacks to happy childhood memories:

> I had fond memories of the place. Mother and I would often shop here ... Everything combined to make the bazaar a pleasant place: the smell of fresh fish, the bright sheen of their skin in the lights; the expression on some of the fish, especially the pampus, which always seemed to be smiling ... the mongers would fish with their nets at night and in the morning present their catches to the customers. The ever-present gulls flapped their wings and made a racket as they feasted on the trimmings the mongers threw into the grated openings in the bazaar floor ... There was no sign of them now.[43]

---

38   Ibid., 191.
39   Ibid., 328.
40   Ibid., 14.
41   Ibid., 378.
42   Ibid., 666.
43   Ibid., 291.

Ecriture feminine is not just the style and how one writes but what one writes about. Cixous' statement of "Women must put herself into the text as into the world and into history by her own movement"[44] indicates that *ecriture feminine*—a strain of feminist literary theory itself—dovetails well with feminists' advocacy for gender equality in all spheres of life and endeavors to raise the status of women and put them in control of their own discourse. Thus, *ecriture feminine* is all about women, femininity, feminism and texts. "Women," "text," "world," "history" and "movement" in Cixous' statement are also present in Zahra Hosseini's *Da* (2014). Zahra Hosseini's effort to raise the status of women begins with writing the memoir, a literary genre that was historically disfavored for men and taboo for women. This sentiment gradually faded away and memoir became a popular genre for male authors. It is interesting to note that memoir also became a favorite tool of expression for Iranian women in exile after the events of the 1979 Revolution and 9/11 so much so that the sudden and rapid increase of its publication turned into a moot point.[45] Elsewhere, I have argued that recounting their own experience of victimhood through memoir has been a post-9/11 strategy to persuade the public in the West that Iranian women are in need of liberation.[46] Despite this popularity for Iranian women in exile, memoir was still a forbidden genre for Iranian women inside Iran until memoirs like Maryam Amjadi's *Maryam's Boots* (2003),[47] Masoumeh Ramhormozi *Eternal Fragrance* (2003)[48] and Zahra Hosseini's *Da* (2008/2014) challenged this sentiment.[49] These are not only women's memoirs written by and about Iranian women but also war memoirs which are supposedly men's genre. *Da* (2014) and others of its ilk are, therefore, part of the movement in bringing women into texts and into the history of the Iran-Iraq war to disrupt the male-inscribed history from which they were either totally absent or had a very insignificant presence.[50] *Da* (2014) includes a series of scenes that are recounted to improve the status of women. Zahra's effort to break the patriarchal and traditional taboo that women should not reveal personal information and family background can be seen on several occasions throughout the

44   Cixous, "The Laugh of Medusa," 875.

45   Esmaeil Zeiny & Noraini Md Yusof, "The Said and Not-Said: New Grammar of Visual Imperialism." *Gema Online Journal of Language Studies*, 16 (1) (2016): 125–141.

46   Esmaeil Zeiny, "From Visual Culture to Visual Imperialism: The Oriental Harem and the New Scheherazades." *The Southeast Asian Journal of English Language Studies*, 23 (2) (2017): 75–86.

47   Maryam Amjadi, *Maryam's Boots*. Tehran: Sureye Mehr Publication, 2003.

48   Masoumeh Ramhormozi, *Eternal Fragrance*. Tehran: Sureye Mehr Publication, 2003.

49   Hosseini, *One Woman's War: Da (Mother)*.

50   Hosseini, *One Woman's War: Da (Mother)*.

memoir. She discloses every member of the family including her sister and mother:

> Father and mother had come to Basra from the Kurdish village of Zarinabad near Dehloran. This was before their marriage, which took place at the end of the 1950s. My four siblings and I were born in the city: Ali in 1961, and afterwards with one year between us Mohsen, myself, and Leila. The last child, born three years after Leila, was Mansur ... We dressed the way the Arabs of the region dressed: in long-sleeved over-shirts known as dishdashas. Mother ... had been living in Basra since she was an adolescent and had long since grown used to the customs of the area.[51]

The incorporation of family background, especially women members of the family, is not frequent in male-produced war memoirs; however, it is a common phenomenon in women's war memoirs.[52] In this fashion, *Da* (2014) establishes and sustains a feminine structure aside from breaking the traditional taboo in a culture that romanticizes feminine silence and restraint. This seems to be the revitalization of feminism in a culture that has been discouraging women's self-revelation and self-referentiality. Through writing a memoir, Hosseini and similar preceding women memoirists generate a movement, a sense of sisterhood and political consciousness in the patriarchal society. What sticks out the most as feminism in *Da* (2014), however, is Zahra Hosseini's choice of words in the title of the memoir: *One Woman's War: Da*. Besides giving significance to women's role in the Iran-Iraq war, "one woman's war" refers to a woman's struggle with the patriarchal culture and the patriarchal grips on war literature. The term "Da," which means "mother" in Kurdish, is simply used to raise the status of mothers in a culture where fathers are predominant. Hence, the words "woman" and "Da" are chosen to extend prominence to women and mothers who have almost always been (under)/(mis)represented in phallogo-centric discourses. In this way, *Da* (2014) epitomizes *ecriture feminine* which endeavors to reconcile with mothers and raise the status of women in general. Moreover, mothers occupy an important place in the notion of *ecriture feminine*; constructing *ecriture feminine* is not possible without returning to the Lacanian pre-oedipal/imaginary phase or what Kristeva (1984) calls a semiotic stage when a child identifies itself with the mother who makes this stage a

---

51   Ibid., 6.
52   Masoumeh Ramhormozi, "Jang va Reveyate Zanan (War and Women's Narratives)." *Ashabe Qalam Quarterly*, (4) (2008).

feminine realm where there is no trace of the-law-of-the-Father.[53] The fluidity, openness and multiplicity of maternality also bear vital significance in *ecriture feminine*.[54]

Zahra Hosseini is constantly questioning the patrilineal culture of society by doing tasks that are usually men's jobs and stands firm against anyone warning her women cannot or should not do the task. For instance, when she wants to dig graves, a man gravedigger tells her: "This is not a playing. You can't dig graves."[55] She gets mad and responds: "Why not? Is that what you men think? We're weak just because we're women?"[56] Another similar instance is when a man tells her that she cannot lift the stones because they are too heavy but she says very defiantly "Yes I can."[57] When Zahra decides to inform the authorities of what is going on and ask for more people to come and wash the corpses, Zeinab asks her: "Who is going to listen to you? ... This is something a man should do, go there and demand new people,"[58] and Zahra responds: "What's wrong with us? We have tongues, don't we?"[59] On many occasions, Zahra defies top military male officers asking her and her friends to leave the front because it is dangerous to which she oftentimes responds: "If it's dangerous, what keeps you here? I'm no different from you,"[60] and "Don't think that only men can fight; women can also,"[61] and "We won't go back ... We're here and we know what we are doing."[62] This is Zahra's way to protest against the presumption that women are weak. These excerpts and many other examples such as taking care of the cemetery at night,[63] accepting responsibility to take care of the family,[64] calming down the uncontrollable crowds at times of invasion,[65] and cleaning and repairing guns and reloading magazines[66] suggest that Zahra has not been dominated by any man; this reinstates her own agency and women's in general. Her tough, tenacious, brave and ready-to-help-at-any-time personalities challenge the stereotypical role of Iranian women.

---

53   Kristeva, *Revolution in Poetic Language.*
54   Cixous, "The Laugh of Medusa."
55   Hosseini, *One Woman's War: Da (Mother)*. 99.
56   Ibid.
57   Ibid., 137.
58   Ibid., 103.
59   Ibid.
60   Ibid., 206.
61   Ibid., 207.
62   Ibid., 257.
63   Ibid., 149.
64   Ibid., 133.
65   Ibid., 197.
66   Ibid., 365–66.

Zahra Hosseini's feminism also comes to the surface with her continuous mentioning of the Blessed Zeinab, Prophet Muhammad's granddaughter, in the memoir. Zeinab is an iconic figure and symbol of piety, strength and sacrifice in Islam, and she is known as the "Heroin of Karbala." Zahra thinks of the Blessed Zeinab when she faces her father's body for the first time,[67] she calls out to her to get "strength to go on,"[68] she admires her composure "in face of tragedy,"[69] and wonders "how could a human being reach such a state of wisdom that she could look beyond the obvious horror and see the blessings in her son's and brother's torments?"[70] Zahra can relate to the sufferings of the Blessed Zeinab as both of them had to endure the martyrdom of a father and their beloved brother. Zahra would like to emulate the Blessed Zeinab's actions, her heroism in times of war, especially in Karbala and her great fortitude. Zahara's brother, Ali also tells her "to be like Zeinab," Abbas's mother,[71] particularly in wartime. The fact that she chooses a woman as a role model agrees well with Cixous' *ecriture feminine* in bringing women into texts and history.

5   *Da* and Nationalism

Zahra Hosseini seems to take feminism up a notch and link it with nationalism as the connection between the two is central to the women's movement in the Middle East. Contrary to Western feminism which is oftentimes more individualistic, Iranian feminism is deeply connected to nationalism. For instance, during the Constitutional Revolution of 1905–1911, Iranian women organized many clandestine associations and meetings in support of the nationalist and anti-imperialist movement, organized street riots and strikes, participated in fights against foreign forces, boycotted the importation of foreign goods, helped in the demolition of a Russian bank, and raised funds for the establishment of the National Bank. These activities were derived from nationalistic pride but they are also qualified as Iranian feminism by virtue of women's concurrent endeavors to gain "equality of all citizens in law" and voting rights. Zahra Hosseini's recounting of her experience in the front is replete with similar instances. Her willingness to go to the front[72] and her insistence that

67   Ibid., 181.
68   Ibid., 244.
69   Ibid., 171.
70   Ibid.
71   Ibid.
72   Ibid., 104.

women are also good fighters to defend the country[73] are not only motivated by nationalistic pride but are also derived from her feminism. Her choice of words for the title of the memoir: *One Woman's War: Da* accentuates women's role in nationalism and highlights women's struggle with the patriarchal culture.

Knowing that nationalist ideologies have deep roots in the patriarchal social system and being aware that nationalism itself is regarded as a masculine project, Zahra Hosseini challenges the existing standards in nationalism. In nationalist discourses, women are represented as "mother and the nation" in need of protection; they are presented as the bearer of "national honor" and men are portrayed as proprietors and guardians of the nation and national honor. Hosseini questions this patriarchal definition and presents a new set of standards in which women are no longer needed to be defended but rather they can stand up for themselves and their country. This marriage of feminism and nationalism can also be located right at the outset of her memoir. Her reading of the book "Women Heroes"[74] at the age of fourteen and her interest in "Djamila Boupacha,"[75] a former militant woman from the Algerian National Liberation Front, disclose her eagerness to interrogate the assumption that nationalism is a masculine project. Just like admiring the Blessed Zeynab in enduring tragedies in Karbala, Zahra Hosseini adores Djamila Boupacha for her strength and endurance, and her entering "into a one-sided struggle against the occupiers of her country."[76] Citing Djamila has also one more significance if one reads between the lines: it draws attention to Gisèle Halimi, the Tunisian lawyer and feminist, and Simone de Beauvoir, the French feminist and social theorist. As important figures in feminism, both of them assisted Djamila with her trial. Halimi acted as a counsel for Djamila and helped her bring her torture case to trial and Simone de Beauvoir assisted in the case publicity by writing an article in the French newspaper, Le Monde.

This is the first example of a series of instances in the memoir that criticizes the traditional belief about the role of women in nationalism. Zahra's knowledge of how to use a G3 assault rifle and the Colt,[77] her wish to go to the front,[78] her carrying the rifle,[79] her willingness to be martyred for the

---

73   Ibid., 207.
74   Ibid., 1.
75   Ibid.
76   Ibid.
77   Ibid., 88.
78   Ibid., 104.
79   Ibid., 237.

country,[80] her firing the RPG,[81] her desire to go back to the front despite her injuries,[82] and her wish to go the front again after marriage[83] exemplify the role of Iranian women in nationalism in addition to supportive positions during the eight-year Iran-Iraq war. Anchored within such discourse, Hosseini is deconstructing the masculinist nationalism and reimagining the nation. According to Ann McClintok "If nationalism is not transformed by an analysis of gender power, the nation-state will remain a repository of male hopes, male aspirations and male privileges."[84] *Da* brings back memories of Iranian women's nationalist movements and their roles in nationalist projects. Women's roles as a continuation of domestic and maternal responsibilities in the 1979 Revolution and the Iran-Iraq war have been widely recognized and accentuated but their roles as real participants in the nation-building projects have not been discussed widely. *Da* delineates that women's role in the Iran-Iraq war was more than mothering soldiers and supportive positions behind the front such as nursing, driving, managing ammunition and cooking. The women she conceives are no different from men in defending the country. This sentiment is echoed in her actions throughout the memoir and her father's advice at the beginning of the invasion: "Yes, today everyone must help. The difference between men and women doesn't matter anymore. Everybody must lend a hand in the defense ... We can't let a foreigner invade our country ... Both men and women must stop this from happening."[85] Hosseini's definition of nationalism can be best described as what Tavakoli-Targhi explains as "the participation of the nation's children (both male and female) in determining the future of the motherland."[86] The connection between nationalism and *ecriture feminine* in *Da* lies not only in deconstructing the masculinist nationalism and including women in nationalist discourses but also in bringing to light women's own cultural negotiations of the nation and nationalism.

---

80   Ibid., 239.
81   Ibid., 468.
82   Ibid., 478.
83   Ibid., 605.
84   Ann McClintok, *Imperial Leather: Race, Gender and Sexuality in the Colonial Contest.* (New York; London: Routledge, 1995), 385.
85   Hosseini, *One Woman's War: Da (Mother).* 69.
86   Mohamad Tavakoli-Targhi, *Refashioning Iran: Orientalism, Occidentalism and Historiography.* (Palgrave Macmillan, 2001), 13.

6   Conclusion

As the *ecriture feminine* in the genre of war literature, *Da* (2014) demonstrates that *ecriture feminine* is not a better or worse, and stronger or weaker writing structure. It is just different writing that bypasses the masculine structure by introducing elements that are strange and perhaps unknown for the general male writers. It is the insertion of these elements that make it vulnerable to critics' attacks. For instance, *Da*'s descriptive passages and foregrounding of the narrator's feelings and emotions might cause contention between critics arguing that the events of the war would be overshadowed. What they fail to understand is that these elements help Hosseini to establish a feminine writing structure of the previously male-produced literature in which women had no significant presence. This feminine writing raises the status of mothers and women, and tends to include women in discourses from which they were absent. *Ecriture feminine* is, indeed, the locus that reconstructs female identity, and brings women back to the fore from the margins. Writings such as *Da* are rebellious against the fixed and definite characterization of phallogocentrism. *Da* (2014) protests against this phallogocentrism and patrilineal culture that inferiorize women. However, unlike the male-produced war literature where women are either excluded or portrayed within the arena of domesticity as mothers and wives of soldiers or martyrs, the men in *Da* share equal presence and importance with women. This implies that although it is feminine writing, *Da* does not exclude men and does not give them a lesser status. This is illustrative of *ecriture feminine*'s disinclination towards essentialism and its affirmation of plurality and multiplicity.

Bibliography

Afary, J. (2009). *Sexual Politics in Modern Iran*. Cambridge: Cambridge University Press.

Amjadi, M. (2003). *Maryam's Boots*. Tehran: Sureye Mehr Publication.

Cixous, H. (1976). The Laugh of Medusa. *Signs*, Vol. 1 (4): 875–893. https://doi.org /10.1086/493306.

Dabashi, H. (1985). "The Poetics of Politics: Commitment in Modern Persian Literature." *Iranian Studies*, 18 (2/4), 147–188.

Daneshvar, S. (1969). *Savushun*. Tehran: Kharazmi Publications.

DeVault, M. L. (1999). *Liberating Methods: Feminism and Social Research.* Philadelphia: Temple University Press.

Ellmann, M. (1994). *Psychoanalytic Literary Criticism*. London: Longman.

E'tessami, P. [1935] (1974). *Divan* [Collected Poems]. Reprint. Tehran: Fardin.

Gilbert, S. [1979] (1986). "Dancing through the Minefield: Some Observations on the Theory, Practice, and Politics of a Feminist Literary Criticism." In *Critical Theory Since 1965*, edited by Adams, H., and Searle, L. Tallahassee: University Presses of Florida.

Holms, D. (1996). *French Women's Writing, 1848–1994*. London; Atlantic Highlands, N. J.: Athlone.

Hosseini, S. Z. [2008] (2014). *One Woman's War: Da (Mother)*. (Paul Sprachman, Trans.). Costa Mesa: Mazda Publishers.

Jones, Ann Rosalind. (1981). Writing the Body: Toward an Understanding of 'L'Ecriture Féminine.' *Feminist Studies,* Vol. 7 (2): 247–263. https://doi.org/10.2307/3177523.

Kristeva, J. (1984). *Revolution in Poetic Language*. (Margaret Waller, Trans.). New York: Columbia University Press.

Lakoff, R. (1973). *Language and Women's Place*. New York: Harper and Row.

McClintok, A. (1995). *Imperial Leather: Race, Gender and Sexuality in the Colonial Contest*. New York; London: Routledge.

Milani, F. (1992). *Veils and Words: The Emerging Voices of Iranian Women Writers*. Syracuse, N.Y.: Syracuse University Press.

Milani, F. (2016), *Furūq-i Farrukhzāā: Zindigī Nāmah-yi Hunarī bā Nāmah hāy-i Muntashir Nashudah [Forough Farrokhzad: A Literary Biography with Unpublished Letters]* Toronto: Persian Circle Publications.

"Pa-ye sohbat-e Simin-e Danesvar" (A Conversation with Simin Danesvar). *Alefba* (Paris), no. 4 (1983), pp. 147–187.

Peksen, S. (2005). Feminine Writing as an Alternative to the Patriarchal Language. *MP: An Online Feminist Journal*, 1 (2): 1–12.

Ramhormozi, M. (2003). *Eternal Fragrance*. Tehran: Sureye Mehr Publication.

Ramhormozi, M. (2008). Jang va Reveyate Zanan (War and Women's Narratives). *Ashabe Qalam Quarterly*, no. 4.

Joanna Scutts. (2020). Feminize Your Canon: Forough Farrokhzad. *The Paris Review*, November 19.

Tavakoli-Targhi, M. (2001). *Refashioning Iran: Orientalism, Occidentalism and Historiography*. Palgrave Macmillan. https://doi.org/10.1057/9781403918413.

Trask, R. L. [1995] (2004). *Language: The Basics*. New York: Rutledge.

Zeiny, E. (2017). From Visual Culture to Visual Imperialism: The Oriental Harem and the New Scheherazades. *3L: The Southeast Asian Journal of English Language Studies*, Vol. 23 (2): 75–86.

Zeiny, E. & Noraini M. Y. (2016). The Said and Not-Said: New Grammar of Visual Imperialism. *Gema Online Journal of Language Studies,* Vol. 16 (1): 125–141.

Index

www.ingramcontent.com/pod-product-compliance
Lightning Source LLC
Chambersburg PA
CBHW061725120626
46550CB00005B/1712